VINTAGE

AMBEDKAR'S PREAMBLE

Aakash Singh Rathore is a philosopher of international repute and the author of seven books, including *A Philosophy of Autobiography: Body & Text*. He is also India's number three Ironman triathlete and a social media influencer.

Rathore has taught at Jawaharlal Nehru University and University of Delhi, as well as at Rutgers University, University of Pennsylvania, University of Toronto, Humboldt University of Berlin and LUISS University in Rome. He is an international fellow at the Centre for Ethics and Global Politics in Rome and a fellow at the Indian Institute of Advanced Study in Shimla.

He is the series editor of Rethinking India (fifteen volumes) and is the co-editor of its first volume, *Vision for a Nation: Paths and Perspectives* (with Ashis Nandy). Rathore is also the series editor of Ethics, Human Rights and Global Political Thought (Routledge), and Religion and Democracy: Reconceptualizing Religion, Culture, and Politics in a Global Context (Oxford University Press). His eighteen books, some of which he has edited, have been published by leading international publishers. These books range from political philosophy, law and religion to literature, sports and wine. His website is www.aakashsinghrathore.com.

PRAISE FOR THE BOOK

'*Ambedkar's Preamble* is a constitutional history that recounts the deep study and deliberations made to conceptualize the great constitutional values of the Preamble. The book captures the immense vision and contribution of Dr Ambedkar to the legal and social framework of our republic. Aakash Singh Rathore deserves special commendation for having chosen a subject hitherto uncharted by others'—Justice K.G. Balakrishnan, former chief justice of India

'An insightful analysis of the origins and implications of the central ideas of the Preamble to the Indian Constitution. There have been many good books on the Constitution, but none that focused on the Preamble and used it to prise open its distinctive conceptual framework. This is a very valuable book on Ambedkar's seminal contribution'—Bhikhu Parekh, member of the House of Lords and fellow of the British Academy

'*Ambedkar's Preamble* is such a significant book. It not only establishes how Ambedkar steered the drafting of the main body of the Indian Constitution but also how he formulated its soul—the Preamble. The book solves several mysteries about who is responsible for the core philosophy of the living Constitution of India. Everyone—students, activists, lawyers and judges—needs this book on their shelves'—Kancha Ilaiah Shepherd, activist and author of the bestselling *Why I Am Not a Hindu*

'Aakash Singh Rathore decodes the "secret" history of the drafting and adoption of the Preamble to the Indian Constitution. He urges that we all make Ambedkar's handiwork "our own too" by adopting it as an agenda of the struggle for justice in our troubled times. The "unity of the nation" may only be achieved by preserving the fraternal dignity of all individuals. His moral reading of the Preamble, to which constitutional law is a massive footnote, is imperative because it contains both the points of departure as well as that of arrival'—Upendra Baxi, acclaimed constitutional expert and author

'Poet Altaf Hussain Hali had said, "*Admiyat seekhte hain is se sab chhote bade, nau-e-insaan me baqa-e-admiyat is se hai.*" An earlier generation captured our human values in the Preamble. The new generations must remember and practise these values, out of which our nation has sprung. As we celebrate seventy years of the republic, I urge everyone to read this captivating book'—Syeda Hameed, women's rights activist and former member of the Planning Commission

'*Ambedkar's Preamble* is a cross between a scintillating detective thriller, a necessary companion to Ambedkar's life and thought, and a sharply focused glimpse into the intellectual foundations of the Indian republic'—Rohit De, *Outlook*

'In another fascinating book, *Ambedkar's Preamble*, Aakash Singh Rathore celebrates Ambedkar's pioneering role as chairman of the drafting committee of the Constitution, arguing that the key concepts of the Preamble owe more to the Dalit leader than we give him credit for. His study acknowledges the centrality of the Ambedkarite legacy to the Preamble, which defines the core values of the Indian state'—*Mint*

'The book challenges the popular notion [or as Rathore calls it, "the UPSC view"] that the Preamble was Jawaharlal Nehru's . . . Rathore, in the course of a fascinating forensic exercise in his book, credits Ambedkar with being the author of the Preamble'—*Deccan Herald*

'Rathore's work makes us understand the indefatigable pre-eminence of Ambedkar's stamp on the whole of the Constitution. The book is more on the philosophy of the Preamble woven with the semantics of its drafting, telling us what Justice, Liberty, Fraternity and especially 'Dignity' mean today, through Ambedkar. The book makes for a refreshing read in a philosophical tone, granting us a deep understanding of the Preamble'—The *Tribune*

AMBEDKAR'S PREAMBLE

A SECRET HISTORY OF THE CONSTITUTION OF INDIA

AAKASH SINGH RATHORE

VINTAGE
An imprint of Penguin Random House

VINTAGE

USA | Canada | UK | Ireland | Australia
New Zealand | India | South Africa | China | Singapore

Vintage is part of the Penguin Random House group of companies whose addresses can be found at global.penguinrandomhouse.com

Published by Penguin Random House India Pvt. Ltd
4th Floor, Capital Tower 1, MG Road,
Gurugram 122 002, Haryana, India

Penguin Random House India

First published in Vintage by Penguin Random House India 2020

10 9 8 7 6 5 4 3 2

This book is a work of non-fiction. The views and opinions expressed in the book are those of the author only and do not reflect or represent the views and opinions held by any other person.
This book is based on a variety of sources, including published materials. It reflects the author's own understanding and conception of such materials and/or can be verified by research. The objective of this book is not to hurt any sentiments or be biased in favour of or against any particular person, region, caste, society, gender, creed, nation or religion.

ISBN 9780143457183

Typeset in Adobe Garamond Pro by Manipal Technologies Limited, Manipal
Printed at Manipal Technologies Limited, India

'The author would like to thank Sunaina Arya for her help with compiling the notes.'

www.penguin.co.in

FSC www.fsc.org MIX Paper | Supporting responsible forestry FSC® C043100

This is a legitimate digitally printed version of the book and therefore might not have certain extra finishing on the cover.

THE CONSTITUTION OF INDIA

PREAMBLE

WE, THE PEOPLE OF INDIA, having solemnly resolved to constitute India into a SOVEREIGN SOCIALIST SECULAR DEMOCRATIC REPUBLIC and to secure to all its citizens

JUSTICE, social, economic and political;

LIBERTY of thought, expression, belief, faith and worship;

EQUALITY of status and of opportunity; and to promote among them all

FRATERNITY assuring the dignity of the individual and the unity and integrity of the Nation;

IN OUR CONSTITUENT ASSEMBLY this twenty-sixth day of November 1949, do HEREBY ADOPT, ENACT AND GIVE TO OURSELVES THIS CONSTITUTION.

I think the Drafting Committee would accept [it], though not openly, at least secretly.

—Naziruddin Ahmad to the Constituent Assembly
25 November 1949

Contents

Preface

Anatomy of a Secret

On 17 November 1949, Bhimrao Ramji Ambedkar, chairman of the Drafting Committee, launched the proceedings of the Constituent Assembly of India, by moving 'that the Constitution as settled by the Assembly be passed'. The transcripts recording these proceedings stated in brackets that there were 'cheers' from the members of the Assembly upon hearing the motion.[1]

Dr Ambedkar's motion was the beginning of the third reading of the draft Constitution by the Assembly. It had, over the course of the previous year, passed through two readings already. This was now to be the final round.

Naziruddin Ahmad, a Constituent Assembly member representing West Bengal, had persistently been a staunch and vocal critic of the draft Constitution ever since it first made its appearance in the Assembly on 4 November 1948, at the time of the first reading. The text of the draft, he asserted, contained a 'number of errors, anomalies, redundancies and repetitions'.[2] He squarely placed the blame on the Drafting Committee for these problems. These outward criticisms of the draft Constitution were fuelled by an inward suspicion of the Drafting Committee itself. Beneath the surface of Ahmad's critique of the text lay his frustrations over the process of its drafting.

Ahmad believed that the Drafting Committee, led by Dr Ambedkar, had engaged in a drafting process that lacked transparency, making changes to the draft Constitution without the knowledge or consent of the Constituent Assembly. He made his private suspicion a public accusation in the Constituent Assembly, enumerating grammatical and syntactical changes that were there for everyone to see. On 25 November 1949, he quipped:

> This is only a punctuation amendment which, I think, the Drafting Committee would accept, though not openly, at least *secretly*.[3]

The evidence that Ahmad produced was primarily to do with syntax. The insinuation, however, extended to semantics—to meaning. Was the Drafting Committee engaged in a secret process of altering the meaning of constitutional words and phrases?

Several others in the Constituent Assembly thought so too. As the transcripts reveal, members K. Santhanam (from Madras), R.R. Diwakar (from Bombay) and Maulana Hasrat Mohani (from the United Provinces), could often be heard grumbling on this point in the Assembly:

> Santhanam: The Drafting Committee . . . I think illegitimately converted themselves into a 'Constitution Committee'. They have taken upon themselves the responsibility of changing some vital provisions adopted in the open House by this Assembly.[4]
>
> . . .
>
> Diwakar: The Drafting Committee and its chairman . . . not only drafted the decisions of the Constituent Assembly but, in

> my humble opinion, it has gone far beyond mere drafting. I may say it has reviewed the decisions, it has revised some of the decisions and possibly recast a number of them.[5]
>
> . . .
>
> Mohani: Ambedkar has gone out of his way. He has not conformed to the 'Objectives Resolution' and I request all of you to see what he had done. Instead of drafting the Constitution in conformity with the 'Objectives Resolution', he wants to make the 'Objectives Resolution' conform to what he is proposing now.[6]

This allegedly clandestine process is one of the secrets that this history of the Preamble unravels. But it is not the only one.

Authorship of the Preamble

Who wrote the Preamble to the Constitution of India? If that sounds like the sort of question you might expect to find in a Union Public Service Commission (UPSC) coaching manual, that's because it is. But the answer that such manuals invariably offer is wrong.

The authorship of the Preamble is shrouded in a cloak of mystery. Unlike for the Constituent Assembly, we have no verbatim transcripts for the Drafting Committee meetings where all sections and articles of the Constitution were presented, discussed, dissected, debated, modified and finalized. Instead of transcripts, we have minutes. And in those crucial Drafting Committee meetings, when the Preamble was up for discussion and finalization, we don't even have all of the minutes. Even worse, the various narratives that we do have today—inside views by those who attended the Drafting Committee meetings, contemporary statements or writings by Constituent Assembly members not privy to the Drafting Committee meetings, or speculative accounts by historians or others familiar with the drafting process—all seem to disagree on the details.

There are four competing narratives about the authorship of the Preamble.

The first, which for the purpose of convenience we can call the UPSC coaching narrative, is that Jawaharlal Nehru was essentially responsible for the Preamble. It was on the basis of his Objectives Resolution that the Constituent Assembly unanimously adopted the 'aims and objectives' of the future Constitution of India. However, the complaint that we just heard from Constituent Assembly member Mohani threw this option open to question.

The second is a sophomoric view of sorts because it mixes advanced knowledge about the history of Constitution-drafting in India with prejudice against Dr Ambedkar. In this account, it is B.N. Rau who is credited with authorship. It was in his role as Constitutional Adviser that he was tasked with putting together a full, working draft Constitution that would form the basis of the Drafting Committee's future labour.

The third account attributes authorship to the Drafting Committee as a collective whole, joyfully adding that each of its members played a part. While this makes for a pleasant historical narrative, useful for evoking that warm and fuzzy national sentiment that we seek to read into the collaborative origins of the Indian Republic, it is belied by the facts. As T.T. Krishnamachari—a member of the Drafting Committee and the author of memoirs and audio-recorded interviews that offer an inside look—himself detailed,[7] out of the seven original members of the Drafting Committee, one died (D.P. Khaitan), one was away in the United States (Krishnamachari was referring to B.N. Rau here, who was not actually a member), one was engaged in the affairs of state (N. Gopalaswami Ayyangar), and two

(Md Saadulla and N. Madhava Rao) could not be in Delhi owing to ill health. In short, Krishnamachari claimed that five of the key persons actually had either little or no contribution in the drafting process:

> So it happened ultimately that the burden of drafting the Constitution fell on Dr Ambedkar, and I have no doubt that we are grateful to him for having achieved this task in a manner which is undoubtably commendable.[8]

As far as the drafting and finalization of the Preamble was concerned, there were only four members present in the early meetings, and only three in the final meeting. One, of course, was Dr Ambedkar himself, who never missed a single meeting.

And thus we come to the fourth view, which grants B.R. Ambedkar authorship of the Preamble—not definitively or particularly, but by default. Given the ubiquity of Dr Ambedkar's designation as chief architect of the Constitution, it seems to follow that he must also be the chief architect of its Preamble. This view is problematic on two accounts. The first problem is that the drafting of the Constitution and the Preamble were two very different, albeit overlapping, processes. This will become clear as we explore its secret history.

The second, which is not the concern of this book, relates to the debates surrounding the distinction between 'author' and 'architect'. While most of this debate, motivated by caste prejudice and identity politics, is not worth attending to, it does necessarily challenge the logic of default authorship of the Preamble. That is, just because a person is the designated 'chief architect' of a document does not necessarily mean that he or she is its 'author' too.

The fine obituary speech for Dr Ambedkar that the then prime minister Jawaharlal Nehru delivered in the Lok Sabha on

6 December 1956 further reinforced the widespread designation of Dr Ambedkar as chief architect. Nehru had said, 'He is often spoken of as one of the architects of our Constitution. There is no doubt that no one took greater care and trouble over Constitution-making than Dr Ambedkar.'[9] Critics, however, are quick to point out that in his own 25 November 1949 concluding remarks regarding the Constitution-making process, Dr Ambedkar liberally portioned out the credit that the Assembly was bestowing upon him to many others, both inside and outside of the Drafting Committee. Of course, the simple exercise of common sense would indicate that for Dr Ambedkar not to spread credit would have been megalomaniacal, which by all accounts was alien to his nature.

But more important than these two problems assailing the view attributing default authorship of the Preamble to Dr Ambedkar was the lukewarm nature of the attribution itself. So much focus has been placed on foregrounding his role in the drafting of the overall Constitution that his authorship, specifically of the Preamble, is blurred in the background.

In what follows, the focus will be different: the Preamble is sharply foregrounded and the rest of the Constitution is somewhat blurred. Ideally, a comprehensive book will appear one day utilizing 'deep focus', with the Preamble and the body of the Constitution fully explored in all of their entangled richness with nothing blurred. Until then, it will be valuable to amplify attention on the Preamble in particular, because the message of this truly wondrous and historic set of eighty-one words—both the immediately discernible message as well as the secretly encoded one—merits as wide a dissemination as possible. Stated succinctly, the Preamble trumpets our collective aspirations as a republic; indeed, it articulates the principles that precondition the possibility for our unity as a nation.

The Preamble after Dr Ambedkar?

Dr Ambedkar's preamble, the original preamble to the Indian Constitution, read:

> WE, THE PEOPLE OF INDIA, having solemnly resolved to constitute India into a SOVEREIGN DEMOCRATIC REPUBLIC and to secure to all its citizens
> JUSTICE, social, economic and political;
> LIBERTY of thought, expression, belief, faith and worship;
> EQUALITY of status and of opportunity; and to promote among them all
> FRATERNITY assuring the dignity of the individual and the unity of the Nation;
> IN OUR CONSTITUENT ASSEMBLY this twenty-sixth day of November, 1949, do HEREBY ADOPT, ENACT AND GIVE TO OURSELVES THIS CONSTITUTION.

This version differed from the present, post-1976 Preamble by being four words shorter. It did not include the three main concepts of 'secular' and 'socialist' and 'integrity' or the conjunction 'and'. Our Preamble today is eighty-five words, not eighty-one as per the 1950 original.

Just as we will not be focusing upon the Constitution in this book but upon the Preamble instead, we are also limiting our exploration to Dr Ambedkar's preamble and not its later trajectories. The Preamble *after* Dr Ambedkar has had an eventful career, not only in terms of its amendment, but also with regard to its adjudication. Courts have ruled diversely on the relationship of the Preamble to the body of the Constitution itself, and how and why it is a part of the 'basic structure' of the Constitution. All of this jurisprudential history, with its reversals and ambiguities and achievements, is fascinating.

Thankfully there is no shortage of literature on it. What this vast body of literature uniformly fails to feature, however, is the historic nature of the moment when the Preamble to the Constitution of India made its first appearance. That moment has a well-documented but scarcely investigated date of birth.

It was born on 6 February 1948.

Who were the parents? What was its genealogy? What was its gestation period? Where was it delivered? Why was it born on that specific day? How did it grow or develop? All of this has remained a secret till now.

Anatomy of a Preamble

There are as many differences between preambles as there are between constitutions, at least when it comes to content. In structure though they all share the same basket of anatomical parts from which they are free to pick and choose.

There is a 'declaratory' part that says who has framed the document and with what mandate. The declaratory part of the original Indian Preamble read:

> WE, THE PEOPLE OF INDIA . . .
>
> IN OUR CONSTITUENT ASSEMBLY this twenty-sixth day of November, 1949, do HEREBY ADOPT, ENACT AND GIVE TO OURSELVES THIS CONSTITUTION

There were lively debates within the Constituent Assembly on the declaratory part, especially the opening phrase—'We, the People'—and fortunately there are several books exploring them.

Preambles also have an 'objective' part that sets out why the document was framed and what its goals are. The objective part of the original Indian Preamble read:

> having solemnly resolved to constitute India into a SOVEREIGN DEMOCRATIC REPUBLIC . . .

In the Constituent Assembly Debates (CAD), a great deal of attention was devoted to the objective part; it was enormously controversial. The proceedings of the Assembly were packed with arguments over whether the term 'sovereign' alone should be used, or whether 'independent' should be added to it, whether the term 'republic' should be used, or the word 'state', whether India was to be a 'union' or 'federation', or something in between. As important as these debates were, and still are today, they will not engage our attention in this book. However, a concise and straightforward, though not uncontroversial, explanation of each of the final choices that were made by the Drafting Committee in this regard is available in Ambedkar's 4 November 1948 speech to the Constituent Assembly. This speech, as I mentioned above, launched the first reading of the Constitution.

But, for now, back to the anatomy of a preamble.

There is a 'descriptive' part that explains how the aims and objectives of the document are going to be realized. This is where we find the basic principles enumerated. The descriptive part of the original Indian Preamble read:

> to secure to all its citizens
> JUSTICE, social, economic and political;
> LIBERTY of thought, expression, belief, faith and worship;
> EQUALITY of status and of opportunity; and to promote among them all
> FRATERNITY assuring the dignity of the individual and the unity of the Nation

And there is an 'invocative' part, which usually invokes the name of God. The original preamble did not include an invocative part, although many in the Constituent Assembly were repeatedly demanding the inclusion of one. The two primary contenders for the invocation were 'god' and 'Mahatma Gandhi', and in some amendments both.

> **Shibban Lal Saksena:** That for the Preamble the following be substituted: 'In the name of God the Almighty, under whose inspiration and guidance, the Father of our Nation, Mahatma Gandhi, led the Nation from slavery . . .'
>
> **Pandit Govind Malaviya:** 'By the Grace of Parameshwar, the Supreme Being, the Lord of the Universe (called by different names by different peoples of the world) . . .'[10]

All of these proposed amendments were, thank God, rejected.

Let's now turn back to the descriptive part. The original preamble consisted of a mere forty-four words, if we leave aside its declaratory and objective parts. From among these forty-four words of the Indian Preamble's descriptive part, this book is about just six. These are:

> to secure to all its citizens
> ***JUSTICE***, social, economic and political;
> ***LIBERTY*** of thought, expression, belief, faith and worship;
> ***EQUALITY*** of status and of opportunity; and to promote among them all
> ***FRATERNITY*** assuring the ***dignity*** of the individual and the unity of the ***Nation***

The scope of this history is thus drastically intensified. Not only do we background the Constitution to foreground the Preamble; not only do we leave the life of the Preamble after Dr Ambedkar for others to interrogate; not only do we hone in on the Preamble's descriptive part (keeping the declaratory and objective [and would-be invocative] parts to one side); but we fix upon six, and only six, words from the Preamble, quarantined from the others.

The reason? So that we can isolate the Preamble's gene. It is these six words that allow us to hack into the DNA of Dr Ambedkar's preamble, gaining access to many of its secrets.

Introduction

A Tale of Four Preambles

On 26 January 1950, over seventy years ago, our Constitution came into force. The supremacy of the Constitution meant the abrogation of the Government of India Act, 1935—which had effectively been the governing document for the country even after independence in 1947—effecting a significant change in status for India. An independent dominion in the British Commonwealth of Nations, India finally became, as the Preamble of the new Constitution declared, a sovereign democratic republic.

The Labyrinth of Dates

But 26 January 1950 is not a date that readers of the Preamble will come across:

> WE, THE PEOPLE OF INDIA . . . IN OUR CONSTITUENT ASSEMBLY this twenty-sixth day of November, 1949, do HEREBY ADOPT, ENACT AND GIVE TO OURSELVES THIS CONSTITUTION.

Why was there a two-month lag between the date of adoption mentioned in the Preamble (26 November 1949, now feebly celebrated as 'Constitution Day') and the date that India celebrates as Republic Day (26 January, a public holiday)?

The reason dates back to almost two decades before the Constitution was completed. In 1929, during the Indian National Congress's (INC) Lahore session, a call was made for complete independence, or *purna* Swaraj, in defiance of the offer of dominion status that the British government had put forth. In his closing statement as chair of the Lahore session, Jawaharlal Nehru had declared, 'Complete independence is our motto.'[1] A year later, M.K. Gandhi published an article on 26 January 1930 that read, 'Today is the day to proclaim that we will not be satisfied with dominion status; we want purna Swaraj, or complete independence.'[2] This bold and defiant move began to be recognized, and routinely celebrated, on 26 January as Purna Swaraj Diwas.

As a callback to this significant demand, the Constituent Assembly determined that the new Constitution, Preamble and all, would come into complete effect on 26 January 1950.

The now-infamous snail cartoon from *Shankar's Weekly* (dated 28 August 1949)[3] represented the oft-murmured public impatience with the long-drawn-out process of drafting and finalizing the Constitution. And while Dr Ambedkar and the other members of the Constituent Assembly in general, and the Drafting Committee in particular, justified the slow pace of completion, the temporary enactment of the Constitution, which delayed it till Purna Swaraj Diwas, indicated the comfort of former prime minister Jawaharlal Nehru—despite the cartoon portraying him as the whipper, hastening the completion of the Constitution—and the other decision makers in sacrificing urgency for ideological impact.

Photo courtesy: *Shankar's Weekly*, issue dated 28 August 1949

The political and legislative history of India was marked by a number of events, such as this, that ultimately came to bear upon the original text of the Preamble. If we were to begin, albeit arbitrarily, with the 1929 formal demand for purna Swaraj, the next salient date to mark might be 16 May 1946, which is when the Cabinet Mission and the then viceroy presented specific recommendations about the future Constitution of India. It was under the terms of the Cabinet Mission's plan that the original 389 members of the Constituent Assembly would be elected, with the ratio of representation according one Constituent Assembly member to one million of the general population. These specifications, of course, altered given the ensuing Partition and the specific clauses of the Indian Independence Act, 1947.

A 'Declaration' by the Experts

A great deal happened between the Cabinet Mission recommendations of 1946 and our 'tryst with destiny' in August 1947. On 22 July 1946, the Experts' Committee tasked by the Congress Working Committee (CWC) with preparing material for the future Constituent Assembly, moved a 'declaration' outlining the objectives of the Assembly. This committee included Jawaharlal Nehru as its chairman, along with some prominent members such as Asaf Ali (an alumnus of St Stephen's College, who would eventually serve as the first Indian ambassador to the United States), K.M. Munshi (who would later be part of the Drafting Committee), N. Gopalaswami Ayyangar (who too became a member of the Drafting Committee), K.T. Shah (an alumnus of the London School of Economics and a prominent socialist who pushed the Constituent Assembly and Dr Ambedkar, without success, to include the terms 'secular' and 'socialist' into the Constitution) and Humayun Kabir (a public intellectual, the author of a book on German philosopher Immanuel Kant, the compiler of Azad's well-known autobiography *India Wins Freedom* and adviser to UNESCO, which consulted him about

India's heritage of human rights during the drafting of the Universal Declaration of Human Rights, 1948).

This 'declaration', though little-known, proved to be life-changing for every Indian citizen by way of its future adaptations and iterations. It read:

> This Constituent Assembly declares its firm and solemn resolve to proclaim India as an Independent Sovereign Republic and to draw up for her future governance a Constitution wherein
>
> the territories that now comprise British India, the territories that now form the Indian States, and such other territories and parts of India as are outside British India and the States and are willing to be constituted into the Independent Sovereign India, shall be a Union of them all; and the said territories, either with their present boundaries or with such others as may be determined by the Constituent Assembly and thereafter according to the Law of the Constitution, shall possess and retain the status of autonomous units, together with residuary powers, and exercise all powers and functions of government and administration, save and except those that are assigned to and vested in the Union, save and except such powers and functions as are inherent in the Union by virtue of the sovereignty of the Union; and
>
> wherein
>
> all power and authority of the Sovereign Independent India, its constituent parts and organs of government, are derived from the people; and
>
> wherein
>
> shall be guaranteed to all the people of India by law and secured to them by declared social objectives and purposes, economic organization and administrative machinery

(a) justice, social, economic and political;
(b) equality of status, of opportunity, and before the law;
(c) freedom of thought, belief, vocation, association and action, subject to law and public morality; and

wherein

adequate safeguards shall be provided for minorities, backward areas, and classes; and

whereby

shall be maintained the integrity of the territory of the Republic and its sovereign rights on land, sea, and air according to Justice and the law of civilised nations,

and

this ancient land attains its rightful and honoured place in the world and makes its full and willing contribution to the promotion of world peace and the welfare of mankind.[4]

Nehru's Objectives Resolution: Three More Freedoms

Nearly five months later, on 13 December 1946, this obscure declaration penned by philosophers, freedom fighters and future statesmen took on historic significance when Jawaharlal Nehru moved what was essentially the same text in the Constituent Assembly, as a 'Resolution Regarding Aims and Objectives'. Nehru's celebrated Objectives Resolution, as it was more familiarly called, consisted of a few cosmetic alterations to the earlier declaration, as well as the addition of three words to supplement the freedoms it enumerated. While the declaration proposed 'freedom of thought, belief, vocation, association, and action', Nehru's Objectives Resolution added 'freedom of expression, faith, and worship'.

A quick glance at the Preamble, as it was adopted in 1950, indicates that Nehru's supplementary concepts proved crucial. The freedoms underlined in the Preamble adopted all of Nehru's additional terms, while dropping most of those originally forwarded in the declaration (that is, vocation, association and action). The relevant line in the Preamble—opting for the term 'liberty' over 'freedom'—read as 'liberty of thought, expression, belief, faith and worship'. Another way of looking at this is to say that all of the freedoms listed in the Preamble originated either from Nehru's Objectives Resolution or from the declaration of the Experts' Committee of the CWC, except that these source documents speak of 'freedom' and not 'liberty'; the latter, as we shall see later, being the term preferred by Dr Ambedkar.

Nehru's 'Resolution Regarding Aims and Objectives' read thus:

> (a) This Constituent Assembly declares its firm and solemn resolve to proclaim India as an Independent Sovereign Republic and to draw up for her future governance a Constitution;
> (b) WHEREIN the territories that now comprise British India, the territories that now form the Indian States, and such other parts of India as are outside British India and the States as well as such other territories as are willing to be constituted into the Independent Sovereign India, shall be a Union of them all; and
> (c) WHEREIN the said territories, whether with their present boundaries or with such others as may be determined by the Constituent Assembly and thereafter according to the Law of the Constitution, shall possess and retain the status of autonomous Units, together with residuary powers, and exercise all powers and functions of government and administration, save and except such powers and functions as are vested in or assigned to the Union, or as are inherent or implied in the Union or resulting therefrom; and
> (d) WHEREIN all power and authority of the Sovereign Independent India, its constituent parts and organs of government, are derived from the people; and

> (e) WHEREIN shall be guaranteed and secured to all the people of India, justice, social, economic and political; equality of status, of opportunity, and before the law; freedom of thought, expression, belief, faith, worship, vocation, association and action, subject to law and public morality; and
> (f) WHEREIN adequate safeguards shall be provided for minorities, backward and tribal areas, and depressed and other backward classes; and
> (g) WHEREBY shall be maintained the integrity of the territory of the Republic and its sovereign rights on land, sea, and air according to Justice and the law of civilised nations, and
> (h) This ancient land attains its rightful and honoured place in the world and make its full and willing contribution to the promotion of world peace and the welfare of mankind.[5]

After eight days of discussion spread across December 1946 and January 1947, the resolution was adopted on 22 January 1947—this was despite the fact that a member of the Constituent Assembly (H.J. Khandekar) moved 'that a resolution of so great importance should be passed on' 26 January, or Purna Swaraj Diwas. This time, however, Nehru did object, stating that the Constituent Assembly was obligated to complete its work as soon as possible, and that delays on such an important matter in the early days would not bode well for the promptness expected in the near future.

What was interesting about the acceptance of the resolution was the peculiar way in which nearly all historians describe its unanimous adoption by the Constituent Assembly—that is, in a *solemn* manner, with all the members standing. It is true. Prior to its adoption, all motions for amendment were withdrawn and the path was cleared for Nehru's Objectives Resolution to shape the inalterable contours of India's future Constitution in general and its Preamble in particular. Championing justice (social, economic, and political), equality (of status, of opportunity, and before the law) and freedom (of thought, expression, belief, faith, and worship), Nehru and the other members of the Constituent Assembly, and through them the hundreds of millions of Indians for whom they spoke, espoused our bedrock principles, the values that we stood for, literally.

Objections to the 'Objectives'

There had, of course, been numerous suggestions for amendments to the Objectives Resolution. The chairman of the Constituent Assembly, Rajendra Prasad, noted on 17 December 1946 that he had a list of over fifty names of members who wished to speak and propose amendments to the resolution.[6] Dr Ambedkar was one of its most articulate critics. Honing in on the irony that a dedicated socialist like Nehru would not so much as mention the term 'socialism' in the resolution, Dr Ambedkar told the chairman, along with Nehru and all those present, that:

> If this Resolution has a reality behind it and a sincerity, of which I have not the least doubt, coming as it does from the Mover of the Resolution, I should have expected some provision whereby it would have been possible for the State to make economic, social and political justice a reality and I should have from that point of view expected the Resolution to state in most explicit terms that in order that there may be social and economic justice in the country, that there would be nationalisation of industry and nationalisation of land. I do not understand how it could be possible for any future Government which believes in doing justice socially, economically and politically, unless its economy is a socialistic economy.[7]

Yet, Dr Ambedkar too refused to stand in the way of the passage of the resolution in the first of many concessions that he made as a member of the Constituent Assembly and later as chairman of its Drafting Committee. He justified these concessions through eloquent appeals to all the members of the Constituent Assembly, especially those heading rival factions (among whom he included himself), garnering an unprecedented clamour of applause from all those who were present:

> Our difficulty is how to make the heterogeneous mass that we have today take a decision in common and march on the way which leads us to unity . . . [I]n order to make us willing friends, in order to induce every party, every section in this country to take on to the road, it would be an act of greatest statesmanship for the majority party even to make a concession to the prejudices of people who are not prepared to march together and it is for that, that I propose to make this appeal. Let us leave aside slogans, let us leave aside words which frighten people. Let us even make a concession to the prejudices of our opponents, bring them in, so that they may willingly join with us on marching upon that road, which as I said, if we walk long enough, must necessarily lead us to unity.[8]

However, Dr Ambedkar's call for magnanimous concessions that would lead to unity did not preclude him from making his own position loud and clear.

Dr Ambedkar's 'Proposed Preamble': Memorandum on States and Minorities

Two months after Nehru's resolution was adopted, Dr Ambedkar submitted a memorandum of over 20,000 words, titled 'States and Minorities: What Are Their Rights and How to Secure Them in the Constitution of Free India',[9] to the Constituent Assembly's Advisory Committee on Fundamental Rights, Minorities and Tribal and Excluded Areas, chaired by Vallabhbhai Patel. However, despite the fact that Dr Ambedkar was a member of two of the Advisory Committee's subcommittees (the Fundamental Rights subcommittee chaired by J.B. Kripalani and the Minorities Subcommittee chaired by H.C. Mookerjee), the committee failed to take cognizance of the memorandum.

Undaunted, Dr Ambedkar published the text as a book in 1947. He elaborated on the title page that this was a 'memorandum on the Safeguards for the Scheduled Castes submitted to the Constituent Assembly on behalf of the All India Scheduled Castes Federation'.[10] But beyond remaining content to frame simple safeguards for the scheduled castes, Dr Ambedkar actually sketched the framework of an entire Constitution, which he dubbed as a 'Constitution for the United States of India'. This Constitution began with a 'proposed preamble' that read:

> We the people of the territories of British India distributed into administrative units called Provinces and Centrally Administered Areas and of the territories of the Indian States with a view to form a more perfect union of these territories do—
>
> *ordain* that the Provinces and the Centrally Administered Areas (to be hereafter designated as States) and the Indian States shall be joined together into a Body Politic for Legislative, Executive and Administrative purposes under the style *The United States of India* and that the union so formed shall be indissoluble

and that with a view:

(i) To secure the blessings both of self-government and good government throughout the United States of India to ourselves and to our posterity,

(ii) To maintain the right of every subject to life, liberty and pursuit of happiness and to free speech and free exercise of religion,

(iii) To remove social, political and economic inequality by providing better opportunities to the submerged classes,

(iv) To make it possible for every subject to enjoy freedom from want and freedom from fear, and

(v) To provide against internal disorder and external aggression,

establish this Constitution for the united states of India.[11]

Dr Ambedkar's proposed preamble, it is important to note, neglected to use the term 'socialist', despite both his critique of Nehru's Objectives Resolution and the fact that, beyond any doubt, Dr Ambedkar's proposed Constitution for the united states of India was state socialist all through. Under Dr Ambedkar's state socialist Constitution, there were provisions for nationalization of industry, as well as state ownership in agriculture, land, insurance and collective farming. None of this made its way into the Constitution that came into effect on 26 January 1950, even though Dr Ambedkar was universally hailed as its chief architect.

The Mystery of Reversal: Three Hypotheses

One may well ask 'Why not?', and to be sure, many already have. There are a lot of differing opinions, but they can broadly be grouped into three types: first is the conspiratorial answer forwarded by prominent public intellectual and author Anand Teltumbde, and recently echoed by emerging young scholar Suraj Yengde; second is the concessional explanation that is probably the most widely shared and has been expertly laid out by political scientist Niraja Jayal; the third, what we might call the constitutionalist explanation, is the one to which I subscribe.

The conspiratorial view is fascinating. In addition to the fact that the socialist structures of Dr Ambedkar's *States and Minorities* failed to materialize in the 1950 Constitution, Teltumbde, and following him, Yengde, base their position on two further statements by Dr Ambedkar after the implementation of the Constitution. The first is his fiery remark in the Rajya Sabha in 1953 that, contrary to the common attribution of Dr Ambedkar as the main author of the Constitution, 'I was a hack. What I was asked to do, I did much against my will.' The second, related to the first, is Dr Ambedkar's admission that he had wanted to burn the Constitution.[12] Despite his explanation later for his remarks and his statement in 1955 that 'the Constitution which has been given to this country is a wonderful document', the conspiratorial account holds that in the retraction of his true feelings, Dr Ambedkar was just being politic:

> The substance of the Constitution comprises the decisions of the Congress party that emphatically represented the ruling classes. When he spoke in the Rajya Sabha [in 1953] disowning the Constitution, it was not an angry outburst, but a painful disclosure of the truth, and when he covered it up two years later by saying that the Constitution was a beautiful temple occupied by demons, it was a strategic retreat.[13]

According to this conspiratorial account, the dedication that Ambedkarites have towards the Constitution should be rethought[14] in light of the discrepancy between Dr Ambedkar's own position in *States and Minorities* and the 1950 Constitution, as well as by his revealing claims of disowning the latter. This rethink would, according to Teltumbde and Yengde, open the door to a more radical agenda for political, social and economic change than what the constitutional-democratic framework permits.[15]

The concessional explanation is far more sober, which possibly accounts for why it is nearly universal in appeal. Although there are dozens of formulations nuancing various aspects of the compromises that Dr Ambedkar had to make and why, Niraja Jayal's assessment is that:

> Ambedkar may have had to enter into political compromises, as he simultaneously fought to secure the rights of Dalits and also for social and economic rights for all citizens. On issues relating to the Dalits—especially untouchability and reservations—Ambedkar made impassioned and decisive contributions to the Constituent Assembly's proceedings. It is possible that he may have been compelled to be less inflexible on other issues.[16]

According to this narrative, Dr Ambedkar's explanation for his disavowal of the Constitution was sincere. There was consistency in his position once all concessions and compromises are accounted for, but despite that he abandoned his commitment to state socialism in bringing forth the 1950 Constitution.

I find both these explanations unsatisfying. The conspiratorial account underestimates Dr Ambedkar's boldness and fearlessness, his irrepressible sense of righteousness. Dr Ambedkar was not 'played' because he sought to retain power and position. He was one of those rare political figures who sought public positions in order to 'secure the blessings of good government', to cite from his proposed preamble, 'for all citizens'. His biography bore this out at every juncture.[17] The concessional account, on the other hand, tends to assume a monolithic Dr Ambedkar; that he had a basket of fixed ideas—A, B, C, D, E and F—and that over time he would concede D, E and F, say, in order to preserve A, B and C. It thus assumes that Dr Ambedkar's pragmatism meant a willingness to compromise in order to get things done. But this is too simplistic. Dr Ambedkar was forever a student, forever engaged in study, discussion and debate, and although he held remarkably strong and consistent fundamental principles, his thinking and practice about how best to achieve those principles were always changing based on new information, new data and exposure to new persons and ideas. His pragmatism was akin to a constant evolution, adapting to changing circumstances, grounding his willingness to consider other points of view and to be able to change his mind.

The preambles, both the proposed preamble from *States and Minorities* and the Preamble to the Constitution, reflect Dr Ambedkar's fundamental principles. As we shall see, he was rather uncompromising when it came to the main concepts. But as far as the specific articles within the Constitution as a whole went, he proceeded pragmatically.

A better alternative to both the conspiratorial and the concessional accounts is what I refer to as the constitutional explanation. That is, the change in Dr Ambedkar's position occurred owing to his experience with the Constituent Assembly and the drafting of the Constitution. The process of engaging with all of the other members gave him a wealth of new empirical information—all extremely cautionary. This view takes into consideration that although Dr Ambedkar was firm on his principles, he was pragmatic about the means and strategies used to secure them. As new empirical information came in, he modified his means accordingly, searching for the most realistic or appropriate way to get his principles realized. And a lot changed between the time *States and Minorities* was written and when Dr Ambedkar relented on the demand for state socialism. The most important of this was the reality of Partition, which led to the Constituent Assembly's numbers, and more importantly its demographic composition, changing radically.

If one keeps in mind that for Dr Ambedkar state socialism had always been in danger of degrading into despotism that violated individual dignity and rights, it is easier to understand why he surmised that in an absolute Hindu-majority nation, which is what India was destined to be, it was going to be difficult to secure basic political rights for minorities and the 'depressed classes'—which is what the Dalits were called then—let alone economic justice through the administrative (Hindu, casteist) state apparatus.

There is a great deal more to be said about Dr Ambedkar's changed position and some of it will be addressed in later chapters. For now, let us return to the ideas that Dr Ambedkar put forward in March 1947, in reaction to Nehru's Objectives Resolution.

In the published 'explanatory notes' appended to *States and Minorities*, Dr Ambedkar wrote a note regarding its 'proposed preamble':

> The Preamble gives constitutional shape and form to the Resolution on objectives passed by the Constituent Assembly on Wednesday the 22nd January 1947.

What did the 'proposed preamble' add to the Objectives Resolution? The rights asserted by Dr Ambedkar in clause [2], to life, liberty and pursuit of happiness, as well as to free speech and free exercise of religion, were in no way inconsistent with clause [5] of the Objectives Resolution. Dr Ambedkar's clause [3] followed Nehru in the tripartite focus on social, economic and political aspects, but instead of speaking of them here as aspects of justice, Dr Ambedkar gave substantive meaning to the term 'justice' by speaking of removing inequalities. That is, where Nehru spoke loftily of securing justice—social, economic and political—Dr Ambedkar shaped 'securing justice' to mean removing social, political and economic inequalities. Similarly, instead of Nehru's clause [6], which stated that 'adequate safeguards shall be provided' for minorities and 'depressed classes', Dr Ambedkar more substantively spoke of 'better opportunities', indicating a teleology in clause [4]: 'to make it possible for every subject to enjoy freedom from want and freedom from fear'.

B.N. Rau's Draft Preamble: A Trusted Placeholder

Dr Ambedkar was not the only one drafting preambles in response to Nehru's Objectives Resolution. Constitutional Adviser B.N. Rau (a well-respected legal savant who went on to serve as judge at the Permanent Court of International Justice in The Hague) had also been preparing a memorandum on the Union Constitution, which was admitted on 30 May 1947. Rau's preamble had the character of a placeholder, a trusted one that served as the working preamble for the draft Constitution right up to 6 February 1948, when Dr Ambedkar replaced it. Rau's preamble from 30 May 1947 read:

> We, the people of India, seeking to promote the common good, do hereby, through our chosen representatives, enact, adopt and give to ourselves this Constitution.[18]

Four days later, thunder struck. The then British prime minister Clement Attlee announced 'the Mountbatten Plan', fixing the terms of Partition. This changed everything: the nature and number of the Constituent Assembly members, as the constituencies from where they came might no longer be in India; the validity of the 16 May 1946 Cabinet Mission recommendations regarding the future Constitution of India; and even the solemnly and unanimously approved Objectives Resolution now needed to be revisited.

Realizing that it would take time to fully appreciate the legal, political, social and other implications of Partition, on 30 June 1947, the Union Constitution Committee of the Constituent Assembly provisionally accepted the draft preamble that B.N. Rau had prepared. Meanwhile, a subcommittee (it was actually a sub-subcommittee appointed by a subcommittee of the Union Constitution Committee) convened to examine how the Objectives Resolution ought to be amended in the light of Partition. This sub-subcommittee, not surprisingly, consisted of many of the members of the Experts' Committee from back in July 1946, who had originally drafted the 'declaration' that had formed the basis, almost word for word, of Nehru's Objectives Resolution. K.M. Munshi and N. Gopalaswami Ayyangar were there again (both of them also became members of the Drafting Committee soon after). But this time, Dr Ambedkar was added, as was Alladi Krishnaswami Ayyar, who would himself become a member of the Drafting Committee, and B.N. Rau, the constitutional adviser.

This sub-subcommittee took an interesting decision. They claimed that since changes to the Objectives Resolution only needed to be made just before the final draft of the future Constitution was created, there was really no reason to amend it right then. Although this decision simply seemed to say 'let's do it later', it was setting a precedent in the minds of the future Drafting Committee members. The precedent was that the Objectives Resolution, irrespective of how solemnly it was unanimously adopted, would only be a guide in how content ought to be framed and not serve as the content itself. It was, and was not, the Preamble to the Constitution of India.

The Drafting Committee

Nehru, about a month before he became prime minister of India, seemed to readily concede this tacit usurpation of prerogative from this merely advisory sub-subcommittee, which itself was just six weeks away from becoming the Drafting Committee for India's Constitution. On 18 July 1947, Nehru told the Constituent Assembly:

> It is proposed to constitute a Drafting Committee which will produce a formal draft for the consideration of the next session of the Constituent Assembly. . . . The Preamble . . . ha[s] been dealt with in the Objectives Resolution . . . and the final Constitution will have to incorporate parts. . . . That Objectives Resolution will have to undergo some modification . . . but the basic principles . . . will remain . . .[19].

On 29 August 1947, the Drafting Committee was appointed through a resolution of the Constituent Assembly. Its stated task was to:

> scrutinise the draft of the text of the Constitution of India prepared by the Constitutional Adviser, giving effect to the decisions already taken in the Assembly and including all matters which are ancillary thereto or which have to be provided

> in such a Constitution, and to submit to the Assembly for consideration the text of the draft Constitution as revised by the committee.[20]

Among the members of the Drafting Committee were Alladi Krishnaswami Ayyar, N. Gopalaswami, B.R. Ambedkar and K.M Munshi. At its first meeting, Dr Ambedkar was unanimously elected the chairman.

Towards the end of October 1947, the Drafting Committee began scrutinizing the draft Constitution prepared by B.N. Rau, who himself sat in on the Drafting Committee meetings.[21] Though the idea was to go through the draft and discuss each article, the committee decided not to begin with the Preamble, but instead with Article 1. They thus held discussions over the Preamble at the end, only after the entire draft Constitution had been examined.

The Birth of the Preamble: Out of the Blue

Four months later, on 6 February 1948, the Drafting Committee met, with Dr Ambedkar as chairman and only three other members in attendance (Alladi Krishnaswami Ayyar, Maulavi Md Saadulla and N. Madhava Rao, who had come in as a replacement for B.L. Mitter). The latter two members were relatively quiet, according to the Constituent Assembly Debate (CAD)[22] records. K.M. Munshi, a stalwart who was absent from these meetings, was of the view that Saadulla and Rao had little to contribute. He, in fact, seemed to have a rather low opinion of them. In his memoirs covering the Drafting Committee, Munshi refused to include them within his descriptions of 'prominent personalities', where other members like Alladi Krishnaswami Ayyar and Dr Ambedkar featured. T.T. Krishnamachari's insider assessment concurs with that of Munshi's.[23] By contrast, Munshi could hardly contain his admiration for B.N. Rau.[24]

Rau, the constitutional adviser, was also in attendance at the meetings, though he was not a member—it was thus at the discretion of the chair, Dr Ambedkar, if Rau was permitted to be heard and whether his vote was counted or not when it came to the decisions of the committee. On the minutes for this day was the consideration of the preamble to the draft Constitution. B.N. Rau's preamble, once again, read:

> We, the people of India, seeking to promote the common good, do hereby, through our chosen representatives, enact, adopt and give to ourselves this Constitution.

The minutes of the meeting of the Drafting Committee for 6 February 1948 laconically read: 'Preamble: It was decided that for the Preamble [cited above], the Preamble as shown in Appendix B to these minutes should be substituted'![25] And what was the preamble as shown in Appendix B? Was it the 'declaration' from 22 July 1946, or was it Nehru's Objectives Resolution sanctified on 22 January 1947, or the 'proposed preamble' from Ambedkar's *States and Minorities* (15 March 1947), or just another repeat of B.N. Rau's 30 May 1947 version?

Interestingly, it was none of them, but in a certain sense it was all of them:

> We, the people of India, having solemnly resolved to constitute India into a sovereign independent state, and to secure to, or promote among, all its citizens: Justice, social, economic and

> political; liberty of thought, expression, belief, faith, worship, vocation, association and action; Equality of status, and of opportunity; and, Fraternity assuring the dignity of every individual without distinction of caste or creed . . . do hereby adopt, enact and give to ourselves this Constitution.[26]

We can easily infer from the minutes of the meeting that the introduction of this completely new text was not contentious at all, even though it seemingly came out of the blue. It was not drafted during the meeting, but brought in, ready-made, from outside. Someone apparently pulled it out from his shirt pocket. Discussions around it occurred within only one of three items on the minutes, and were listed along with consideration of as many as eight other constitutional clauses. It seemed as though it may have been discussed for just ten minutes out of the three-and-a-half hours of meeting time. Perhaps it was not contentious because it was simply introduced and then quickly assented to by all to function as the new working draft, to be put aside for closer scrutiny and debate in ensuing sessions.

However, only one person on that committee wielded the authority and clout to introduce new, home-spun text like that, and to have it 'decided' that his own version of the preamble 'should be substituted' for B.N. Rau's. That person was, of course, the chairman.[27]

It was not just the procedure of adoption that singled out the author. The content, too, revealed Dr Ambedkar's composition. The closing line: 'Fraternity assuring the dignity of every individual without distinction of caste . . .' had Dr Ambedkar's fingerprints all over it. And his pragmatic genius as well.

If we dissect this first iteration of the new, Ambedkarian draft preamble, we can see traces of every document mentioned till now. Notably, from the 'declaration' we have freedom of thought, belief, vocation, association and action; supplemented by the freedoms introduced by the Objectives Resolution, and expression, faith, and worship. Also, from both these predecessors, there was the 'solemn resolve', the 'sovereign independent', the 'Justice, social, economic and political', and the 'Equality of status, and of opportunity'. From B.N. Rau's draft, there was 'We, the people of India', and the 'adopt, enact and give to ourselves this Constitution'. Dr Ambedkar thus gave something to all the stakeholders present. In the process, he added terms that could not have been anticipated: 'fraternity', 'dignity' and 'caste'.

From the 'proposed preamble' of *States and Minorities,* we see how the impulse arose for Dr Ambedkar to add to the Nehruvian phrase 'to secure to', the more active supplement of 'or promote among'. If you recall, where Nehru's Objectives Resolution spoke of securing justice (social, economic and political), Dr Ambedkar reshaped the role of the state into a more active one—to remove social, political and economic inequalities, which it would do by promoting affirmative action policies, and hence, Dr Ambedkar's introduction of the word 'caste'.

Footnotes and Further Concessions

The committee met again on 9 February 1948, with the same people present as in the previous meeting. This time, the draft of Dr Ambedkar's preamble was up for debate. Concessions seem to have been granted by Dr Ambedkar to both the left and the right wings, specifically, to the expression 'without distinction of caste or creed' the leftist notion of 'class' was inserted, and to the expression 'dignity of every individual' the nationalist idea of 'unity of the nation' was added. However, both of these ostensible concessions actually had histories within

Dr Ambedkar's own thought and work. 'Class' had always been his foremost concern, as was clear from his assiduous efforts at leading the Independent Labour Party, his labour law reforms, and a lot more that is outlined in the next chapter. As for the call for the unity of the nation, this was a constant demand with Dr Ambedkar throughout the period that the Constituent Assembly existed. But, as we shall later learn, what Dr Ambedkar understood by the term 'nation' was quite unique.

The amended draft preamble, as of 9 February 1948, read:

> . . . and to secure to all its citizens: Justice, social, economic and political; Liberty of thought, expression, belief, faith, worship, vocation, association and action; Equality of status, and of opportunity; and to promote among all its citizens, Fraternity, without distinction of caste, *class* or creed, so as to assure the dignity of every individual *and the unity of the nation* . . .[28]

The following day, the same sparsely attended committee meeting again took up the preamble. No changes were made to the text, but it was decided to append a footnote to the preamble clarifying that 'the Committee has followed the Objectives Resolution in drafting the Preamble.'[29] Presumably, this was only for the benefit of the Constituent Assembly and there was no serious intention for our Constitution's Preamble to be annotated! There are, as B.N. Rau would have surely interjected, no known constitutional preambles anywhere in the world with footnotes.

The next two Drafting Committee meetings, on 11 and 13 February 1948, welcomed even fewer members. N. Madhava Rao did not attend, leaving only Dr Ambedkar and two others discussing the draft. There is, very mysteriously, no mention of the preamble in these minutes.

The Final Version and Changes None

During the 21 February 1948 closing meeting of the committee, on the day that Dr Ambedkar forwarded the draft Constitution to the president of the Constituent Assembly, some more changes were made to the draft preamble, mostly terms being deleted for simplification.[30] The version sent to the Constituent Assembly read:

> WE, THE PEOPLE OF INDIA, having solemnly resolved to constitute India into a SOVEREIGN DEMOCRATIC REPUBLIC and to secure to all its citizens: JUSTICE, social, economic and political; LIBERTY of thought, expression, belief, faith, and worship; EQUALITY of status and of opportunity; and to promote among them all FRATERNITY assuring the dignity of the individual and the unity of the nation . . ..[31]

This version was not significantly different from the radically innovative text that Dr Ambedkar had originally penned and introduced on 6 February 1948, totally out of the blue. And as difficult as it may be to believe, this 21 February 1948 version turned out to be the final version adopted nearly two years later, on 26 January 1950. The Constitution, including its Preamble, was discussed, criticized and debated across three separate readings by the Constituent Assembly throughout 1948 and 1949. However, no amendments were accepted by the Drafting Committee and ultimately no changes were made to it at all.[32]

Why Dr Ambedkar's Preamble?

The CAD did throw up some important points, both in their appreciation as well as their critique of Dr Ambedkar's draft.

These will be taken up in the chapters that follow. For now, we have traced the evolution of the Preamble itself, and in so doing, it has become apparent that the Preamble to the Constitution of India is Dr Ambedkar's preamble.

It is Dr Ambedkar's preamble not only because of the processes by which it came to be, but also because of its conceptual content—it is Dr Ambedkar's preamble both procedurally and substantively. Unlike for B.N. Rau, or even for Nehru, each and every one of its central concepts—justice, liberty, equality, fraternity, dignity and nation—has a decisive and inimitable provenance in Dr Ambedkar's writings and speeches. This is not only true for the concepts that were unique to his draft, and used almost exclusively by him, but also for the ones that had made appearances in earlier sources like the Objectives Resolution. As it turned out, the new concepts that Dr Ambedkar introduced altered the centre of gravity for all of the previously appearing concepts too.

In what follows, we shall discover exactly why and how this came to be. Through six eponymous chapters, this book gives voice to the secret backstories of these six constitutional (or, to use the better though uglier term, 'preambular') concepts. Together, we will uncover little-known aspects of modern Indian intellectual and constitutional history, and spotlight moments of Dr Ambedkar's revolutionary social, political and jurisprudential thought, hitherto hidden from conventional accounts.

1

Justice: The Story of B.R. Ambedkar

On 21 February 1948, Dr Ambedkar, in his capacity as chairman of the Drafting Committee, was ready to submit the first draft Constitution that had been prepared over the forty-two sittings. The meetings began on 27 October 1947, the first since the one on 30 August when Dr Ambedkar had been elected chairman. He sent it to the president of the Constituent Assembly, Rajendra Prasad, who had it widely published on 26 February, so that interested members of the public could consider it. The draft was also sent to all members of the Constituent Assembly, asking them to submit their views by 22 March 1948. A number of amendments were suggested, some specific to the Preamble, but not one of them was about the concept of justice.

The Drafting Committee reconvened on 23, 24 and 27 March 1948 to evaluate the many comments and suggested amendments they had received. Since the committee had introduced both phraseology and substance that seemed to depart from the Constituent Assembly's earlier decisions, president Prasad decided to assemble a high-powered Special Committee to look carefully into the matters in question—the draft Constitution, the numerous amendments suggested, the Drafting Committee's opinions on them, and so on. The Special Committee was chaired by Jawaharlal Nehru and consisted of the who's who of the Constituent Assembly. It included members of the Drafting Committee, of course, but also principal members of the Union Constitution Committee, as well as the Provincial Constitution Committee. Meeting on 10 and 11 April 1948, many of the names who subsequently enlivened the CAD included Bhogaraju Pattabhi Sitaramayya, Khushal Talaksi Shah, Jivatram Bhagwandas Kripalani, Kanaiyalal Maneklal Munshi, Thakur Das Bhargava, and, of course, B.R. Ambedkar, who never missed a Drafting Committee or related meeting. Also present was Naziruddin Ahmad, whose suspicion that the Drafting Committee was prone to taking 'secret' and unilateral decisions was now beginning to crystalize.

The minutes of the Special Committee meeting on 10 April 1948 were unusually curious. They began:

> The committee considered the matters referred to in the letter of the Chairman of the Drafting Committee to the President of the Constituent Assembly of India, dated the 21st February 1948.
>
> Preamble: The consideration of the amendments to the Preamble was held over and it was decided that the final settlement of the Preamble should be left to the decision of the Constituent Assembly.[1]

This was unusual because the entire reason behind assembling the Special Committee was to try and scrutinize the changes that the Drafting Committee had introduced to the draft Constitution, one of the most crucial being the unanimously adopted Objectives Resolution. As we shall soon discover, one of the earliest points in Dr Ambedkar's letter to the president of the Constituent Assembly was to do with the unilateral changes introduced by the Drafting

Committee into the Preamble. It appears that Nehru was true to his word and that he ensured—rather to the displeasure of Naziruddin Ahmad—that the Drafting Committee was given the latitude to adapt the Objectives Resolution to the changing times.

But as far as the formulation of the 'justice' clause was concerned, Dr Ambedkar's letter indicated no departure from the Constituent Assembly's decisions and there were no suggested amendments to this clause for the Special Committee to consider.

Indeed, throughout the numerous Constituent Assembly Debates on the draft Constitution in general, and the Preamble in particular, no member specifically targeted the line on 'Justice, social, economic and political', at least not for rephrasing. There were critiques that the terms needed fleshing out, that they were unsubstantial; but such critiques were grounded precisely on the tripartite expression of justice, demanding that each of the terms—social, economic and political—be accorded full strength in equal measure, rather than on any demand to dismantle the phraseology.

A distinguished member of the Drafting Committee, Alladi Krishnaswami Ayyar (known as a brilliant legal mind, and who was a member of eight other committees apart from the Drafting Committee, including the Advisory Committee and the Sub-Committee on Fundamental Rights), defended the clause robustly:

> There was a further comment as to the reference to 'justice, social, economic and political' being too thin. The expression 'justice, social, economic and political', while not committing this country and the Assembly to any particular form of polity coming under any specific designation, is intended to emphasize the fundamental aim of every democratic State in the present day. The Constitution framed will, I have no doubt, contain

> the necessary elements of growth and adjustment needed for a progressive society.[2]

The Constituent Assembly agreed. The clause stood as is.

The 42nd Amendment

It was not until 1976, when a bill on the 42nd Amendment to the Constitution was introduced in the Lok Sabha, that any suggestions for rephrasing the 'justice' clause were raised. The amendment added three terms to the Preamble: 'secular', 'socialist' and 'integrity', giving us the Preamble as we know it today. It began:

> WE, THE PEOPLE OF INDIA, having solemnly resolved to constitute India into a SOVEREIGN SOCIALIST SECULAR DEMOCRATIC REPUBLIC and to secure to all its citizens JUSTICE, social, economic and political . . .

This meant that, in the end, no change was made to the 'justice' clause, despite several motions coming up in both the Lok Sabha and Rajya Sabha, even in 1976.

For the most part, all of these rejected motions had sought to add more layers to species of justice beyond social, economic and political, or more elaborate specifications of how that justice was to be realized.

For example, some members proposed adding the term 'religious', so that the 'justice' clause would read: 'Justice, social, political, economic and religious'. Others sought to add substantively to the clause, so that after 'Justice, social, economic and political' various modifying clauses would be added, such as: 'thereby creating a social order in which there would be no unemployment', or 'the State shall ensure equality of educational opportunities', or 'thereby creating a social order in which there shall be no distinction made by the State between citizen and citizen . . .'.[3] Again, none of these amendments were accepted and the Preamble was only amended to add the three terms mentioned above.

Ambedkar's Authority

Returning to the focus on Dr Ambedkar's preamble, it was remarkable, at least at first blush, that Dr Ambedkar had no problem with the formulation of the 'justice' clause. At least it would seem remarkable from the point of view of so many intellectuals, politicians and activists who routinely attributed the origination of the tripartite division of justice (as social, economic and political) to Dr Ambedkar. As we have seen, this formulation dates back to before Nehru's own 'resolution' to the 'declaration' upon which the Objectives Resolution was based; indeed, it went back to before the 'declaration' too, as the expression 'justice, social, economic and political' was believed to have been a catchphrase of the Russian Revolution of 1917. The next chapter will illustrate how the tripartite division of justice, sourced from the Russian Revolution, had parallels with the tripartite articulation of social democracy as consisting of liberty, equality and fraternity, which was borrowed from the French Revolution.

That Dr Ambedkar enjoyed full authority to alter the 'justice' clause hardly seems contentious. With so few members in attendance, and with so much of the responsibility for the drafting falling upon his shoulders, the minutes of the Drafting Committee often revealed that on several clauses, especially those wherein the Congress did not have vested interests, Dr Ambedkar's word was law. This is corroborated through numerous accounts of the process, both in terms of drafting and later in terms of the follow-up with the Constituent Assembly:

> Several members of the drafting committee used to remain absent to many meetings and Dr Ambedkar had to shoulder considerable burden of the responsibility. His work did not end with preparing the lengthy draft; he had to reply to debates in the Constituent Assembly. He had to decide whether to accept or reject amendments suggested during the article-wise discussions; many times, new phrases were put forward which had to be taken into consideration. The Constituent Assembly was a legislative body; and to pilot such a huge piece of legislation through the extensive debates, responding to various points and winning approval, was perhaps a record performance.[4]

It is therefore suggestive that Dr Ambedkar left the justice clause untouched. Despite being rightly regarded as the preeminent advocate of social justice in India in the twentieth century, he had no special conceptual fascination for the term 'justice'. At one point, in fact, he stated prosaically, 'In short, justice is simply another name for liberty, equality, and fraternity.'[5] Throughout the voluminous writings and speeches of Dr Ambedkar, he nowhere seeks to technically or too rigidly define the meaning of 'justice' as a term of art, which was not the case with other terms like 'dignity', 'nation', 'fraternity', and so on. He used the term as frequently as he used its opposite—injustice—but his usage for the most part relied upon the general understanding: he spoke of 'injustice' as a harm one suffered. As for justice, on the one hand he spoke of it often in its legal sense, as in legal remedy and 'doing justice to X'; and, on the other hand, he spoke of justice in the political sense, as aspirational, what inspires us to engage politically, and as a feeling or moral sense, that which motivates us to act.

Justice was not by any means merely affective for Dr Ambedkar. The specifications and determinations of the meaning, and the urgent necessity of social justice, economic justice and political justice have been spelt out in numerous places throughout Dr Ambedkar's works. There is an abundance of literature available on his conception of social justice, and to some extent economic justice and political justice. What Dr Ambedkar's writings and their numerous expositions in the secondary literature[6] show is that for him the demands of justice dictate proactive and long-arm policies of the state, implemented by coordinated institutions at several levels simultaneously; not passivity and neutrality.

Political Justice

Justice is a complex and multifaceted concept, and none of its components or constituent aspects are necessarily exclusive of the others. If we distinguish political justice from social, legal, economic or gender justice, it is only for the sake of focus and spotlight, and not because of any sort of essentialist claim. Political justice is not axenic, but it does evoke a general range of broadly definable concerns. For example, some questions central to political justice include:

a. What are the basic political rights of individuals, or of communities?
b. What is the proper role of government or the state?
c. What are the basic principles of democracy?
d. Why are all citizens equal and in what ways should that equality be manifested?

e. When is political power legitimate or illegitimate, and what duties do those enjoying power have?
f. Should some political communities be superior to others?

Dr Ambedkar addressed each of these and some related questions about political justice throughout his works. A few of his salient texts include his early 'Evidence before the Southborough Committee' (1919); his speech at the Round Table Conference (1930); *Annihilation of Caste* (1936); *What Congress and Gandhi Have Done to the Untouchables* (1945); *States and Minorities: What Are Their Rights and How to Secure Them in the Constitution of Free India* (1947); *Thoughts on Linguistic States* (1955); and the lecture titled 'Buddha and Karl Marx' (1956).[7]

Dr Ambedkar was deeply committed to democratic modes of resolving social and political disagreements. He understood democracy to be a political association of equal and free citizens engaged in the process of defining itself in the indefinite future. He was committed to designing democratic institutions for post-colonial India as a politician, lawyer and, of course, as the chairperson of the Drafting Committee.

Social Justice and Economic Justice

We know that Dr Ambedkar was widely regarded as the preeminent authority in modern India when it came to social justice. Since his first academic writing, *Castes in India: Their Mechanism, Genesis and Development*, to his powerful booklet *Annihilation of Caste*, to his more reflective writings like *Philosophy of Hinduism*,[8] right up to the essays and speeches till the end of his life, Dr Ambedkar was incessantly preoccupied with social justice, the ways to achieving it, and the social and ideological, and political and economic, hindrances. With respect to the fundamental issues of social justice, Dr Ambedkar's preoccupations during the first half of the twentieth century remain our preoccupations in the first half of the twenty-first century.

And while social justice was his concern all along, it was actually economic justice (and legal justice) that were closer to the primary areas of his academic expertise and training. Although Dr Ambedkar was a polymath who made pioneering innovative contributions to fields as diverse as political science, sociology, historiography, religious studies, and so on, law and economics were the two disciplines in which he was formally credentialed. Among other degrees, Dr Ambedkar earned an MSc and DSc in economics, as well as the Bar-at-Law (barrister) degree.

Over the course of his life and vocation, Dr Ambedkar's understanding of the nature of economic justice evolved, but his commitment to it never faltered. He envisaged a proactive role for the state and public policy to intervene in order to support the disadvantaged and marginalized sections. While he supported the state's intervention in the economy, he also stressed the need to adopt strong policies for affirmative action that would reshape the state and make it representative, responsive and accountable.

While, as mentioned before, Dr Ambedkar was concerned about the terminology of liberty, equality and fraternity, he was not concerned—at any point during the drafting or finalizing of the Preamble—with modifying the justice clause's components of social, economic and political justice. The reason for raising this point here is that there is a very real sense in which the notion of justice, for Dr Ambedkar, got spelt out robustly, not by tracing the conceptual history of the term within his lifetime of writings and speeches but by bearing witness to his life itself—his labour, work and action, which cannot be better characterized than as a lifelong quest for justice.

Hence, to get a proper sense of the man behind the Preamble, we shall now turn to a brief outline of the biography of the Constitution's chief architect. We shall do so through a chronology that periodically overlaps and intersects with, and therefore fleshes out, the epoch—from 26 January 1930 to 26 January 1950—that was detailed in the Introduction.

Living Justice

Dr Ambedkar's life offered unique vantage points for sustained reflection on the concerns of justice and its connection to other human values. His story perfectly depicted an irrepressible spirit on a lifelong, contagiously inspiring quest. Ironically, Dr Ambedkar's comprehensive life story actually remains untold in the English language. While Marathi biographies are more complete, textured and nuanced, for Anglophone readers there are just two main approaches to telling Dr Ambedkar's story. The first approach has been reverential, if not hagiographic, (e.g., Gail Omvedt's *Ambedkar: Towards an Enlightened India*).[9] For readers who are already sympathetic to Dr Ambedkar and what he stood for, accounts such as these are wonderful and worthwhile. However, for those who are resistant to aspects of the Ambedkarite movement, hagiographic biographies fail to provide a neutral and objective foundation for them to comfortably stand on, and are indeed no hook at all for bringing them into the fold of sympathizers.

The second approach is the polar opposite of the first: callous character assassination (e.g., Arun Shourie's *Worshipping False Gods*).[10] The appeal of the second approach is utterly baffling to anyone informed about the life of Dr Ambedkar. This approach actually feeds upon, and is fuelled by, the absence of widespread information about him. What we require is a vivid life portrait of this foremost persona of the twentieth century, a personality-driven narrative covering the period from his birth to death, along with salient aspects of his contemporary legacy, in order to lay bare the bold and inspirational nature of his story, revealing the blood with which the Preamble was written. Unfortunately, no such thing can even be remotely approximated here. Here, we can at most signal to a few select events from Dr Ambedkar's profoundly consequential life. His life was riveting, one that often seemed to unfold as a series of trials and struggles; it was a tale of his remarkable tenacity and talent that led to, in nearly all cases, his eventual triumph. In this way, Dr Ambedkar's story was exemplary, much like the Preamble that can be seen to distil it.

It is interesting to note at the outset that in many ways the world was both ready, and not ready, for Dr Ambedkar. He had his predecessors in nineteenth-century social reformers such as Mahadev Govind Ranade, Pandita Ramabai and Jyotirao Phule. In this respect the world was ready for him. However, Dr Ambedkar profoundly intensified, radicalized and widened their critiques, channelling social action into other domains, disrupting them—political, juridical, economic, historiographical, sociological, religious—for this, the world was clearly not ready for him. In some certain respects, it remains unready for him even today.

From Young Bhim[11] to Dr Ambedkar

Sometime around 1935, Dr Ambedkar wrote about thirty pages of an unfinished autobiography, now known as *Waiting for a Visa*.[12] It consisted of a series of brief stories about the discrimination and humiliation that he suffered throughout his childhood and early years. Several of these motifs (e.g., inability to find drinking water, exclusion from school) eventually transformed into major issues that the mature Dr Ambedkar addressed structurally and nationally.

There were also signs of things to come during the school years (1900–08), when Dr Ambedkar graduated from Elphinstone School to Elphinstone College. Noteworthy was young Bhim's defiance of his casteist college teacher who told him that the Mahars (the 'untouchable' caste to which Dr Ambedkar belonged) had no business seeking higher education. Within fifteen years of that early confrontation, Dr Ambedkar emerged as the most highly educated Indian in pre-Independence history, eventually earning advanced degrees from Columbia University and the London School of Economics.

It is worth pausing for a moment to speak about Dr Ambedkar's years at Columbia University, because of how central they turned out to be for his intellectual trajectory.[13] In 1930, reflecting on his time in New York City, Dr Ambedkar wrote, 'The best friends I have had in my life were some of my classmates at Columbia and my great professors, John Dewey, James Shotwell, Edwin Seligman and James Harvey Robinson.'[14] Among these great professors, the most lasting influence was certainly that of the pragmatist philosopher John Dewey.[15]

Decades after he was in New York City, having attained international acclaim for his work on the Constitution of India, Dr Ambedkar was invited by Columbia University in June 1952 to receive an honorary doctorate. He was particularly looking forward to meeting John Dewey. But as luck would have it, Dewey died on 2 June 1952, while Dr Ambedkar was transiting through Rome on his way to New York City. As Ambedkar wrote in a poignant letter to his wife, 'I am so sorry. I owe all my intellectual life to him. He was a wonderful man.'[16]

After Dr Ambedkar returned to India in 1917, with his years at Columbia University and London School of Economics behind him, he began working in the service of Baroda state to repay the scholarship he had received for studying abroad. Due to caste prejudice, he was unable to find a room to even sleep in. He finally had to pose as a Parsi to be given access to a rat-infested attic. However, he soon had to flee from there after an encounter with an armed Parsi mob that had discovered his deception. He left Baroda immediately and returned to Bombay (now Mumbai).

Back in Bombay, Dr Ambedkar joined the faculty of Sydenham College as a professor of political economy. But despite his academic credentials far exceeding that of the other faculty members, he suffered constant humiliation and was asked not to use the same utensils as the rest of the staff. In 1919, he gave evidence before the Southborough Committee regarding franchise. In doing so, he attracted the attention of the Prince of Kolhapur, Chattrapati Shahu Maharaj, who offered him financial assistance. Dr Ambedkar was thus able to launch his fortnightly *Mook Nayak*, and began organizing large-scale conferences, such as the All-India Depressed Classes Conference in Nagpur.

With the money saved from his salary and assistance from Shahu Maharaj, Dr Ambedkar was finally able to return to London in 1920 to earn his MSc and DSc (Economics), as well as his law degree. He also did a stint in Germany (Bonn and Berlin) to learn Sanskrit as he knew that doing so in India would have been impossible for him.

After completing his formal education, Dr Ambedkar returned to Bombay once again, where he sought to start a legal practice but did not have the money to pay the registration fee of the Bombay High Court. His friend Naval Bhatena loaned him the required 500 rupees. Dr Ambedkar then took on some noteworthy cases, often hopeless ones where he championed the underdog. This led him into early conflict with some prominent and powerful people, including Bal Gangadhar Tilak.

With the cooperation of Gandhian satyagrahi P.N. Rajbhoj and others, Dr Ambedkar launched a series of satyagrahas, including the monumental march to Mahad (in present-day Maharashtra) in 1927 to allow untouchables to drink from the public well, and several important temple-entry campaigns (e.g., Kalaram Temple Satyagraha). He was shocked to realize that far from receiving the support he was promised from the INC, some party members actually sabotaged his satyagrahas. In another related landmark event in 1927, Dr Ambedkar publicly burnt the *Manusmriti*. He also launched the newspaper *Bahishkrut Bharat*, through which the word 'Dalit' began to gain prominence.

In 1927, Dr Ambedkar was appointed as a member of the legislative assembly (MLA) from Bombay Province for five years (it was renewed in 1932 for another five years). In this capacity, he submitted a statement before the Simon Commission on 29 May 1928. It is noteworthy because it was a radical departure from all other submissions by pontificating on the nature of constitutional democracy and within that framework highlighting the plight of untouchables. This was the launch of the era of his political prominence.

Dr Ambedkar's strong performance while representing the 'depressed classes' at the 1930 Round Table Conference in London catapulted him on to the national, and indeed the international, stage. The second Round Table Conference in 1931 saw the beginning of the lifelong feud between M.K. Gandhi and Dr Ambedkar. The Communal Award that Dr Ambedkar had fought so hard for at the Round Table Conference was granted in 1932, providing for a scheme of separate electorates for the untouchables. Gandhi resorted to a fast-unto-death against the award, which placed Dr Ambedkar in an impossible predicament.

Blackmailed into it, Dr Ambedkar signed a pact with Gandhi in 1932, with terms that were quite disagreeable to him. Dr Ambedkar thus characterized Gandhi not as Mahatma, but as a dangerous opponent, famously quipping about this period that Gandhi 'showed me his fangs'.

Dr Ambedkar's Gandhi[17]

> I know Gandhi better than his disciples. They came to him as devotees and saw only the Mahatma. I was an opponent, and I saw the bare man in him. He showed me his fangs.[18]

Gandhi's relationship with other epoch-makers of his time, be it allies like Jawaharlal Nehru, friends like Rabindranath Tagore, or antagonistic rivals like Muhammad Ali Jinnah, was never straightforward, uncomplicated, or free of turbulence. Among the most controversial relationships was that between Gandhi and Dr Ambedkar. Scrutinizing it is of crucial importance to arrive at a proper understanding of both these pioneering figures, despite their notorious rivalry. As Upendra Baxi put it, 'our understanding of leading historic figures like Gandhi or Nehru is bound to remain incomplete, both in the sense of biography and history, in the absence of the grasp of their relations with Ambedkar.'[19]

The rivalry between Gandhi and Dr Ambedkar lives on through polemics in street-corner debates, newspaper columns, blogs, books, documentaries, theatre plays, and so on, often with aggressive insults parlayed between the pro-Ambedkar, anti-Gandhi group, and the pro-Gandhi, anti-Ambedkar group. Indeed, the numerous differences between Gandhi and Dr Ambedkar during their own lifetimes are always evoked in support of the currently sustained enmity between their followers.

Ramachandra Guha has well capsulated many of the differences between Gandhi and Dr Ambedkar:

> Gandhi wished to save Hinduism by abolishing untouchability, whereas Ambedkar saw a solution for his people outside the fold of the dominant religion of the Indian people. Gandhi was a rural romantic, who wished to make the self-governing village the bedrock of free India; Ambedkar an admirer of city life and modern technology who dismissed the Indian village as a den of iniquity. Gandhi was a crypto-anarchist who favoured non-violent protest while being suspicious of the state; Ambedkar a steadfast constitutionalist, who worked within the state and sought solutions to social problems with the aid of the state.[20]

What Guha has captured here would seem to be the bases for a perfectly amicable dispute. The Gandhi–Ambedkar dispute was far from cordial. It was, at times, an existential battle, a life-or-death struggle.

The 1932 Poona Pact remained a thorn in Dr Ambedkar's side until he died and the details of its unfolding continue to irk Dalits and Ambedkarites till date, and for good reason. Gandhi's fast in defiance of the communal voting rights that the British had awarded to the untouchables presented Dr Ambedkar with an agonizing dilemma. He had to choose between letting Gandhi starve to death in order to permit the untouchable communities to retain essential voting privileges within democratic elections or giving in to Gandhi's demand of undivided general elections for the untouchables, thereby undermining their political representation but saving Gandhi's life.

Ultimately, Dr Ambedkar gave in to Gandhi, the Poona Pact was signed and Gandhi broke his fast. After this, Dr Ambedkar understandably became increasingly bitter towards Gandhi's movement and his biopolitical methods.

Many historians view this unfortunate event as the paradigmatic conflict between Gandhi and Dr Ambedkar. In reality, the situation is far more complicated.[21] In an interview for BBC radio in 1955, Dr Ambedkar, nearing the end of his life, spoke candidly about Gandhi, withholding none of the acrimony that had accumulated over the years. Answering the interviewer's question, 'So you would say Gandhi was an orthodox Hindu?' he answered:

> Yes, he was absolutely an orthodox Hindu. He was never a reformer. He has no dynamics in him, you see. All this talk about untouchability was just for the purpose of making the untouchables drawn into the Congress; that was one thing. And secondly, he wanted that the untouchables would not oppose his movement of Swaraj. I don't think beyond that he had any motive of uplift.[22]

In the same interview, he characterized Gandhi as a cunning politician, rather than as a mahatma. He suggested that Gandhi's decisions and declarations about the untouchables were based on calculated politics rather than appreciation of the inherent injustices of the caste system and the urgent humanitarian need to address it. As far as Dr Ambedkar saw it, Gandhi's deeper motivation was to pack together Hindus by including the numerous scheduled castes within this section, as against independent communities like Sikhs and Muslims.

For his part, Gandhi sought without success to continue to lure Dr Ambedkar into his own fold. In a letter to Dr Ambedkar (dated 6 August 1944), Gandhi wrote:

> I know to my cost that you and I hold different views on this very important question [i.e. untouchability]. And I know, too, that on broad politics of the country we see things from different angles. I would love to find a meeting ground between us on both the questions. I know your great ability and I would love to own you as a colleague and co-worker.
>
> But I must admit my failure to come nearer to you. If you can show me a way to a common meeting ground between us I would like to see it. Meanwhile, I must reconcile myself to the present unfortunate difference.[23]

As is apparent from Dr Ambedkar's 1955 assessment, the 'present unfortunate difference' to which Gandhi had to reconcile was not reconciled in any subsequent events. The politics of the era pitted Gandhi and Dr Ambedkar as antagonists on too many issues, and on issues so crucial to their persons and personalities that bridging the divide remained impossible.

Dr Ambedkar firmly believed that Gandhi was attached to an idealized version of the varna system, a system against which he was inalterably and profoundly opposed, and was intent on completely annihilating. Dr Ambedkar's systematic polemic writings against Gandhi, including *Mr Gandhi and the Emancipation of the Untouchables* and *What Congress and Gandhi Have Done to the Untouchables*,[24] were full of citations about Gandhi on the question of varna, quoted with venomous disdain and contempt. He sketched the progression of Gandhi's ideas on the subject from his early South Africa days to the end of his life, attempting to show that Gandhi's subtle differentiation between caste and varna amounted to mere rhetoric.

Moreover, in the starkest possible contrast to Gandhi's romanticist nostalgia for a pre-modern organization of human social and political economy, Dr Ambedkar was an irrepressible pro-enlightenment modernist. This difference was not simply theoretical, but practical in every way. Indeed, it even became a fundamental issue in the framing of the Constitution.

In the Constituent Assembly

As mentioned at the outset, the draft Constitution prepared by the Drafting Committee on 21 February 1948 was sent to the Constituent Assembly and wider public for comments. It underwent a great deal of scrutiny through various bodies and the newly established Special Committee (which met from 10 to 11 April 1948). The Drafting Committee met again between 18 and 20 October to assess all the new submissions and decisions of the Special Committee. After all these processes were completed, the draft Constitution was resubmitted to the Constituent Assembly—along with all collated suggestions and related notes—on 4 November 1948 in a motion by Dr Ambedkar that inaugurated the first reading of the draft Constitution (from 4 to 9 November 1948). One of the primary concerns throughout the debates of the first reading was the failure of the draft Constitution to reflect Gandhian thought, especially the centrality of his ideal village republic.

As will be explored in the next chapter, Gandhianism was a spectre that haunted the CAD. The very day that the Constituent Assembly convened for the first reading, its president, Rajendra Prasad, began the proceedings with what was apparently a mandatory homage to the 'Father of the Nation'. The CAD transcript runs:

> Honourable Members, before we take up the items on the Order Paper, I bid you to rise in your places to pay our tribute of homage and reverence to the Father of the Nation who

> breathed life into our dead flesh and bones, who lifted us out of darkness of despondency and despair to the light and sunshine of hope and achievement and who led us from slavery to freedom. May his spirit continue to guide us. May his life and teaching be the torchlight to take us further on to our goal.[25]

In his address on 4 November 1948, Dr Ambedkar gently explained to the assembly that village and district panchayats were not taken as the fundamental basis because members of the Constituent Assembly, in the written submissions received throughout 1948, had recorded adverse opinions regarding grounding all authority in them. Then, dropping this gentler cover under the jurisprudential aspect, in open defiance of the 'Father of the Nation who breathed life into our dead flesh and bones', Dr Ambedkar proffered his own assessment of the Indian village that was in total contrast to that of Gandhi's. He stated that village republics cannot be justified only because of their longevity, that 'the village is a sink of localism, a den of ignorance, narrow mindedness and communalism.'[26]

Many Gandhians within the Constituent Assembly were shocked, and throughout the ensuing days of the first reading, Dr Ambedkar's remarks were critiqued relentlessly. Constituent Assembly member Damodarswarup Seth typified the criticisms while moving an amendment to the draft Constitution:

> I want to ask whether there is any mention of villages and any place for them in the structure of this great Constitution. No, nowhere. The constitution of a free country should be based on 'local self-government'. We see nothing of local self-government anywhere in this Constitution. This Constitution as a whole, instead of being evolved from our life and reared

> from the bottom upwards is being imported from outside and built above downwards . . .
>
> Mahatma Gandhi emphasized the fact that too much centralization of power makes that power totalitarian and takes it towards fascist ideals.[27]

From early works like *Hind Swaraj* to those near the turn of the century to later writings on 'village swaraj', Gandhi maintained a utopian village ideal as the apogee of Indian life. Aiming to convince the CWC that was working on the 1946 'declaration' which would give shape to the basic orientation of the Constitution, Gandhi wrote to Nehru: 'You will not understand me if you think that I am talking about the villages of today . . . My villages . . . exist in my imagination':[28]

> My idea of Village Swaraj is that it is a complete republic, independent of its neighbours for its own vital wants and inter-dependent for many others in which dependence is a necessity. Thus every village's first concern will be to grow its own food crop and cotton for its cloth. It could have a reserve for its cattle, recreation and playground for adults and children. Then if there is more land available, it will grow useful money crops, thus excluding ganja, tobacco, opium and the like. The village will maintain a village theatre, school and public hall. It will have its own water works ensuring clean water supply.[29]

The real village and the village of Gandhi's imagination differed analogously to the way that caste, as it was practised, and Gandhi's ideal of *varnashrama* did. Obviously, Dr Ambedkar was not convinced by either. For Dr Ambedkar, and Nehru shared much with Dr Ambedkar on this, the Indian village was precisely characterized as 'a sink of localism, a den of ignorance, narrow-mindedness, and communalism'.

Further, with regard to Dr Ambedkar and Gandhi's rival conceptions about the causes and cures of the 'disease of untouchability', the former sought to underscore the reality of social life in Gandhi's 'so-called republic':

> Indian villages represent a kind of colonialism of the Hindus designed to exploit the untouchables. The untouchables have no rights. They are there only to wait, serve and submit. They are there to do or to die. They have no rights because they are outside the village republic and they are outside the so-called republic because they are outside the Hindu fold. This is a vicious circle.[30]

In absolute contrast to Gandhi, Dr Ambedkar viewed the village as paradigmatic of the oppressive social system and the lack of social, political and economic mobility of the untouchables. While Gandhi portrayed the village in utopian terms, Ambedkar portrayed it as a prison and ghetto:

> The Hindu society insists on segregation of the untouchables. The Hindu will not live in the quarters of the untouchables and will not allow the untouchables to live inside the Hindu quarters . . . It is . . . a cordon sanitaire putting the impure people inside the barbed wire into a sort of cage. Every Hindu village has a ghetto. The Hindus live in the village and the untouchables live in the ghetto.[31]

Gandhi and Dr Ambedkar remained fixed in these fundamental beliefs. Thus, although both of them understood themselves to be champions of the emancipation of the untouchables, their conceptions *from what* and *into what* the untouchables were being emancipated were radically and fundamentally at odds.

Despite this, many scholars believe that Gandhi's ideas came closer to Dr Ambedkar towards the last decade of his life. Harold G. Coward claimed that because 'of continually having to contend with Ambedkar's critique' Gandhi's ideas on the political activity of the untouchables and indeed his ideas on varna changed from the 1940s.[32] Coward specially mentioned Gandhi's support for appointing Dr Ambedkar to chair the Constituent Assembly's constitutional Drafting Committee, even in the face of opposition from Congress leaders smarting under Dr Ambedkar's incessant criticisms, as well as sundry remarks made by Gandhi, such as appointing a 'chaste and brave Bhangi girl' as President of the new India.

These and similar arguments about Gandhi's changing position towards the end of his life raise perhaps a reasonable doubt about the issue of varnashrama constituting one of the principal bedrocks for the irreconcilability of Gandhi and Dr Ambedkar. But one cannot fail to mention that Dr Ambedkar himself was unconvinced of this argument. Perhaps he deserves the last word over whether his understanding of Gandhi's later position was more reconcilable with his own.

In fairness, it should be noted that a larger share of Gandhians have indeed come over to Dr Ambedkar's position on the need to annihilate caste in order to establish egalitarian justice and, at least in this respect, the contemporary Gandhian and Ambedkarite camps have far less justification for mutual antagonism.

From Dr Ambedkar to Babasaheb

In 1936, Dr Ambedkar wrote a long speech, 'Annihilation of Caste', to address a Lahore-based organization for social reforms. The organization, however, objected to certain passages. Dr Ambedkar later published the controversial speech as a booklet that attracted attention from all corners, also adding fuel to his long-standing debate with Gandhi regarding the casteist nature of Hinduism.

In August 1936, Dr Ambedkar founded the Independent Labour Party (ILP), which was based not on caste but class. He joined hands with the left and attempted to apprise the Marxists about their shared interests. Dr Ambedkar was a champion of labour rights at a time when the concept of workers' rights did not exist. In India, much before other nations even started thinking about instituting just and fair conditions for workers, Dr Ambedkar (back in 1942) successfully led the struggle for reducing working hours from twelve to eight hours. His commitment to labour rights was evident through Article 19(C) of the Constitution that guarantees the fundamental right to form associations or unions.[33]

In November 1939, Dr Ambedkar's ILP floated a bill on 'birth control'. Dr Ambedkar argued that a population policy was necessary for the eradication of poverty. The bill was regarded as scandalous, however, because it spoke explicitly about sexuality and contraception, and received no support from any party other than Dr Ambedkar's own.

He was also inextricably connected with the Reserve Bank of India (RBI). The RBI was created on the basis of guidelines he had presented back in 1925 to the Royal Commission on Indian Currency and Finance, and under the influence of his definitive book *The Problem of the Rupee—Its Problems and Its Solution.*[34]

Around that period, in 1937, the cry of 'Jai Bhim!' was heard for the first time. It was coined by an ILP MLA from Kamptee (Nagpur), Babu L.N. Hardas. The expression remains a mainstay salutation amongst the former Mahar community specifically and can be heard on the lips of Ambedkarites globally.

From Babasaheb to Bodhisattva Ambedkar

Throughout 1946–47, Dr Ambedkar was responsible for establishing the Central Water Irrigation and Navigation Commission. He also played an important role in establishing the Damodar Valley Project, Hirakud Project and the Bansagar Dam. As a child, he was constantly denied drinking water. In Baroda, the office peons refused to give him water. As a faculty member at Sydenham College, he was asked not to drink the water meant for the faculty. He was arrested for drinking water from a Mahad public tank. After all this, in 1947, he acquired the authority to be able to ensure water for everyone. Dr Ambedkar thus was, in some respects, the father of the democratization of water—a concept and concern that has persisted well into the twenty-first century and beyond.

In August 1947, Dr Ambedkar joined the Nehru cabinet as law minister. He had hoped to be given the portfolio for development, so he could pursue projects in electricity, transportation, health, and so on, to improve the quality of life for the millions of destitute. Nevertheless, he accepted the law portfolio, thereby launching his uneasy tenure in the Union cabinet, from which he resigned in protest after four years.

On the personal front, Dr Ambedkar had several health problems by the late 1940s, his loneliness exacerbating them further. In 1948, he married Dr Sharada Kabir (thereafter known as Dr Savita Ambedkar), a physician, who also happened to be a Brahmin. Many members of his community were displeased, and indeed the conspiracy theories surrounding his late, inter-caste marriage continue to proliferate to this day. However, Dr Ambedkar was reported to have taken comfort in the fact that Gandhi would have been proud of his decision.

As law minister, Dr Ambedkar spearheaded the introduction of the Hindu Code Bill that gave rights of inheritance and property ownership to women. Both he and Nehru believed it was a 'vital step in the introduction of true democracy in India, and would remove the practices and the logic that underpinned the caste system'.[35] Yet, all diverse factions from the right united to defeat the bill, as well as to vilify and attack Dr Ambedkar personally. When Nehru himself withdrew support from the bill due to political expediency, Dr Ambedkar resigned from the cabinet.

Dr Ambedkar was one of the most prominent voices advocating the empowerment of women. As far back as his first academic paper (1916), he had addressed the position of women in India. In his later works, he posited a thesis that women traditionally enjoyed a high status in ancient India, but reactionary developments—represented through the patriarchy of the *Manusmriti*—led to a systematic decline of their stature. Thus, women in India were accorded no rights to education, property, or divorce, and were themselves reckoned as property.[36]

In January 1952, Dr Ambedkar was defeated in his bid to becoming a member of Parliament (MP) by N.S. Kajrolkar of the Congress. It appeared that the latter may have enlisted the support of V. Savarkar and the Hindu Mahasabha to ensure Dr Ambedkar's defeat. Shortly before his death, Dr Ambedkar sketched out the constitution for a new national party, the Republican Party of India. Though it made a promising start, soon after his death it split up into a number of factions, remaining heavily splintered even today.

In the final decade of his life, Dr Ambedkar was hard at work on a manuscript that would eventually prove to be one of his most controversial publications, *Riddles in Hinduism*.[37] Although people often consider this as nothing more than a motivated attack on Hinduism, what they fail to understand is that Dr Ambedkar turned his razor-sharp rationalism to Buddhism just as much as he did to Hinduism. His monumental work *The Buddha and His Dhamma*[38] stands testament to his relentless demand that religion be rational and promote values of unity rather than division.

Beginning around 1948, Dr Ambedkar had turned to Buddhism as a personal faith as well as an ideology that offered an alternative to Hinduism. On 14 October 1956, he formally converted to Buddhism, alongside hundreds of thousands of his followers. In doing so, he fulfilled the vow that he had made publicly in Yeola (in present-day Maharashtra) in 1935, that although he was born a Hindu, he would not die a Hindu. To the Navayana, or new, Buddhists, now numbering in the millions, Dr Ambedkar was nothing less than a bodhisattva, leading all towards the path of liberation.

In a touching anecdote, the head of the Western Buddhist Order, Sangharakshita, described his final encounter with Dr Ambedkar shortly before the latter's death. He described Dr Ambedkar as very ill and unable to speak clearly—a shocking change from his usual booming voice. Dr Ambedkar was repeating something in an impassioned manner, but inaudibly, to Sangharakshita. He placed his ear close to Dr Ambedkar's lips to be able to hear what he was saying. Dr Ambedkar's last words to the monk to whom he entrusted the Buddhist education of the hundreds of thousands of new converts were: 'There is still so much to be done . . . So much to be done.'[39]

This life sketch, though incomplete and brief, nevertheless serves to reveal the character, the tenacity, the temperament of B.R. Ambedkar, to whom we owe the Preamble to the Constitution of India. During its drafting, there were terms that Dr Ambedkar felt necessary to insert, and terms that he was comfortable leaving as inherited from previous foundational and historical sources. 'Justice' was one term that he let stand, in the Nehruvian dress that the concept came clothed in.

When first faced with this formulation in 1946, Dr Ambedkar had decided to redraft and reformulate the way the concept of justice was presented. In an effort to frame the Objectives Resolution, Dr Ambedkar had put forth his own 'Proposed Preamble', which although following Nehru in the tripartite division of social, economic and political, gave substantive meaning to the term 'justice' by speaking of the removal of inequalities. That is, where Nehru's text spoke of securing justice, social, economic and political, Dr Ambedkar's text interpreted 'securing justice' to mean *removing* social, political and economic inequalities.

And that was how Dr Ambedkar's life was spent, from an early age until death: fighting to secure justice for the people of India, which is to say, to deploy every means available to him to remove social, political and economic inequalities, especially for minorities and the 'depressed classes' (or Dalits).

Hence, while subjecting the preambular concept of justice to closer scrutiny, I chose to take a detour from its conceptual history and turn instead to Dr Ambedkar's lived experiences. His life was a life lived justly. Beyond simply tracing the concept, the abstract idea of justice, we see in Dr Ambedkar a concrete embodiment of the true meaning of that word.

2

Liberty: Swaraj Is Whose Birthright?

Dr Ambedkar's preamble, which seemed to have appeared out of nowhere on 6 February 1948, was finalized by the Drafting Committee and submitted to the Constituent Assembly. It then underwent scrutiny and critique throughout 1948 from circles both inside and outside the newly emerging corridors of power. The week-long first reading of the draft Constitution (inaugurated by Dr Ambedkar on 4 November 1948 through a motion for its consideration in the Constituent Assembly), debated its broader framework and principles. There were confrontations over the non-Gandhian character of the Constitution, which Dr Ambedkar staunchly defended, with support from Jawaharlal Nehru. The next week, a clause-by-clause reading began. Referred to as the second reading, this session began on 15 November 1948 and continued till 17 October 1949, and saw the once-again amended draft Constitution being scrutinized—this period of the second reading gave us some of the most fascinating discussions of the CAD. The Preamble was taken up for debate not on the first day of the second reading, but on the last, i.e., 17 October 1949.[1]

The 'Freedom' Clause

As mentioned in the previous chapter, the concept of a tripartite formulation of justice had not been commented upon throughout the course of the debates. However, another staple tripartite division (of liberty, equality and fraternity) did invite a number of interventions and proposed amendments. Although Dr Ambedkar had left Nehru's 'justice' clause from the Objectives Resolution untouched, he did tweak the 'freedom' clause. In the Objectives Resolution (adopted on 22 January 1947), the freedom clause read:

> (5) WHEREIN shall be guaranteed and secured to all the people of India . . . freedom of thought, expression, belief, faith, worship, vocation, association and action . . .[2]

In Dr Ambedkar's 'Proposed Preamble' from *States and Minorities* (15 March 1947), there were a couple of clauses that were of potential relevance to the 'freedom' clause of the Preamble to the Indian Constitution. The 'Proposed Preamble' read:

> (ii) To maintain the right of every subject to . . . free speech and free exercise of religion . . .
> (iv) To make it possible for every subject to enjoy freedom from want and freedom from fear . . .[3]

Again, in the final version of the Preamble, as drafted by the Drafting Committee in February 1948 and adopted in November 1949, the 'liberty' clause ultimately read:

> LIBERTY of thought, expression, belief, faith, and worship . . .[4]

So how did the freedom/liberty clause evolve, marking a great departure from its predecessors?

Red Rights or Blue Rights

There were several changes that took place, but the clearest of them all was a rather drastic reduction of the list. Starting with the positive freedoms of thought, expression, belief, faith, worship, vocation, association and action (on Nehru's list), as well as speech and religion (on Dr Ambedkar's list), and adding the negative freedoms from want and fear (on Dr Ambedkar's list), the number of freedoms enumerated in the final Preamble's 'liberty' clause was whittled down from twelve to five, ending with thought, expression, belief, faith and worship. Even if speech and religion are redundant, as expression and faith are synonymous with them, of the ten freedoms and liberties that could have been included, only half made it through.

But the reduction was not really a question of quantity; it was a question of quality, of type. Each of the freedoms and liberties that were removed belonged more to the genre of social freedoms (commonly referred to as red rights), than they did to the genre of political liberties, or blue rights. Freedom of vocation, association, action, freedom from fear and want—these are the freedoms that have traditionally been championed by labour and leftist movements. They are also the ones far more difficult to find remedies for; to understand how to adjudicate.

There were long-running debates within the Constituent Assembly, originating in the Sub-Committee on Fundamental Rights and spilling over into the Constituent Assembly itself. These were to do with problems associated with rights and remedies: which rights ought to be fundamental and which ought to be included into other sections of the Constitution, like the Directive Principles of State Policy. The latter, after tempestuous negotiations, ultimately became a sort of repository for all the articles that were too controversial to achieve large-scale agreement over. The issue was articulated as one where justiciable and non-justiciable rights should be demarcated in the Constitution. Civil and political rights are justiciable, as they mostly require the state to refrain from taking action; but social and economic rights are held by many to be non-justiciable because they require positive action by the state. The majority of the members of the Drafting Committee, including Constitutional Adviser B.N. Rau, favoured the division of these rights. This was how the distinction between fundamental rights and Directive Principles of State Policy happened. The main components of economic justice, and many of social justice, were relegated to the Directive Principles as they were considered too controversial for inclusion into other binding sections of the Constitution. Similarly, the more robust, labour-related freedoms were dropped from their privileged place in the Preamble. Thankfully, however, most of the terms found a place within the body of the Constitution itself, with some eventually being included as fundamental rights.[5]

Freedom or Liberty?

Running parallel to the selection of particular freedoms and liberties, which were largely based on juridical questions—for which rights can people seek remedies in courts, and for which can they not—was the issue of very basic nomenclature that has not been brought out into the light yet. That is, the term that appears in the Preamble is not 'freedom', but 'liberty'. This requires a closer look.

Nehru's Objectives Resolution spoke of freedoms and not liberties, while Dr Ambedkar's 'Proposed Preamble' from *States and Minorities* employed both terms: 'freedom' and 'liberty'.[6] However, as we shall soon see, there was a wider context that urged Dr Ambedkar to ultimately prefer the term 'liberty' over 'freedom'. Indeed, the finally adopted Preamble, diverging from the Objectives Resolution, employed the term 'liberty' in place of 'freedom'.

Why so?

There are two surface explanations: first, as we have ourselves been using the terms, they are largely interchangeable, although they do have their own distinctive etymologies and emerge from different traditions of sociopolitical history and thought ('liberty' is Latinate and 'freedom' Germanic); second, and related, Dr Ambedkar's addition of the term 'fraternity' to the Preamble more or less compelled him to opt for 'liberty' instead of 'freedom', given that with the well-known catchphrase of the French Revolution—*liberté, égalité, fraternité*—it would sound discordant for the Preamble to say 'freedom, equality and fraternity'.

But there are also deeper reasons that explain this.

A 'Gandhian Constitution'

We can begin to discern these reasons by recalling the central contentions of the first reading of the draft Constitution—Gandhian, village-based and Swaraj-focused, as opposed to the Ambedkarian version, which was that of a modern social democracy. The Gandhi–Ambedkar debate began in the 1930s after their clash at the Round Table Conference in London, reached a crescendo with the Poona Pact and was present even during the drafting of the Constitution. It had been Nehru's job, and also that of the other authors of the Objectives Resolution, to preclude the romantic and regressive Gandhian impulses from finding their way into the 'Swaraj' Constitution. However, Dr Ambedkar still had to contend with its fallout, which littered the CAD all through its three readings, spanning over nearly two years.

During one of the interventions of the second reading, when the Preamble was being discussed on 17 October 1949, J.B. Kripalani, a close confidant of Gandhi's and chairman of the Sub-Committee on Fundamental Rights, spoke at length, making the following remarks specifically about the 'liberty' clause:

> I want, at this solemn hour to remind the House that what we have stated in this Preamble are not legal and political principles only. They are also great moral and spiritual principles . . . And I submit that the principle of non-violence, is a moral principle. It is a spiritual principle. It is a mystic principle . . . We have said that we will have liberty of thought, expression, belief, faith and worship. We must understand the implications of this also. All these freedoms can only be guaranteed on the basis of non-violence. If there is violence, you cannot have liberty of thought, you cannot have liberty of expression, you cannot have liberty of faith or liberty of faith or liberty of worship.[7]

Kripalani—'the conscience-keeper of Gandhian principles'[8]—made a rather mild and harmless invocation of the Gandhian backdrop of the freedom struggle, pointing to its spiritual and even mystical qualities. There were far more direct and pointed confrontations within the Constituent Assembly with respect to the need to orient the Constitution back in line with Gandhian ideas. Several of these were to do directly with the Preamble. During the first reading on 4 November 1948, Dr Ambedkar had rejected the clamour of the Gandhians who sought to make the Constitution of free India a Gandhian one, to have it tallying with the Constitution of Gandhi's dreams, the one that had been evoked over and over again since 26 January 1930 (Purna Swaraj

Diwas). Right from 26 January 1930 up to the decision to delay the effectiveness of the Constitution until 26 January 1950, the spirit of the Gandhian Swaraj movement continuously haunted its drafting, even if the spectre of it was recognized as nothing but a hollow threat. Recall how the 4 November 1948 session of the Constituent Assembly began:

> Honourable Members . . . I bid you to rise in your places to pay our tribute of homage and reverence to the Father of the Nation . . . who led us from slavery to freedom. May his spirit continue to guide us.[9]

The conceptual association of 'freedom' with 'Swaraj' was prevalent throughout the first half of the twentieth century. Within this broader historical context, both terms were suspect for Dr Ambedkar. The spiritualization of the concept of 'freedom', by way of its association with the Hindu majoritarian undertones of the nationalist movement put Dr Ambedkar off—whose freedom, whose Swaraj would be won, Dr Ambedkar wondered, as long as the nationalist movement remained ideologically pegged to Brahmanical Hinduism?

Almost a century later, political historians still follow the conceptual pattern that Dr Ambedkar sought to disrupt. For example, observe how political theorist Gurpreet Mahajan launched the chapter on 'Freedom' in her popular 2013 book (*India: Political Ideas and the Making of a Democratic Discourse*) on the core political ideas of modern India:

> For a people living under colonial rule, freedom was a spiritual longing, defining what it means to be a human being. As the social and political conditions for the exercise of the enjoyment of freedom did not exist, this longing often employed a spiritual

> idiom to give voice to an inner desire that remained unrealized, if not stifled, under the British Raj. The desire to be free was not an aspiration to be an autonomous individual, it was the longing to be a self-determining political community, and it was this that was represented through the term *swaraj*.[10]

This spiritualization of freedom grounded its ineluctable association with Swaraj and imbued the idea with a taint of exclusivist Hindu nationalism within the overall discourse of modern India. It was not for nothing that Mahajan's chapter on freedom failed so much as to mention the name B.R. Ambedkar, focusing instead on the likes of Tilak, Aurobindo and Vivekananda, and of course Gandhi.

In very much the same vein, Ananya Vajpeyi's oft-cited book, *Righteous Republic*, focused on Swaraj as being essential to the project of the construction of the Indian Republic.[11] Yet, her chapter on Dr Ambedkar *was totally silent* on his critique of Swaraj. This was despite Vajpeyi's own claim in the Introduction to the book that the term 'Swaraj' was what bound her book together on modern India. As usual, irrespective of the motive, Dr Ambedkar was impossible to integrate into the heart and logical core of spiritualized narratives about Swaraj and the freedom movement. Gurpreet Mahajan too employed that trope, equating freedom for all Indians with the narrower interests of the predominantly Hindu Swaraj movement. She wrote:

> The political freedom that was being desired and fought for was, as Bal Gangadhar Tilak so evocatively put it, one's birthright.[12]

In stark contrast, Dr Ambedkar had once quipped, 'If Tilak had been born among the untouchables, he would not have raised the slogan "Swaraj is my birthright", but he would have raised the slogan "Annihilation of untouchability is my birthright".'[13] We know whose birthright the preambular concept of 'liberty' is, but *whose* birthright is Swaraj?

Freedom as Inequality[14]

If Indians were slaves under imperialism, as Gandhi and others had often claimed, then the untouchable communities whom Dr Ambedkar represented were the 'slaves of slaves'.[15] There was necessarily a tension, at times outright antagonism, between Swaraj being understood as freedom for a Hindu-majority India, and the more focused interests of the 'depressed classes', or Dalits.

Once again, the idea of freedom, just as we saw in the previous chapter when looking at justice, recapitulates one of the numerous irreconcilable differences (as Dr Ambedkar viewed them) between Gandhi and himself. For the latter, freedom for all, if that was what Swaraj claimed to promote, would have to be preconditioned upon liberty for the Dalits, or Dalit Swaraj. Dalit Swaraj then was not just a precondition for Swaraj, or true Indian independence; rather, it became the mark, measure and metric of Swaraj as such. It was not just straightforward home rule then, it acquired more nuanced moral and spiritual denotations, such as those mentioned by Kripalani and other Gandhian members of the Constituent Assembly.

Gandhi, in his own idiosyncratic way, was emphatic about this now and again. He wrote in *Young India* in 1920:

> Non-cooperation against the Government means cooperation among the governed, and if Hindus do not remove the sin of untouchability, there will be no Swaraj in one year or one hundred years . . .[16]

A decade later, at the Round Table Conference, Gandhi again said:

> Just as the Congress considered Hindu–Muslim Unity, thereby meaning unity amongst all classes, to be indispensable for the attainment of Swaraj, so also did the Congress consider the removal of the curse of untouchability as an indispensable condition for the attainment of full freedom.[17]

However, at other times, he vacillated:

> A correspondent indignantly asks me . . . what I am doing for the (untouchables): 'Should not we the Hindus wash our bloodstained hands before we ask the English to wash theirs?' This is a proper question reasonably put. And if a member of a slave nation could deliver the suppressed classes from their slavery without freeing myself from my own, I would so do today. But it is an impossible task.[18]

As far as Dr Ambedkar was concerned, he believed that words such as these showed that Gandhi and the Congress were insincere when they said that removal of untouchability had to precede Swaraj. But not relying on words alone, Dr Ambedkar also set out to show in his writings that Gandhi's words were never followed through with the required action.

For this, Dr Ambedkar provided three bundles of evidence. First, he documented the farce that was made out of the Bardoli Programme, which was a constructive plan of the Congress drawn up in 1922 for recruiting members, raising funds, and spending the funds on social and political endeavours. The fourth point of action of the plan was 'to organise the Depressed Classes for a better life, to improve their social, mental and moral condition and to induce them to send their children to national schools and to provide for them the ordinary facilities which the other citizens enjoy'.[19] The subcommittee set up to implement the fourth point of action did not receive the funds required, and thus its head, Swami Shradhanand of the Arya Samaj, resigned. With neither funds nor a subcommittee head, the Working Committee, meant to oversee the implementation of the Bardoli Programme, decided that instead of implementing the fourth point of action it would pass off this work to the All-India Hindu Mahasabha. In 1923, it asked the Mahasabha 'to take up this matter and to make strenuous efforts to remove this evil [untouchability] from amidst the Hindu community'.[20] Dr Ambedkar sardonically concluded his account of these events saying: 'Thus came to an end the Constructive Programme undertaken by Mr. Gandhi and the Congress for the Untouchables'.[21]

Second, Dr Ambedkar organized the satyagrahas at Mahad and Nasik, mentioned in the previous chapter, for establishing the depressed classes right to draw water from a public tank and to enter temples, respectively. Since these satyagrahas were organized by the untouchables against the Hindus, and not by Indians against the British, Gandhi opposed them and the Congress did not lend support.[22] The satyagrahis were isolated and demoralized with supply lines cut off.

The third piece of evidence Ambedkar pointed to in order to show that neither the Congress nor Gandhi were sincere about Dalit liberty as a precondition for Swaraj was to do with the Round Table Conference, specifically Gandhi's vociferous objections to the demands made there by Dalit representatives about the Indian Constitution containing two political safeguards: the right to 'adequate representation', or what today we refer to as reservation; and, separate electorates for a period of ten years. How these details were decided on later through the Poona Pact has been widely discussed in terms of creating a chasm between Gandhi and Ambedkar. For now we shall return to some of these points with regard to Ambedkar's understanding of 'freedom' to imply 'Swaraj'.

Freedom or Swaraj

Dr Ambedkar's discomfort with Swaraj, both as a term and what it signified, is fairly well known. Far less known, however, are the subtle ways in which he appropriated this term from time to time. There are more than 215 uses of the word within the corpus of Dr Ambedkar's writings and speeches. Indeed, if one follows the development of his thought from the 1920s to the 1950s, it is apparent that he mastered a powerful rhetorical use of the term, ultimately deploying it to justify his deeply controversial conversion to Buddhism in 1956.

But a great deal happened before that moment. To begin with, one of the most articulate and direct expositions of Dr Ambedkar's understanding of Swaraj can be found in his opening address at the Round Table Conference held in London in 1930. It is cited here at length as it allows us to enter directly into the crux of Dr Ambedkar's understanding of both the problems and the promise inherent in Swaraj.

> The depressed classes . . . one-fifth of the total population of British India . . . form a group by themselves . . . and, although they are included among the Hindus, they in no sense form an integral part of that community. It is one which is midway between that of the serf and the slave . . . This enforced servility and bar to human intercourse, due to their untouchability . . . works out as a positive denial of all equality of opportunity and the denial of those most elementary of civic rights . . .

> . . . The Depressed Classes had welcomed the British as their deliverers from age long tyranny and oppression by the orthodox Hindus . . . Has the British Government done anything to remove it? Before the British, we could not enter the temple. Can we enter now? Before the British, we were denied entry into the Police Force. Does the British Government admit us in the Force? Before the British, we were not allowed to serve in the Military. Is that career now open to us? . . . There is certainly no fundamental change in our position.
>
> . . . We must have a Government in which men in power . . . will not be afraid to amend the social and economic code of life which the dictates of justice and expediency so urgently call for. This role the British Government will never be able to play. It is only a Government which is of the people, for the people and by the people that will make this possible.
>
> . . . We feel that nobody can remove our grievances as well as we can, and we cannot remove them unless we get political power in our own hands . . . It is only in a Swaraj constitution that we stand any chance of getting the political power into our own hands, without which we cannot bring salvation to our people.
>
> . . . The idea of Swaraj recalls to the mind of many of us the tyrannies, oppressions and injustices practised upon us in the past and fear of their recurrence under Swaraj. We are prepared to take the inevitable risk of the situation in the hope that we shall be installed, in adequate proportion, as the political sovereigns of the country along with our fellow countrymen.[23]

This moving speech touched upon the central dilemmas of freedom or Swaraj. The first was that though the Dalits were included among the Hindus, it was done in a way that simultaneously cast them out of the fold. They were excluded from within, which is why they naturally feared that after the coming independence they would be 'included out'. Having been always excluded, the Dalits had earlier falsely invested hope in the British thinking that they would be their liberators. But the British preserved the social system they found and carried on permitting the untouchables to be excluded from social and civic life. Thus, Swaraj *was* desirable, despite the fact that it brought back to mind the oppression and tyranny that the untouchables faced for centuries at the hands of the Hindus. Now, to prevent being excluded even after Swaraj, the government in India needed to be *of* the people and *by* the people: that is, Dalits (at that time one-fifth of the population) must be permitted a share of political sovereignty.

Finally, Dr Ambedkar made it clear that the Dalits themselves must own and address their grievances—it is not to be done *for* them, but *by* them. It was a vicious irony, however, because they needed Swaraj in order to empower themselves and, at the same time, to empower themselves was to achieve Swaraj.

Gandhi was well aware of the double bind that Dr Ambedkar found himself entangled in. Not only did he describe the situation in detail, but he also advised Dr Ambedkar that there was only one way out, which was to find salvation in Hinduism:

> There are three courses open to these down-trodden members of the nation. [1] They may call in the assistance of the slave-owning Government. They will get it, but they will fall from the frying pan into the fire. Today they are slaves of slaves . . . They will be used for suppressing their kith and kin. Instead of being sinned against, they will themselves be the sinners . . . [2] The second is rejection of Hinduism and wholesale conversion . . . [3] Then, . . . self-help and self-dependence, with such aid as the non-Panchama Hindus will render . . . The better way . . . is

> for the Panchamas heartily to join the great national movement that is now going on for throwing off the slavery of the present Government.[24]

Thirty years later, Dr Ambedkar reflected upon this advice:

> When Gandhi demanded Swaraj, I supported him. I asked him just one question: what will be the position of the Dalits in his so-called Swaraj? Will our people have some standard of life, will we be educated, will there be no harassment of untouchables in Swaraj?[25]

But in the interim, at least until Gandhi's fast-unto-death, which forced Dr Ambedkar into signing the Poona Pact, the latter had actually paid some heed to Gandhi's advice. For example, it was reported that when Dr Ambedkar affirmed that he would attend the Round Table Conference in London in 1930, despite the Congress boycott, he had said, 'I will demand what is rightful for my people, and I will certainly uphold the demand for Swaraj.'[26] That was the curious, plain statement of the dilemma: the double bind: What was rightful for Dr Ambedkar's people (since they are both Dalits *and* Indians) was both Swaraj and not Swaraj.

Whose Swaraj?

Chittaranjan Das had once remarked that Swaraj was undefinable. But that did not prevent him and countless others from impregnating the term with all kinds of meanings. This could be banal and literal—such as, 'Purna Swaraj means complete independence'[27]—or sarcastic and ironic—such as Swaraj is 'the highest bliss and the greatest stimulant'.[28] Gandhi's understanding was surely the most rich and complex. We are aware of the double sense of Swaraj as home rule, as well as individual self-mastery, both political and moral. Beyond that, Gandhi spoke of it in terms of agency: India must 'generate sufficient power to be able to assert herself'. Swaraj thus had these elements of power and self-assertion. Gandhi then evoked the image of 'paralysis' as the opposite of Swaraj: 'What can a paralytic do to stretch forth a helping hand . . . but to try to cure himself of his paralysis?'[29] And, finally, there were interpretations of others' use of the term. For example, Dr Ambedkar argued that Gandhian Swaraj was a 'paradox': It stood for freedom from foreign domination, which means destruction of the political order. But it kept intact the social order, which permitted one class to dominate the other—indeed, on a hereditary basis, which was permanent domination. This was the paradox of Swaraj.[30]

For some, Swaraj suggested not freedom, but tyranny and slavery, something to fear. Dr Ambedkar closed his well-known *Annihilation of Caste* with words to that effect:

> In the fight for Swaraj you fight with the whole nation on your side. In this [eradication of caste] you have to fight against the whole nation and that too, your own [nation]. But it is more important than Swaraj . . . Swaraj for Hindus may turn out to be only a step toward [our] slavery.[31]

Dr Ambedkar, therefore, fought tirelessly to 'make sure that Swaraj does not become a strangle-hold for the Untouchables'.[32] The Dalits must be protected 'against the tyranny of the majority under the Swaraj constitution'.[33] This motif was repeated several times throughout his writings and speeches:

> Swaraj would be the substitution of domination by the British for domination by the Hindus. Without ensuring protection of

all their rights, in a free India [Dalits] would not be free. Swaraj meant Hindu Raj.[34]

So, in conclusion, Dr Ambedkar queried:

> What good can the Congress brand of Swaraj bring to [the servile classes of India]? They know that under the Congress brand of Swaraj the prospect for them is really very bleak . . . If it is [Gandhism] it will mean the spread of charkha, village industries, the observance of caste, Brahmacharya (continence), reverence for the cow and things of that sort. If it is left to governing classes to make what it likes of Swaraj the principal item in it will be the suppression of the servile classes . . .[35]

Dr Ambedkar believed that it was not only the untouchables who feared Swaraj. He cited evidence to show that many other minority communities had their apprehensions. He indicated, for example, that a letter written by an Indian Christian reproduced in *Young India* illustrated the attitude of the community to Swaraj:

> How comes it then that the Indian Christian born and bred on the soil of India and of ancestry purely Indian, has not learnt to cherish the ancient history of this country . . .? . . . Again how comes it that both Hindus and Mahomedans regard the Indian Christian sentiment towards their aspirations as lukewarm if not positively hostile, and conversely why is it that the ever-growing height of the national spirit in India makes the Indian Christian feel dwarfed and helpless and suspicious of his security in the future.[36]

Dr Ambedkar suggested that, notwithstanding a few prominent members, the Indian Christian community, far from taking active part in the struggle for Swaraj, was really suspicious and afraid of it.

Indeed, Dr Ambedkar recognized that Swaraj meant different things to different communities. Citing Gandhi: 'To the Musalmans, Swaraj means, as it must mean, India's ability to deal effectively with the Khilafat question.'[37] He also went into a long analysis of Savarkar's understanding of Swaraj for the Hindus:

> Swaraj to the Hindus must mean only that in which their 'Swaraj', their 'Hindutva', can assert itself without being overlorded by any non-Hindu people.[38]

As part of his idea of Swaraj, Savarkar insisted upon the retention of the name 'Hindustan' for India, the retention of Sanskrit as the sacred language; Hindi, written in Devanagari, as the national language. Dr Ambedkar summed up Savarkar's position:

> . . . the scheme of Swaraj formulated by Mr Savarkar will give the Hindus an empire over the Muslims and thereby satisfy their vanity . . . But it can never ensure a stable and peaceful future for the Hindus, for the simple reason that the Muslims will never yield willing obedience to so dreadful an alternative.[39]

What was interesting was that not only did Dr Ambedkar contrast his own understanding of Swaraj from that of Gandhi's, but also from that of Savarkar's. This will prove to be of crucial importance when another preambular concept is discussed, that of the 'nation' (Chapter Six).

Dr Ambedkar also referred to Chittaranjan Das's idea of Swaraj, and several others. As we shall see, he also evoked Jyotirao Phule's take on Swaraj and chose to align himself with Mahatma Phule. None of this was presented systematically in

Dr Ambedkar's writings, but we can endeavour to reconstruct a concise and coherent picture.

Swaraj: From Arya Samaj to Mahatma Phule

There can be no doubt that Dr Ambedkar was well aware of the range of meanings attributed to the term 'Swaraj': from political to moral, from religious to ontological. He cited at length a letter of Shradhananda Sanyasi of the Arya Samaj, whom he respected for his forceful stand that 'the curse of untouchability' needs to be 'blotted out of the Indian society', and that this was a precondition for the Congress to succeed 'in their efforts for the attainment of Swaraj'. In this letter, the swami's peculiarly biopolitical, yet spiritual, understanding of Swaraj was abundantly clear: 'National self-realization and virile existence is impossible without Swaraj. I, as a Sanyasi, should devote the rest of my life to this sacred cause—the cause of sexual purity and true national unity.'[40]

Dr Ambedkar also went into a lengthy discussion of Chittaranjan Das's understanding of Swaraj, primarily to argue that both he and Gandhi obfuscated its meaning to suit their political agendas: if they wished to advocate dominion status for India rather than total independence, then Swaraj would mean something deeper than independence. In Das's words, 'Independence, to my mind, is a narrower ideal than that of Swaraj.' He continues, 'India may be independent tomorrow in the sense that the British people may leave us to our destiny but that will not necessarily give us what I understand by Swaraj.'[41]

Despite Dr Ambedkar's critique, it appeared that Das's understanding of Swaraj was in fact quite complex and profound. Further, I think Das's sense of Swaraj seemed to come close to Dr Ambedkar's own at certain points. Consider this:

> To my mind, Swaraj implies, firstly, that we must have the freedom of working out the consolidation of the diverse elements of the Indian people; secondly, we must proceed with this work on National lines, not going back two thousand years ago, but going forward in the light and in the spirit of our national genius and temperament.[42]

Das here prioritized India's internal harmony to its independence from British rule. He also offered a future-oriented conception of Swaraj, one that did not leap back into some golden age but rather one that pushed forward. If by 'diverse elements' Das could be understood to refer to the Dalits, in addition to the Muslims, then the authorship of this text could easily be attributed to Dr Ambedkar himself. It was consistent with Dr Ambedkar's remarks at the Round Table Conference. It was often said of Das that he pursued Swaraj 'for the masses and not for the classes'. In his own talk on 'What is Swaraj?' and in other speeches, Das distinguished bourgeois revolution from the truly mass revolution that Swaraj, to be authentic, must be. Nevertheless, despite the similarities, Dr Ambedkar had nothing complimentary to say either about Das or his understanding of Swaraj. For Dr Ambedkar, Das was simply toeing the Gandhian line and such words meant next to nothing, since no substantive action for the downtrodden ever followed from them.

In stark contrast was Mahatma Phule's notion of Swaraj. Dr Ambedkar's radical socio-historical work *Who Were the Shudras?*[43] was dedicated to the memory of Phule. It is fascinating to read the way that Dr Ambedkar attributed to Phule his own position with regard to Swaraj, and the primacy of social equality and emancipation over home rule. This is clear in the dedication, where Dr Ambedkar referred to Phule as:

> The Greatest Shudra of Modern India who made the lower classes of Hindus conscious of their slavery to the higher classes and who preached the gospel that for India social democracy was more vital than independence from foreign rule.[44]

Five Hindu Attitudes towards Swaraj

Dr Ambedkar's dedication to Phule, and his positioning of Phule as a social emancipator, over and above a Swarajist, foreshadowed a division that Dr Ambedkar made later in the preface to *Who Were the Shudras?* He divided the Hindus into five classes, and I believe that we can read these five classes as articulating the five different attitudes towards Swaraj:

> [1] There is a class of Hindus, who are known as orthodox and who will not admit that there is anything wrong with the Hindu social system. To talk of reforming it is to them rank blasphemy. [2] There is a class of Hindus who are known as Arya Samajists. They believe in the Vedas and only in the Vedas . . . [3] There is a class of Hindus who will admit that the Hindu social system is all wrong, but who hold that there is no necessity to attack it. Their argument is that since law does not recognize it, it is a dying, if not a dead system. [4] There is a class of Hindus, who are politically minded. They are indifferent to such questions. To them Swaraj is more important than social reform [5]. The fifth class of Hindus are those who are rationalists and who regard social reforms as of primary importance, even more important than Swaraj.[45]

Clearly the fifth class called back Dr Ambedkar's dedication to Phule. The first group was the *sanatanis*, perhaps the Rashtriya Swayamsevak Sangh (RSS) too. The latter was suggested in

Dr Ambedkar's quip that these 'meek and non-violent looking' Hindus can become very violent when someone attacks their sacred books.[46] The second group might include Savarkar's notion of Hindu Swaraj. It certainly included Swami Shradhananda's biopolitical idea of Swaraj. Dr Ambedkar said that the book 'treads heavily on the toes' of this second group.[47] While he did not further define or describe the third group in his text, the fourth group was clearly the Congress of Gandhi and also C.R. Das. About this group, Dr Ambedkar wrote that 'as to the politically-minded Hindu, he need not be taken seriously'.[48] This curt dismissal was surprising because Dr Ambedkar spent decades dedicated to the effort of bringing this fourth group around to his point of view. His more elaborated opinion about this group can be found in his work on Partition:

> Under the leadership of Mr. Gandhi, the Hindu Society, if it did not become a political mad-house, certainly became mad after politics. Non-cooperation, Civil Disobedience, and the cry for Swaraj took the place which social reform once had in the minds of the Hindus. In the din and dust of political agitation, the Hindus do not even know that there are any evils to be remedied. Those who are conscious of it, do not believe that social reform is as important as political reform, and when forced to admit its importance argue that there can be no social reform unless political power is first achieved.[49]

It was the fifth group of Hindus whom Dr Ambedkar thought would be likely to welcome the book. It was to them that he addressed his arguments. This was the group of people who believed in the urgency of social reform, despite the fact that the problem would certainly require not just enormous effort, but also a great deal of time.[50] This group by definition included

Dr Ambedkar himself, for he was at this time willy-nilly also a Hindu. But though it represented his lexical priority of Dalit emancipation over the others' preferences for Swaraj, it did not exhaust his own conception of Swaraj. What we do notice though is that for Dr Ambedkar, Swaraj was just too important an issue to be left in the hands of the Congress. As he succinctly put it: 'Do they not know that in the Swaraj of India is involved the fate of 60 millions of Untouchables?'[51]

Dalit Swaraj

One of the finest articulations of Dr Ambedkar's own authentic sense of Swaraj became visible through his critique of the petty scheming being carried out by both the Hindu elements within the Congress and the Muslim League:

> Is Swaraj to be an opportunity to serve the people or is it to be an opportunity for Hindus to conquer the Musalmans and for the Musalmans to conquer the Hindus? Swaraj must be a Government of the people by the people and for the people. This is the *raison d'etre* of Swaraj and the only justification for Swaraj. If Swaraj is to usher in an era in which the Hindus and the Muslims will be engaged in scheming against each other, the one planning to conquer its rival, why should we have Swaraj and why should the democratic nations allow such a Swaraj to come into existence? It will be a snare, a delusion and a perversion.[52]

In Dr Ambedkar's view, nationalism was a means to an end and not the end in itself. The worth of Swaraj was determined by the nature of the society constructed thereby.[53] The end of Swaraj, its sole justification, was in bringing government to the people, low-born as well as high, having a government *by* these people and not just *for* these people. Recall that not only for Gandhi, but for Dr Ambedkar too, agency was at the heart of Swaraj. In Gandhi's conception, however, the agency was attributed to caste Hindus, that they should do penance for their sin of untouchability—and thus, for example, the Harijan Sevak Sangh should consist primarily of caste Hindus and the Harijans should not work in it.[54] For Dr Ambedkar, however, Swaraj was more profoundly democratized, tied up with the agency of the untouchables, and it was crucial that the Dalits owned and themselves agitated their own grievances and the injustices they suffered.

In contrast with the democratic orientation of his own position, Dr Ambedkar cited several examples of the contempt that the Congress leadership, the upper classes, had for the lower classes. Even Bal Gangadhar Tilak, reputed to be the 'Father of the Swaraj movement', said in 1918, when the backward classes had started an agitation for separate representation in the legislature, that he did not understand why the oil-pressers, tobacco shopkeepers, washermen, and so on, should want to go into the legislature. He said, 'Their business was to obey the laws and not to aspire for power to make laws.'[55] This was the starkest possible contrast to Dr Ambedkar's own agency-centred understanding of Swaraj for the people. Thus Dr Ambedkar reiterated that unless the Dalits agitated and owned their fight, 'Swaraj will not be government *by* the people, but . . . government . . . by the governing class; . . . and government *for* the people will be what the governing class will choose to make of it'.[56]

But Dr Ambedkar was quite specific, nonetheless, that it was the profound impoverishment of the masses that pushed him to side with the Swarajists against the British, despite the fact that, as he humorously described it, when Dalits hear the upper castes speak on Swaraj, it seems to them like they are hearing the Devil cite the scriptures. But, as Dr Ambedkar touchingly remarked, without Swaraj 'no Indian can feel that upward impulse which is the source of elevation witnessed in a self-governing community'.

Dalit Swaraj, or free and equal participation in the political sovereignty of a free and sovereign nation, worked Dr Ambedkar and the Dalits out of the double bind that they found themselves ensnared in for so long. At any rate, one of the strangleholds—British rule and external domination—had already dissolved itself by the time the Preamble was drafted. In that long, arduous, complicated and bloody process, Dr Ambedkar never did manage to win separate electorates for his people. The untouchables were no longer slaves of slaves. But what about internal domination? Were they still slaves?

Buddhism As Dalit Swaraj

Gandhi, when speaking of the untouchables' quandary, had said that they had only three options. From among those options, he had warned them of the dangers of siding with the British. He had also ruled out the second option, the idea of embracing Christianity or any other religion on the basis of insincerity and opportunism. What he advised as the best option was that the untouchables find salvation in Hinduism, by entering more completely into the Hindu fold. Until now we have spoken only of the first and third options—Dr Ambedkar's Scylla and Charybdis—and the way they manifested themselves for Dr Ambedkar and the Dalits as an irresolvable dilemma or double bind. But Dr Ambedkar also had the second option before him. And he took it.

The previous chapter chronicling Dr Ambedkar's life story ended at the point where he converted to Buddhism. When

Dr Ambedkar was asked what advantage he would gain by converting, he replied:

> What will India gain by Swaraj? Just as Swaraj is necessary for India, so also is change of religion necessary for the untouchables. The underlying motive in both the movements is the desire for freedom.[57]

With Dr Ambedkar deploying the idea of Swaraj to justify his controversial decision to convert, we should realize that at that moment he had mastered the powerful and rhetorical use of the term. Dr Ambedkar picked up and preserved what he found valuable in the concept, even as he cancelled and overcame what was retrograde to his aims and intentions.

Not only was the justificatory terminology that Dr Ambedkar used a liberating appropriation, but the very act itself—the autonomous act of conversion, the refusal to accept the paternalism of Hindu Swaraj—was an expression of Dalit Swaraj. Buddhism dissolved the tension of the double bind. It was Swarajist insofar as the religion originated on Indian soil. It was thus not a search for liberation through the British or alien ideas and practices. As a religion, its holy sites were not located outside of the Indian subcontinent, unlike Christianity (Rome, Jerusalem), Judaism (Israel), or Islam (Mecca, Medina). In this respect, he anticipated and deflected the critique that would emerge from the followers of Savarkar's idea of Hindu Swaraj. But at the same time, Buddhism was the destination for the transit out of Hindu bondage, it was Swaraj as freedom from alien rule, Swaraj as freedom from Hindu domination.

Dr Ambedkar hinted at this in various ways throughout the preface of 1948 that he had authored for Laxmi Narasu's *The Essence of Buddhism*:[58]

> Prof. Narasu was the stalwart of the 19th century who had fought European arrogance with patriotic fervour, orthodox Hinduism with iconoclastic zeal, heterodox Brahmins with nationalistic vision and aggressive Christianity with a rationalistic outlook—all under the inspiring banner of the unflagging faith in the teachings of the Great Buddha.[59]

Dr Ambedkar's long search for a resolution to the predicament took so long that one of the coils of bondage was undone of its own accord. The other remained. The political system had changed; the social system abided all change. Towards the end of his life, Dr Ambedkar had found a way out of the social system that did not—to call back Gandhi's warning—take the Dalits from the frying pan into the fire. This was conversion to Buddhism. This was Buddhism as Dalit Swaraj.

Not Swaraj, Not Freedom, but Liberty

The surface explanations of the preference for the term 'liberty' over 'freedom' in Dr Ambedkar's preamble are certainly valid. Liberty is more political than metaphysical and it fits the tripartite formula better than freedom would have. But it is important to keep in mind the wider context within which Dr Ambedkar was making his specific decisions and choosing his words with utmost care. The long history of the national movement, the conceptual status of Swaraj within it, the mystification of the term 'freedom' in relation to Swaraj, and the almost universal exclusion of the untouchables from the predominant understanding of both concepts (a phenomenon which continues unabated in contemporary political and conceptual histories) were among the overarching factors that provoked Dr Ambedkar to eschew those easy associations in his newly conceived preamble.

If the concept of 'freedom' was contaminated by a Brahmanically imbrued 'Swaraj', then why risk its residue in the very document that articulates liberation from caste oppression as every Dalit's birthright? Liberty, forget Swaraj, is every Indian's birthright—Dalits and non-Dalits alike.

Liberty, then, was far more preferable than freedom. Dalit liberation, which preconditioned and provided the barometer for the achievement of every Indian's freedom, both seventy years ago and today, was, in Dr Ambedkar's view, the very essence of the revolution that was signalled by the Preamble to India's Constitution.

3

Equality: The Constitution As Revolution

The 'equality' clause in the Preamble to the Constitution of India today reads exactly as it did on 26 January 1950, and indeed exactly as it did when drafted by the Drafting Committee in February 1948:

> EQUALITY of status and of opportunity . . .[1]

It seems sparse. And sure enough, if we look back at one of its earliest predecessors, we see that some words were dropped from it. In Nehru's Objectives Resolution (January 1947), the 'equality' clause read:

> (5) WHEREIN shall be guaranteed and secured to all the people of India . . .equality of status, of opportunity, and before the law . . .[2]

It may come as some surprise, however, that in Dr Ambedkar's 'Proposed Preamble' from *States and Minorities* (March 1947), there was not really an 'equality' clause at all, at least not a positive one. Instead, there was an 'inequality' clause:

(iii) To remove social, political and economic inequality by providing better opportunities to the submerged classes.[3]

Equality in the Constitution of India

The reason for the lack of an 'equality' clause in Dr Ambedkar's 'Proposed Preamble' was the same as the one behind the economy of expression in the Preamble as it reads today. That is because both Dr Ambedkar's 1947 Constitution from *States and Minorities* and the 1950 Constitution of India entailed extremely detailed and robust enumerations of the equalities guaranteed therein. Our Constitution—in the main articles beyond the Preamble—among several other guarantees, made illegal the state's discrimination between citizens on the grounds of religion, race, caste, sex, or place of birth (Article 15); throws open all public spaces to all citizens equally (15[2]); abolishes untouchability (17); abolishes titles of honour (18); offers equality of opportunity in public employment (16); and, guarantees equality before the law and equal protection of the law, as justiciable rights (14). With all of these specific, justiciable rights appearing in the body of the Constitution, the Preamble was relieved of the burden of recounting them. It then only stated their essence in a sparse fashion.

This choice for a succinct 'equality' clause in the Preamble had the benefit of preventing debate on this phrase within the Constituent Assembly; however, what was spared the Preamble only fuelled more argument when it came to the articles of the Constitution itself. Questions at that time were centred on the same issues as today: What exactly are we seeking to equalize when pursuing equality?

Controversies around equality in India have existed since the birth of the Republic of India on 26 January 1950 right up till the present day. This is evident in the earliest and the latest amendments: the very first amendment to the Constitution, back in 1951 (concerning Article 15, especially clause [4]), and the quite recent amendment to the Constitution (concerning Articles 15 and 16, especially clause [6]) centre on equality and both have been extremely controversial. The principle of radical equality that we find in the Constitution has been a constant and enduring struggle for us over the last seventy years.

And not just the last seventy years. Equality has been of crucial concern for forefront critics of the origin, perpetuation and persistence of caste and gender inequalities in India, going as far back as twelfth-century author Basaveshwara and on with Kabir, Ravidas, Tukaram, Guru Nanak and Jyotirao Phule, to recent thinkers-activists such as Periyar, Iyothee Thass and, of course, Dr Ambedkar himself. What Dr Ambedkar incorporated into the Preamble was, in a way, the distillation of this long history of critique.

But Dr Ambedkar dated the struggle for equality much further back than the twelfth century. We can see this in the title he chose for a set of books he planned to write about the history of equality. It was to be called *Revolution and Counter-Revolution in Ancient India.* Thus, he dated the origins of the struggle for equality in India all the way back to ancient India.

Revolution and Counter-Revolution in Ancient India

If we follow Dr Ambedkar's line of inquiry about the nature and status of equality in India, we will see that nearly all of India's recorded civilizational history can be reorganized and rewritten as a millennia-long struggle for equality. If you can believe it, that was precisely what he decided to undertake in his very last years.

Dr Ambedkar was widely regarded as one of the most radical egalitarians of the twentieth century. The concept of equality was so close to his heart that, at the fag end of his life, he outlined a multi-volume history of equality in India (*Revolution and Counter-Revolution in Ancient India*). This set of books was intended to trace the rise of Buddhism in ancient India as the moment when the principle of equality took root in the subcontinent. The decline and fall of Buddhism, according to the thesis of Dr Ambedkar's book, occurred as a result of an inegalitarian counter-revolution that was complex. It was initiated:

(a) Politically, by Pushyamitra Shunga (when he overthrew the Mauryan dynasty),
(b) Legally, by the *Dharmashastras*, and most crucially the *Manusmriti*, and
(c) Ideologically, stabilized by caste-rigid orthodox philosophy (especially Mimamsa and Vedanta) and the pan-Indian spread of religious precepts (i.e., *Varnashramadharma*).

This counter-revolution, according to Dr Ambedkar, lasted from the penning of the *Manusmriti* right until it was finally vanquished in a new egalitarian revolution through the penning of a basic law that abrogated and annihilated it: the 1950 Constitution of India.

Challenging the Marxist View of History

If the second portion of Dr Ambedkar's book-project title took us all the way back to the ancient world, what did the first portion refer to? In the nineteenth century, Friedrich Engels had published a series of articles, with contributions from none other than Karl Marx. These were entitled 'Revolution and Counter Revolution'. A book was later published under the authorship of Marx and Engels called *Revolution and Counter-Revolution in Germany*.[4] Closer home, prominent Marxist M.N. Roy (who later reformed, disavowing Marxism), wrote a book titled *Revolution and Counter-Revolution in China*.[5] Dr Ambedkar knew Roy personally and had read his work. But although he regarded Roy as inadequately informed about the problem of untouchability, Roy's own writings many a time presented contrarian positions remarkably similar to Dr Ambedkar's own. It is beyond dispute that Dr Ambedkar had Roy in mind on many occasions during his composition of *Revolution and Counter-Revolution in Ancient India*.

Unlike the principal thesis of Marxist historiography, it was not class antagonism but caste antagonism that fuelled the history of India as Dr Ambedkar saw it:

> . . . the history of India is nothing but a history of a moral conflict between Buddhism and Brahmanism. So neglected is this truth that no one will be found to give it his ready acceptance.[6]

Within the category of 'no one', Dr Ambedkar was obviously including the Marxist historians. And sure enough, there is abundant evidence to show that he was taking a shot at the Indian Marxists while both conceiving of his ambitious project as well as executing it. As we shall see, while working on this magnificent manuscript, Dr Ambedkar had one eye firmly fixed on the Hindu orthodoxy; those who would stand in virulent opposition to his efforts to democratize Hindu personal law, inheritance, succession, and so on, and who saw to it that his pioneering Hindu Code Bill would fail in Parliament. His other eye, meanwhile, was firmly fixed on the Indian Marxists, whom he regarded as ideologically suspect and socially dangerous, given that his decades of experience of trying to strategically ally with them had always ended in disaster.

This was thanks to the casteism that, Dr Ambedkar believed, the individuals in the Communist movement could never manage to shake off.[7]

Marxist Ambedkarites like Anand Teltumbde—or, to use his preferred nomenclature, followers of Marxian Ambedkarism—have suggested that we need to retrieve the radical in Dr Ambedkar. 'Radical' here means the revolutionary potential that has remained untapped in Dr Ambedkar's legacy. But it is apparent from this unfinished project of Dr Ambedkar's that he himself regarded his own position as being revolutionary, and in several ways more satisfactory, than that of the Indian Marxists. This comes out by comparing it to a work of M.N. Roy's that runs very much along the same themes as those of Dr Ambedkar's. But Roy's critiques were suggestive only, and he did not incorporate them into his essential principles of Indian history.

In his text entitled *Materialism*, Roy wrote:

> The spiritual revolt represented by the Indian materialists eventually culminated in the rise of Buddhism which all but liquidated the Vedic natural religion and freed India from Brahmanical domination for several hundred years. Internal evidence proves that the Vedanta Sutras were composed for combating Buddhism. Therefore, they could not be regarded as the direct outcome of the speculative thought recorded in the Upanishads. The composition of earlier Upanishads and Vedanta Sutras must have been separated by several hundred years, during which period the spiritual development of India was in the direction of materialism, represented by Kanada, Kapila and many others, and of rationalism, represented by the Buddhists and Jains subsequently. It was only after the defeat of the Buddhist revolution that Vedantist metaphysics and pantheism were revived as the ideology of Brahmanical orthodoxy.[8]

Dr Ambedkar's premises overlapped with that of Roy's. He also posited, just as Roy stated, that a Buddhist revolution brought to the fore rationalist and materialist thought and practice that 'liquidated the Vedic natural religion and freed India from Brahmanical domination for several hundred years'. And Dr Ambedkar agreed with Roy that this revolution was defeated and Vedanta emerged 'as the ideology of Brahmanical orthodoxy'. As Dr Ambedkar put it:

> Buddhism was a Revolution. It was as great a Revolution as the French Revolution. Though it began as a Religious revolution, it became more than a Religious revolution. It became a social and political revolution.[9]

But a crucial difference between Dr Ambedkar and M.N. Roy's account was that for the former equality was the principle of the revolution, specifically gender and caste equality. All of Indian history, dating back millennia, can be understood as a struggle for gender and caste equality. In this long history there have been egalitarian revolutions, and there have been inegalitarian counter-revolutions. This was not, as Marxists argue, about class; it is about Brahmanism, which has as its essence the doctrine of graded inequality.

Graded Inequality

Graded inequality is a doctrine of hierarchy and ranking that is—very unlike the duality of Marxist class struggle, bourgeoise versus proletariat—internally complicated by replicating antagonism between castes, but also encouraging cooperation between them. In the Brahmanical doctrine, at the top were Brahmins, with the Kshatriyas below them but above the Vaishyas, who in turn were below the Kshatriyas but above the Shudras, and as supplemented later in history, all of these castes were above the untouchables.

Simple inequality, such as that of Marxist class antagonism, generates discontent that may easily sow the seeds of revolution. Graded inequality, on the contrary, invites all people in a society to celebrate inequality and share in its spoils. It thus makes revolution rare, while also accounting for the long stability of orthodoxy and inequality throughout the long history of India—a history where Marxist revolution makes little sense, as it concerns class and not caste. Under the stable and profoundly inegalitarian system of graded inequality, every caste has another community that it may freely and legally exploit, even as it suffers from exploitation.

Only the untouchables, those outside of the varna system that gave birth to the caste system,[10] have no group below them. Yet this potential source of caste revolt is tempered by patriarchy as part and parcel of the system of graded inequality. Brahmanical patriarchy also places men over women, further internally complexifying graded inequality—Brahmin women are subjugated to Brahmin men but stand higher than Kshatriya men. Moving along we find that untouchable men also have a group to tyrannize and exploit: untouchable women. This is Brahmanical patriarchy, where all castes and genders are ranked and kept in place by having the burden of their inequalities compensated by the benefit of exploiting their subordinates. Untouchable women, at the bottom of the bottom, then are the only ones who get no solace in the system, but as the most vulnerable they are least in a position to topple it.

Brahmin men, who get the most from the system, have been the chief architects of its political existence (revolutions like those that brought down the Buddhist reign of the Mauryas), its legal enforcement (in *Manusmriti*) and its ideological hegemony

(Brahmanical philosophy and literature, which dictates through its various forms that caste duty is dharma). However, everyone in between also finds their place and thus they do their part to maintain status quo. In this respect, it must be noted that the concept of Brahmanical patriarchy does not refer to the patriarchal practices followed by Brahmin men; instead, it represents the graded nature of patriarchy in India. Anyone, regardless of his or her caste or gender, who believes, practices, preaches or encourages any kind of discrimination based on this hierarchical structure of graded inequality is following Brahmanism irrespective of his or her hereditary caste. Just as it does not require a man to practice misogyny, it is not necessarily the Brahmins who practice Brahmanism.[11]

In his analysis of caste, Dr Ambedkar regarded patriarchy as the twin sister of Brahmanism.[12] That is, caste and gender were employed together to maintain endogamy (the absence of intermarriage), the essence of the caste system,[13] which had been imposed through various means in Indian history (child marriage, enforced widowhood, sati), all of which functioned to control women's sexuality and hold the entire structure of inequality in India securely in place.

This helps to understand why Dr Ambedkar spearheaded the introduction of the Hindu Code Bill, giving rights of inheritance and property ownership to women. He believed it was a 'vital step in the introduction of true democracy in India, and would remove the practices and the logic that underpinned the caste system'.[14] But as mentioned in the first chapter, various factions from the right united to defeat the Bill, as well as to vilify and attack Dr Ambedkar personally. When Nehru himself withdrew support from the Bill due to political expediency, Dr Ambedkar resigned from the cabinet. It was soon after this resignation towards the end of 1951 that Dr Ambedkar began drafting specific chapter plans for the magisterial history of India (*Revolution and Counter-Revolution in Ancient India*), which remained unfinished at the time of his death.

The Scheme of Books

We know that Dr Ambedkar had been working on this enormously ambitious project for years, as attested in his personal letters. In June 1956, just five months before his death, he referred to the book by name and called it urgent. But due to the vastness of the project, it remained incomplete.

In the 'schemes of books' discovered in Dr Ambedkar's library after his death, the following structure was found, some of it typed out, some handwritten:

Revolution and Counter-Revolution in Ancient India
Table of Contents

Book I	The Age of Racial Conflict
Book II	The Conflict over Inequality
Book III	How Conflict lead to Revolution
Book IV	Results of Revolution
Book V	The Birth of Counter-Revolution
Book VI	Results of Counter-Revolution
Book VII	The Present Age is the Age of Counter-Revolution

For example, under Book II and Book III, there were chapters like:

Book II	**Part One: The Rise of Inequality**
Chapter 3	Graded Inequality the Essence of Chaturvarna
Chapter 4	The Shudra under Graded Inequality
Book III	**Part One: The Revolution and its Principles**
Chapter 1	The Rise of Buddhism as a Revolutionary Force
Chapter 2	Equality as the Principle of the Revolution[15]

Not much of these schemes, tables of contents and chapterizations match the written material that we have today, which seems to be around a third of all of the contents projected in the scheme of books. Dr Ambedkar had been working on some aspects of this massive project since at least 1950, if not earlier. During this long period of studying, thinking and composing, there was a distinct difference in the mood and orientation of Dr Ambedkar's writing—both in style and content—between the first main phase (1952–1953) and the second main phase (1954–1956). Starting from 1951, Dr Ambedkar was deeply anguished and frustrated after resigning as law minister due to the failure of the Hindu Code Bill. His primary protagonist from this phase, then, was the Hindu orthodoxy of the right. But by the time of the second main phase of his writing, the Hindu Code Bill had been passed piecemeal and the Untouchability Offences Act had also been adopted in 1955. Further, Dr Ambedkar was accelerating his process of conversion to Buddhism. This process included the writing of his historic *The Buddha and His Dhamma*. In this latter phase, his primary protagonist was the Marxist orthodoxy of the left.

Hence, Book VII (*The Present Age is the Age of Counter-Revolution*), from which we have absolutely no written material available, was clearly conceived in the darker, first phase of 1953, at a point when he could envision devoting an entire part of the book to the Constitution as a document of counter-revolution. This stood in direct contrast to what Dr Ambedkar had implied during his 25 November 1949 address to the Constituent Assembly, where he said that the democratic system established through the new Constitution was a resurrection of principles and practices of the Buddhism of ancient India. In 1950, as in 1955, the Constitution reflected the egalitarian principle of the revolution.

Dr Ambedkar's writing project evolved, some parts took on more prominence than others. This, of course, is to be expected in something so enormously ambitious. But the driving thesis stood throughout: Buddhism was a revolution against the inequities of caste and gender inequality, and equality was the fundamental principle of that revolution; throughout Indian history, the principle of equality in Buddhism had been subject to the counter-revolution of Brahmanical Hinduism and Brahmanical patriarchy. Now, this counter-revolution against equality had finally met its match:

(a) Politically, with the emergence of the Indian Republic, and
(b) Legally, with the Constitution and its preambular principle of equality.

What remained woefully lacking, however, was the crucial challenge:

(c) Ideologically, which Dr Ambedkar would pursue through igniting resurgent interest in Buddhist philosophy, and by promoting a more rational and egalitarian literature than the reactionary canon of Brahmanism. This also aided in translating the political and juridical achievements into the social realm.

Dr Ambedkar's Historiographical Method

The opening paragraphs of Dr Ambedkar's manuscript reveal the peculiar methodology that he employed: What Brahmanical literature presented as myths were read as containing basic historical facts that have been mythologized; the devas, along with Yaksha, Gandharva, Kinnaras—all of these will be shown, Dr Ambedkar said, to have been actual humans, not gods or mythical creatures. Now why would Dr Ambedkar adopt such a curious strategy?

In 1955, German amateur revisionist historian Werner Keller published *The Bible as History*, a book found on the shelves of Dr Ambedkar's personal library.[16] This book introduced a now-universal way of understanding religious scriptures the world over—where historical facts were mythologized, humans made super-human, men made gods. *The Bible as History* revealed the historical truths, facts and archaeological corroborations of the facts that underlie the Bible as scripture, myth and ritual. The same way, Dr Ambedkar's *Revolution and Counter-Revolution* sought to give the same underlying historical, all-too-human basis for the myths, legends, rituals, gods, and so on, of ancient India.

Brahmanical literature presented the asuras as monsters, the rakshasas as non-human and the nagas as serpents, but Buddhist literature presented a more nuanced picture. The devas came frequently to the Buddha to ask questions. The Nagas in Buddhist literature were presented in two different ways: as those born from woman and as those born from eggs. Thus, the term acquired a two-fold meaning that was exploited by Brahmanical writers. The asuras too appeared in Buddhist literature as *jaan-vishesh*, as special, but still human beings.

Dr Ambedkar pointed out that in the *Satapatha Brahmana* the asuras were descendants of Prajapati, and that they fought with the devas for possession of the earth. Thus, we may infer at the very least that there was some sort of a territorial battle happening. Dr Ambedkar launched into his grand history by trying to understand what sort of battle this might have been, what historical facts may have been erased and superseded through mythologization, and the clear preference in that mythology for who was good and who was evil.

The struggle, of course, slowly revealed the prehistory and early history of the subcontinent, from pre-Vedic to Vedic times, with all the social and political strife that would have accompanied the civilizational changes—whether narrated as Aryan vs non-Aryan, Aryan vs Dravidian, or as Dr Ambedkar preferred to characterize it, Aryan vs Naga. What this ultimately revealed was that behind ancient India's caste struggle was an even more primordial racial struggle that preceded it, and that despite the victory of the Aryans and their triumph in the Vedic period, elements of atavistic discord continued unabated and morphed into other forms of political, cultural and social struggle.

What we eventually learn, much later in Dr Ambedkar's long-wending historical narrative, is that the nagas were a non-Aryan people whom the Aryans were unable to conquer. And they were not just anybody. Dr Ambedkar wrote, 'Whatever fame and glory India achieved in ancient times in the political field, the credit for it goes entirely to the non-Aryan Nagas.'[17] He mentioned the kingdom of Magadha, founded by Shishunaga, a naga. His dynasty was usurped by Mahapadmananda, whom ancient and modern historians assert was of 'low birth', but Aryan nonetheless. The Nanda dynasty ruled till Chandragupta emerged to form the Mauryan dynasty. What's fascinating was that Dr Ambedkar claimed that Chandragupta was related to the last of Shishunaga's line, and thus in overthrowing the Nandas, the Mauryas were actually reinstating the naga lineage. But as we shall see, it was not the naga lineage that prevailed ultimately, for the Mauryas themselves were wiped out through the machinations of Pushyamitra Shunga. And Buddhism too was wiped out with the last of that dynasty. But all this comes later.

Dr Ambedkar presented the triumph of the Vedic Aryans (part of India's early history) using the analogy of the French Revolution, as the *ancien régime*. The first part of Dr Ambedkar's history of struggle was to evaluate the culture of the ancient regime, which he dissected in terms of its mores—especially the addiction to gambling and predilection for bloodshed and violence—and of course its dictates and practices regarding caste and gender.

Then Dr Ambedkar systematically elucidated how the emergence of Buddhism challenged these basic mores, practices and dictates of Vedic Aryan dominance, citing from numerous Buddhist texts of the Pali canon. These Buddhists texts—in Pali and not in Sanskrit—revealed the anti-violence, anti-caste, pro-gender equality principles emanating from the Buddhist revolution recorded in the earliest literature. That revolution was not just religious or social, but as we see from the history of the Mauryan dynasty, it became political and juridical too.

The Mauryas, however, collapsed and this brought to a close the political and juridical incorporation of Buddhist egalitarian doctrines. From this point of drastic drop, a continuous decline of Buddhist influence followed over the centuries. But what about its social and religious influence? How were these obliterated? Mainstream histories have highlighted the role of later Islamic incursion into the subcontinent as a primary factor for the demographic destruction of Buddhism in India. While this narrative seemed to play nicely into the hands of Hindu nationalist historiography, Dr Ambedkar found it unsatisfactory primarily because it failed to explain the total annihilation of Buddhism in all of its variegated forms: political, legal, ideological, social, cultural and aesthetic. Thus, Dr Ambedkar postulated that only the steady decline of Buddhism over the centuries was explained by mainstream history. Its complete fall, collapse and obliteration, however, could only be understood as the result of a counter-revolution that was total and systematic.

Dr Ambedkar provided a comprehensive picture of the counter-revolution in terms of politics, of law, and of philosophy and religion, displaying the full breadth and magnitude of his unparalleled polymath learning, well beyond his formal training in economics and law. In turning to this brief sketch of the grand history that Dr Ambedkar composed, a proper understanding emerges of the unknown backstory of what the term 'equality' in the Preamble actually signified for Dr Ambedkar.

The Ancient Regime and the Rise of Reformers

The Buddha (circa 563 BCE–483 BCE) was presented by Dr Ambedkar as a pre-eminent social reformer of ancient India. Dr Ambedkar's narrative here followed that which he presented in another of his pioneering but unfinalized books, *Buddha and His Dhamma*.[18] In that religious text, being composed by Dr Ambedkar during the same years as this historiographic one, Gautama was shown as being 'oppressed by the evils and misery'[19] of Aryan society, which is why he decided to renounce the world. This, of course, ran counter to the orthodox Buddhist account of Siddhartha Gautama's renunciation on account of the four sights.[20]

Dr Ambedkar then narrated the rapid and wide spread of Buddhism, and augmented his claim that the Buddha was a social reformer in the process. Of course, Dr Ambedkar did not discount that Buddhism swiftly spread far and wide due to the Buddha's own charisma and virtues, his nobility and so on. But what he wanted to emphasize was that what the Buddha was doing was shining the light of his virtues in a dark and debauched environment. It was this that added such appeal to the new dhamma that he propagated.

Dr Ambedkar presented Aryan society, the ancient regime, as being debauched not only socially, but also religiously and spiritually. Not only were social evils abundant, they were not contraindicated by the scriptures. On the contrary, many of these evils were sanctified by the scriptures. Dr Ambedkar provided dozens of pages of citations from the Vedas, the epics, and the *Brahmanas* to illustrate his point.

The Mahabharata, he maintained, was replete with evidence: Gambling was an obsession, and human lives—not just money—were on the line. Drinking (soma, a sacrificial wine only permitted to Brahmins and Kshatriyas; and *sura*, a grain-fermented liquor consumed by all) was ubiquitous. Class strife was rampant and the contradictions inherent within the varna system imposed unjust and chafing hierarchies.

In this era, the Brahmins and Kshatriyas vied for supremacy, with many disputes recorded and bloody battles fought. However, both joined forces to oppress the Vaishyas, whom Ambedkar characterized as the milch cows (the source of tax revenue), and the Shudras, who served as the beasts of burden. Then there were also outcastes like the Chandalas and Shwappakas, not technically untouchables, who would emerge later in history, but rejects of Aryan society all the same.

According to Dr Ambedkar's account, in Aryan society sexual license was pronounced and sanctified; bestiality was not just practiced but also approved. And throughout all this, the priests produced the most elaborate, baroque, absurd sacrificial rituals; orgiastic and void of spiritual meaning. The holy books reinforced all of these vices through depictions of the acts of all the gods. The Aryan religious practices were as debauched and unethical as its social practices.

Buddhist Suttas As Social Reform

In the context of the ethics and politics of his time, the Buddha's teachings took on a special social reformative significance. The Buddha taught by example. To illustrate this, Dr Ambedkar excerpted the first main section (the frame story and the elaboration of the *silas*) of the *Brahmajāla Sutta*, the first sutta in the Dīgha Nikāya (Long Discourses).

This sutta elaborated on the core doctrines of Buddhism—the Ten Precepts (Cula-sila), the Middle Precepts (Majjhima-sila) and the Great Precepts (Maha-sila)—but it did so in a manner that was unusual. That is, it introduced them by way of negating any special fascination for them. But these formal aspects of the Sutta were not Dr Ambedkar's concern. And indeed, unlike the case with other suttas that Dr Ambedkar cited in full in *Revolution and Counter-Revolution*, he did not include the second and third parts (on beliefs and doctrines) of the *Brahmajāla Sutta* at all, focusing exclusively on the ethical practices that the Buddha introduced to Aryan society.

There is no shortage of commentary on this important sutta, which appeared in ancient Tibetan and Mongolian editions as well, and was deemed as the means through which Buddhism spread to Burma in particular. It is, in fact, a major work in the Buddhist canon. However, Dr Ambedkar's interest was historiographical rather than philosophical. For him, the import of this sutta was that it detailed what the Buddha undertook in contradistinction to what the Brahmins undertook, providing contemporary historical evidence of what practices were common during the Vedic-Aryan period. In other words, this sutta reinforced the reading of the Mahabharata and the *Brahmanas* that Dr Ambedkar had cited in order to show the profound moral dilapidation of society under early Vedic Brahmanism.

Most religious commentary on the sutta naturally explored its teachings, the dogmatics, the unique structure of the text, and the like. In so doing, it also commented on parallels with Brahmanical philosophy. This is useful to look at, to gain some perspective on the alternative way that Dr Ambedkar read the text. For example, Buddhist scholar Alexander Syrkin stated:

> We can suggest a possible reference to the four main principles of behavior in Hindu ethics (*purusartha—dharma, artha, kama, moksa*) . . . [Thus] we have interesting testimony [to] the set of life's principle values, so important in Hindu tradition, [that] can be said to have been applied (with natural modifications within the framework of new dogmatics), by early Buddhism.[21]

This is interesting because Syrkin went on to clarify that the *Brahmajāla Sutta* belonged to the fifth to third centuries BCE (although it was written in 80 CE), whereas religious scholars generally posit that Hindu texts finally brought all four *purusartha*s together (*moksa* was added last) no earlier than the first century CE. Although as a modern scholar, Syrkin took for granted the standard interpretation that tenets of Brahmanism influenced Buddhist thought and practice, he was actually providing evidence for the Ambedkarian revisionist thesis, which we saw earlier were also supported by the claims of M.N. Roy. According to this revisionist thesis, Buddhist thought posed a revolutionary challenge to Brahmanism, and thus elements of the former were appropriated in later Hindu thought in order to vanquish it in a counter-revolution.

After his reproduction of the *Brahmajāla Sutta* excerpts, Dr Ambedkar did point to some of the positive precepts (the sila) that the Buddha taught and practised. He wanted to rub it in, that such 'a high standard of moral life was quite unknown to the Aryan society of his day'.[22] Dr Ambedkar then listed not only the Pañcasīla prescribed for the laity, but also five additional precepts for the monks, but he stressed on the first, not to kill. This was not a passive precept, not merely ahimsa, but was to be actualized in *metta* (loving kindness), a concept (as we shall see in the next chapter) that held a prominent place in Dr Ambedkar's preamble.

The precept not to kill may obviously be seen in a doctrinal way, as articulating a basic Buddhist norm. But seen from the perspective of the social context—Aryan society—this first and fundamental Buddhist precept constituted a serious challenge to the protocols of Vedic-Aryan sacrifice, the yajna. Thus, Dr Ambedkar presented the Pañcasīla not only as a positive doctrine of ethics valuable in its own right, but simultaneously as a moment of revolutionary challenge striking at the core of yajna, thereby undermining the hegemonic authority of the Vedas.

To buttress his case, Dr Ambedkar next appended an excerpt from the *Jatakamala* (the tenth story) and the *Kutadanta Sutta*, clearly revealing the Buddha's opposition to yajna.

Violence: Jatakamala and Kutadanta Sutta

In one charming Jataka tale, the Buddha was born as a great king of virtue who ruled justly over a peaceful and prosperous land. A year of drought afflicted his kingdom. He consulted the religious leaders who advised him, in accordance with Vedic practice, to sacrifice a thousand animals. But as a person who held on to rational principles and moral precepts, he did not believe that shedding the blood of a thousand animals would in any way solve the problem. Instead of contradicting his Brahmin advisers, he decided to trick them and everyone else, by announcing the sacrifice of a thousand humans—but only wicked humans. After this proclamation, people became virtuous under the threat of death, and over time, virtue for the sake of its own boons and benefits, rather than out of fear, became the norm. The king then revealed his true plan and, at the same time, his superior wisdom. In place of a sacrifice, he established alms halls across the kingdom so that the poor would be fed and no one would be wanting in basic needs. As poverty disappeared and virtue flourished, the land was once again prosperous and the period of drought passed.

In reproducing this text, Dr Ambedkar was again deploying his two-fold strategy: the positive moral virtue was foregrounded, the precept that one must not kill, signifying that kindness was superior to sacrifices; at the same time, the inherent violence of Vedic prescriptions was exposed, which not only mandated the killing of a thousand animals, but even tolerated without objection the plan that a thousand humans be killed instead.

Dr Ambedkar then turned to *Kutadanta Sutta* to reveal more about the Buddha's attitude towards sacrifice, citing Thomas Rhys Davids' translation in full. Interestingly, Rhys Davids may have been one of the primary catalysts for Dr Ambedkar's understanding of the role of Buddhism in social and religious transformation. In his Introduction to the translation, Rhys Davids wrote:

> On the question of caste or social privileges, the early Buddhists took up, and pushed to its logical conclusions, a rational view held also by others. And on this question of sacrifice their party won. The Vedic sacrifices of animals had practically been given up when the long struggle between Brahmanism and Buddhism reached its close. Isolated instances of such sacrifices are known even down to the Mohammedan invasion. But the battle was really won by the Buddhists and their allies. And the combined ridicule and earnestness of our Sutta will have had its share in bringing about the victory.[23]

This sutta recounts the transformation of the Brahmin Kutadanta, who was preparing a huge animal sacrifice, by listening to a story of the Buddha. The Buddha taught Kutadanta that sacrifices of alms giving, generosity and promoting the happiness of others was far superior to killing animals to appease the gods. Kutadanta then decided to set all the animals free and follow the path that the Buddha taught.

Caste and Gender Equality: *Ambattha Sutta* and *Lohikka Sutta*

Once Dr Ambedkar established the Buddhist overturning of the Brahmanical paradigm of killing animals for sacrifice (and the benefits that the priests enjoyed thereby), he moved on to the social revolution effected by the Buddha's denunciation of caste. Now, this was not the caste system in its rigid later form, where inter-dining and intermarriage were prohibited. However, caste still meant inequality. It was this inequality at the heart of caste that the Buddha opposed. As we saw in the 'schemes of books', Dr Ambedkar made it quite clear that equality was in some sense the essence of the Buddhist revolution in ancient India. For evidence, he cited the *Ambattha Sutta* in its entire length.

The *Ambattha Sutta* is truly amazing in several respects. First, it reveals a social struggle between Kshatriyas and Brahmins, establishing the superiority of the aristocrats over the priests. This itself functioned within Dr Ambedkar's grander narrative of counter-revolution, since the overwhelming Brahmanical assertion (counter-revolution) that came about a few centuries later included not only the exile of Buddhism from India, but also the social victory of the priestly classes over the aristocracy. Second, the Buddha's supernatural powers are appealed to here, indicating that he was able to summon powerful gods and make his bare body visible through his clothes and so on.

Dr Ambedkar's interest in the text, however, concerned the disavowal of caste as a central revolutionary feature of Buddhism. This is found in the verse that the Buddha cited as representing his own view:

The Khattiyas are best of those people
who take clan as the standard.
But one accomplished in knowledge and conduct
is best of gods and humans.[24]

That is, while it might be true that the Kshatriyas are superior amongst castes, the concern of tribal thinking, what was truly best was not reducible to birth, varna, caste—it was the attainment and practice of right knowledge and conduct.

In the sutta, the Brahmin student Ambattha was sent by his famous teacher Pokkharasaati to find out if the acclaimed Gautama was really the great man that he was said to be. Ambattha was to particularly ascertain if the Buddha bore the thirty-two marks of a great man. Ambattha went to meet the Buddha and behaved insultingly towards him, arrogating himself to a higher position as a Brahmin over the lower-born Sakyas (Kshatriya). The Buddha humbled Ambattha, educated him, and the student returned to his teacher to narrate what had occurred. Pokkharasaati was angered, he kicked Ambattha and took off in the middle of the night to confront the Buddha. However, upon encountering the Buddha and seeing that he did indeed bear all the marks of a great man, he engaged with the Buddha openly and ended up as a convert and supporter of the sangha.

In his commentary on the *Ambattha Sutta*, Dr Ambedkar emphasized that in practice, the Buddha ignored the birth origins of the people who came before him, permitting the Shudras to be bhikkhus and just as well as Brahmins. Dr Ambedkar mentioned Upali (formerly a barber), Sunita (from the Pukkusa tribe), Sati (from a fisherman community), Nanda (formerly a cowherd) and many other examples of lower caste and outcaste people who played prominent roles in the Buddhist texts.

In Dr Ambedkar's reading, not only did the Buddha elevate the status of the lower castes but also that of women. While in Aryan society, women were ineligible for *sanyas*, the Buddha accepted them as bhikkhunis. In Brahmanical literature, women were often equated to the Shudras, but in Buddhism, their position was uplifted in line with the principle of equality. We should note that since the time of Dr Ambedkar's writing on the emancipatory orientation of early Buddhism, there has been important debate regarding the persistence of misogynistic practices and beliefs in the sanghas. Dr Ambedkar's essential point, however, was that the very possibility and actuality of women's inclusion into the order, as introduced by Buddhism, was revolutionary. The new revolutionary principle of equality implicit to Buddhism grounds our own critique of its faulty implementation within the sangha.

Also, in line with this revolutionary account of Buddhism was that, according to Dr Ambedkar, the Buddha critiqued the Brahmanical exclusion of the Shudras and women from the privilege of learning. In support, he cited Rhys Davids' introductory commentary from his translation of the sutta:

> that everyone should be allowed to learn; that everyone, having certain abilities, should be allowed to teach; and that, if he does teach, he should teach all and to all; keeping nothing back, shutting no one out.[25]

In light of these assertions, Dr Ambedkar cited from the *Lohikka Sutta*. The sutta gave the Buddha's views on good and bad teachings, as well as on who is entitled to be a teacher. In it, the Brahmin Lohikka held the view that if someone discovered new knowledge, he should keep it to himself. The Buddha interrogated the assumptions behind Lohikka's position and replaced it with an enlightened view of knowledge and the teaching of knowledge over birth or status.

The Decline of Buddhism: Mainstream View

Historians are yet to provide a satisfactory answer to the eradication of Buddhism from India, in contradistinction to its flourishing all over northern and South East Asia. To address it, Dr Ambedkar first made a subtle distinction between 'the fall of Buddhism' and the total '"downfall" of Buddhism'.[26] The standard reasons for the fall that are provided by mainstream historians are obvious and unobjectionable; but the reasons for the total 'downfall' are not so obvious.

Dr Ambedkar agreed that the fall of Buddhism may be attributed to factors such as its steady decline subsequent to its losing political and juridical support after Pushyamitra Shunga and the ensuing dynasties from the first century onwards, and this culminated centuries later with the Muslim invasions and the enmity of Islam toward *but*s (idols). Dr Ambedkar posited that the very term 'but' was derived from the name 'Buddha'. A recent historian of Buddhism, Peter Harvey, himself confirmed this:

> From 986 CE, the Muslim Turks started raiding northwest India from Afghanistan, plundering western India early in the eleventh century. Forced conversions to Islam were made, and Buddhist images smashed, due to the Islamic dislike of idolatry. Indeed, in India, the Islamic term for an 'idol' became 'budd'.[27]

The Muslims identified Buddhism as being idolatrous and set about destroying idols and images, and decimating the religion from Bactria and huge tracts across Asia.

But how did the equally idolatrous Brahmanism survive the onslaught that Buddhism could not withstand? Dr Ambedkar offered three reasons:

(a) Brahmanism had state support; Buddhism did not.
(b) Muslims were able to massacre the Buddhist bhikkhus (who were celibate), but not the Brahmin priesthood, as any person born to Brahmins could refill the ranks naturally.
(c) Buddhist laity was tortured by Brahmins and that disposed them to convert to Islam when pressured by the Muslims to do so.

Dr Ambedkar spent a lot of time defending these controversial claims. To his mind, they helped to explicate how the mainstream view of Buddhism's total downfall paid too much attention to the actions of the Muslims and too little attention to the social and cultural logic of Brahmanism that was always at play.

With reference to various histories of the era, Dr Ambedkar tried to establish that between 1000 CE and 1200 CE, almost all the major kingdoms were ruled either by Brahmins or by the Kshatriyas and Rajputs who were adherents of orthodox Brahmanism (counter-intuitively, but that is how graded inequality operates).

The Buddhist universities (Nalanda and others) were ransacked and viharas everywhere were destroyed. The bhikkhus were massacred, with no relief or protection to be found from any ruling king. Hence those who survived fled to the north and east. But in Brahmanism, any sundry Brahmin by birth could be recruited to the priesthood, and thus every male member of the population would need to be annihilated in order to successfully wipe out the priesthood. This was unlike Buddhism, where the priests, monks and nuns had to be ordained in accordance with the rites by those already ordained. Once the ordained priests were wiped out, the priesthood was wiped out.

Attempts to hurriedly refill the ranks of the Buddhist priesthood led to further problems. 'The paucity of Bhiksus brought about a great change . . .' such that artisans like masons, painters, goldsmiths, etc., had to be recruited. Plying their trade, they had little time to study the scripture. Yet they were expected to lead and guide the lay community.[28]

> They could not be expected to raise the declining Buddhism to a higher position through their endeavors nor could they check its course towards its ruin through the introduction of salutary reforms.[29]

As for the conversion of Buddhist laity in large numbers to Islam, the fact that much of north-eastern areas converted, i.e., largely Buddhist regions converted, is linked to the oppression by Brahmin rulers there. The bloodthirsty Mihirkula as well as Shashanka, the notorious hater of Buddhism, are two kings adduced as evidence. Dr Ambedkar cited Vincent Smith's *Early History of India*:

> Shashanka . . . burnt the holy Bodhi tree at Buddha Gaya . . . broke the stone marked with the footprints of Buddha at Pataliputra; destroyed the convents, scattered the monks, carrying his persecutions to the foot of the Nepalese hills.[30]

We can conclude then that Dr Ambedkar conceded that the fall of Buddhism was largely due to Muslim incursion, as presented in the mainstream view. But he supplemented this with a fuller understanding of how the Buddhists converted to Islam to escape oppression by the Brahmanical Rajput and Brahmin rulers. But the question still remains about Buddhism's total downfall, total eradication, and even disappearance.

The Counter-Revolution

The real explanation behind the total eradication of Buddhism from India is to be found in a systematic and long-standing counter-revolution against the egalitarian revolution that Buddhism had inaugurated. This counter-revolution was launched politically, and can even be dated. The villain of Dr Ambedkar's history was Pushyamitra Shunga, the Brahmin commander-in-chief of Brihadratha (the last ruler of the Mauryan dynasty), who, in 185 BCE assassinated the Mauryan king, usurped his throne and inaugurated the Shunga dynasty.

Now, historians generally buy into the broad outlines, at least of the anti-Buddhistic and pro-Brahmanical manoeuvres of Pushyamitra, in his coup d'état against the Mauryans. Dr Ambedkar set about amplifying all the ways in which Pushyamitra subverted Buddhist doctrines, starting with the brutal and bloody sacrifices that had been abolished under the Mauryans.

As we have a date for the launch of the political counter-revolution (185 BCE), a lot of the rest of Dr Ambedkar's revisionist account of the history of India hangs upon this date. Dating is of course the centre of so much controversy in the study and writing of history. As far as the various kingdoms and dynasties that Dr Ambedkar mentioned are concerned, the historians are in general conformity—within a year or two of difference—as well as in conformity with Dr Ambedkar. That is, as far as the broad strokes of political history are concerned, Dr Ambedkar did not challenge the dating of mainstream historiography. He did, however, hone in on several points that were generally glossed over by the professional historians—the varna (and *gotra*) of the dynastic heads of, for example, the Magadhas, the Mauryans, the Guptas, etc. A fair amount of the evidence supporting the logic of revolution and counter-revolution hangs upon these caste identities.

The political counter-revolution was institutionalized through a legal one with the drafting of the *Manusmriti*. The *Manusmriti* introduced a totally radical juridical regime of Brahmanism and graded inequality, going so far as to justify the right of Brahmins to commit regicide, thereby retroactively legitimizing Pushyamitra's crime. This raises the issue of *its* dating. For his part, Dr Ambedkar provided dates based on numerous secondary sources as well as on internal evidence within the works under discussion. It would be fruitful to compare his results with some mainstream historians, none of whom show familiarity with Dr Ambedkar's historiography—and thus are free from his influence—in their own writings. Three good points of comparison are Romila Thapar,[31] Upinder Singh[32] and Peter Robb.[33] As far as Dr Ambedkar's claim regarding the dating of the *Manusmriti* just after the 185 BCE coup of Pushyamitra is concerned, this turns out to not be problematic for any of these three historians, all of whom mention in their own work a range of 200 BCE to 100 BCE.

Brahmanical Ideology: The Philosophy and Literature of Counter-Revolution

Things get more complicated, however, with the next phase of the counter-revolution; that is, with respect to its ideological stabilization through the vast literature of Brahmanism which, Dr Ambedkar claimed, flourished *after* the political triumph of Pushyamitra. He divided this literature into several categories, which he then set about to comment upon only insofar as the decline of Buddhism was concerned:

a) The *Bhagavad Gita*
b) Shankaracharya's *Vedanta* (although Dr Ambedkar actually only addresses Mimamsa and the *Vedant Sutras*)
c) The Mahabharata
d) The Ramayana
e) The *Puranas*

Again, the controversial point to flag here is Dr Ambedkar's claim that these works/collections came after Pushyamitra, at least in the editions that come down to us. Among our sample of professional historians, there is far less uniformity when it comes to dating this literature. Peter Robb has offered the second century as the probable date for the *Bhagavad Gita*, though he is willing to accept a date as late as 100 CE. Upinder Singh is comfortable with a range closer to that of Dr Ambedkar's; that is, as late as 200 CE. With the Mahabharata, Robb offers a BCE date whereas Singh will go as recent as 400 CE. For Robb, Valmiki's Ramayana is dated 300 BCE whereas for Singh it is 400 CE. Tulsi Das' *Ramayana* is dated 1600 CE by all three historians. There is also no disagreement on Shankaracharya's *Vedanta* from any of the historians or Dr Ambedkar.

As far as the *Puranas* are concerned, there is again no challenge to the dates that Dr Ambedkar prescribed; that is, all dates are around and after the Gupta era. The counter-revolutionary role that Dr Ambedkar attributed to the *Puranas*, especially to the *Maha Puranas*, in undergirding the ritualistic world-view of Brahmanism, is hardly controversial even amongst mainstream historians. Dr Ambedkar was trying to reorient that truism into something more socially and politically powerful—his argument was that the *Puranas* in all their variations and diverse geographical origins were functioning to bring about a pan-Indian resurgence of Brahmanism, as a follow-up to Manu's reactionary juridical revolution.

The only major problem with the dating that Dr Ambedkar proposed is with respect to the *Vedanta Sutras*; specifically, the rival writings of two salient traditions, that of Jaimini (the reputed founder of Mimamsa) and Badarayana. But getting into these details would take us too far afield from the main thesis of *Revolution and Counter-Revolution*, and the fundamental role played by the concept of 'equality' within Dr Ambedkar's thought and writing.

So, at last, how did Dr Ambedkar's claim fare, that all of the literature mentioned was either authored or significantly redacted after Pushyamitra, when compared to the dating of professional historians? In the end, Singh and Thapar (but in a few cases not Robb) would accept Dr Ambedkar's dating for the *Gita*, Shankaracharya's *Vedanta*, the Ramayana, the Mahabharata and the *Puranas*, although the details regarding Mimamsa and the *Vedanta Sutras* may be problematic.

The Hegemony That 'Equality' Is Up Against

Why was it so important to Dr Ambedkar for this vast literature to be consequent to the political revolt of Pushyamitra? Because once Dr Ambedkar pegged the revolt and uprising against Buddhism at the political moment of Pushyamitra, the rest of the Brahmanical literature in question functioned as the philosophical, theological and social counter-revolution to supplement and secure the political one. It was a brilliant thesis and an awe-inspiring, even if incomplete, tome that Dr Ambedkar produced. In its heft and comprehensiveness, it could be compared to Edward Gibbon's

Decline and Fall of the Roman Empire,[34] but in its ultimately philosophical and dialectical vision, what Dr Ambedkar managed to produce was the only known rival in India to German philosopher G.W.F. Hegel's *The Philosophy of History*,[35] incorporating the entire history of philosophy.

For Hegel, the grand march of history had revealed the slow and tortuous journey of the emergence of freedom.[36] But for Dr Ambedkar, history revealed the slow and tortuous journey of the emergence of equality. The 'equality' clause as it appears in the final draft of the Preamble may seem to be stated sparsely, as we noted initially. But as was revealed by an exploration of Ambedkar's *Revolution and Counter-Revolution in Ancient India*, the clause can be understood to encapsulate the entire march of the civilizational history of India's egalitarian revolution.

And that is its real significance in Dr Ambedkar's preamble.

4

Fraternity: Affection for Everyone, Hatred for None

Despite Jawaharlal Nehru supporting the deviations from the Objectives Resolution during the drafting of the Preamble, and irrespective of the fact that the Drafting Committee itself was packed with members who had been authors of the 'declaration' that had—nearly word for word—been the source of Nehru's Objectives Resolution, nearly all the clauses that appeared in the Preamble finalized by the Drafting Committee on 21 February 1948, and submitted by Dr Ambedkar to the president of the Constituent Assembly, came under attack in the Constituent Assembly for veering away from the unanimously and solemnly passed Objectives Resolution. There was one glaring exception to this: the 'fraternity' clause.

The 'fraternity' clause elicited universal and effusive praise from the Constituent Assembly. It was a subject of discussion in each of the Assembly's three readings, from the moment it was introduced to the world in February 1948 right until Dr Ambedkar's famous final speech on 25 November 1949 that led to the Assembly's vote to adopt the Constitution the next day. During the contentious first reading, when Dr Ambedkar was parrying criticism for refusing to introduce Gandhian ideas into the constitutional draft, he was also occasionally lauded. Constituent Assembly member Thakur Das Bhargava (from East Punjab), whom Dr Ambedkar later identified in his famous final speech as one of the always-contrarian 'rebels' who kept him on his toes throughout the drafting process, had this to say during his speech on 6 November 1948:

> I think, Sir, that the soul of this Constitution is contained in the Preamble and I am glad to express my sense of gratitude to Dr. Ambedkar for having added the word 'fraternity' to the Preamble. Now, Sir, I want to apply the touch-stone of this Preamble to the entire Constitution. If Justice, Liberty, Equality and Fraternity are to be found in this Constitution, if we can get this ideal through this Constitution, I maintain that the Constitution is good. In so far as these four things which are contained in the Preamble are wanting, then I am bound to say that the Constitution is wanting, and from this angle I want to judge the Constitution.[1]

The clause also excited J.B. Kripalani who had always condemned the Drafting Committee for forsaking even the most minor of attempts to incorporate Gandhian principles. With the 'fraternity' clause, however, he was able to read in a certain spiritually uplifting morality that gave him solace:

> Again I come to the great doctrine of fraternity which is allied with democracy. It means that we are all sons of the same God, as the religious would say, but as the mystic would say, that there is one life pulsating through us all, or as the Bible says, 'We are one of another'. There can be no fraternity without this. So I want this House to remember that what we have enunciated are not merely legal, constitutional and formal

> principles, but moral principles; and moral principles have got to be lived in life. They have to be lived whether it is private life or it is public life, whether it is commercial life, political life or the life of an administrator. They have to be lived throughout. These things, we have to remember if our Constitution is to succeed.[2]

Gratitude to Dr Ambedkar

It is worth noting that Thakur Das Bhargava expressed his 'gratitude to Dr Ambedkar', as opposed to the Drafting Committee, 'for having added the word "fraternity" to the Preamble'. Indeed, it was Dr Ambedkar who personally added the word 'fraternity' to the Preamble.

The draft preamble, which Dr Ambedkar had apparently pulled out from his shirt pocket on the morning of 6 February 1948, included a 'fraternity' clause without any precedent. If you check any history of the Constitution of India, any commentary on the Preamble, they all vaguely gloss over the appearance of this term. This elision gives the impression that the term simply came from nowhere, it seemingly fell from the sky.

And though totally erroneous, there is pretty good reason to believe this. After all, the Congress Working Committee's (CWC) Expert Committee 'declaration' of July 1946 did not mention the word 'fraternity'. Nehru's Objectives Resolution passed on 22 January 1947 did not mention it. B.N. Rau's preliminary draft Constitution, which formed the basis of what the Drafting Committee was meant to work with, did not mention it. Indeed, in every source document that was influential, either in terms of borrowed clauses and articles, or in terms of historical significance, the term 'fraternity' was absent. This included the 1930 Indian National Congress' famous 'Declaration of Purna Swaraj', which influenced the date the Constitution of India was adopted, and the 1935 Government of India Act from which our Constitution liberally borrowed.

The word 'fraternity' did not even feature in any of the unofficial alternative constitutions that were being drafted by various outliers, minority parties and rivals to the Congress. For example, *The Gandhian Constitution of Free India* that was published in 1946 by Shriman Narayan Agarwal and included a foreword by M.K. Gandhi.[3] Then there was M.N. Roy's *Constitution of Free India: A Draft*, published in 1944 under the auspices of the Radical Democratic Party. Again, in March 1948, right in the midst of the Constituent Assembly and the drafting of our Constitution, the Socialist Party of India prepared its own draft entitled *Draft Constitution of the Indian Republic*, with a foreword by Jayprakash Narayan.[4] The Socialist Party, who sought to nationalize industry, condemned the Constituent Assembly's draft Constitution because it 'fell short of economic and equalitarian ideas', but the party followed the Constituent Assembly's draft very closely in terms of structure and headings.[5] It included a preamble, 'fundamental rights', and even 'Directive Principles of State Policy'.[6] But what it did not include, like its rivals from among the Gandhians or M.N. Roy, or anybody else for that matter, was the term 'fraternity'.[7]

This addition, as we saw, turned out to be universally appreciated within the Constituent Assembly itself. But this does not mean that it was an easy ride for Dr Ambedkar to bring it in to the process of drafting within the Drafting Committee. The hiccups are apparent from the various iterations of the fraternity clause over time.

On 6 February 1948, the clause first read:

> Fraternity, assuring the dignity of every individual without distinction of caste or creed.[8]

This is purely the Ambedkarian formulation of fraternity, quite in line with the history of Dr Ambedkar's articulation of the concept in his own writings, dating back to the 1930s, as we will soon explore. It drew upon fraternity as a resource for upholding individual dignity, which remains perpetually degraded due to the distinctions of caste. In the formulation of the first day, 6 February, when Dr Ambedkar slipped his new preamble into the folio, with its unprecedented fraternity clause, there was no concession with regard to the interests of the left-leaning members of the Drafting Committee, who would have been inclined to introduce their quintessential principle of class conflict, not caste conflict, wherever possible in the draft. Nor was there any hint of concession to the interests of either the right-leaning or nationalist members of the Drafting Committee, who would have been inclined to give prominence to the idea of the nation, and not just the individual, wherever possible in the draft.

Ambedkar's Pragmatism

And this is precisely what unfolded. On 9 February 1948, upon salvos from the other Drafting Committee members, a new, more concessional 'fraternity' clause emerged, with conciliatory inclusion of the terms 'class' and 'nation':

> Fraternity, without distinction of caste, class or creed, so as to assure the dignity of every individual and the unity of the Nation.[9]

Now Dr Ambedkar had managed to bring every Drafting Committee member on board, a masterstroke of diplomacy and inclusive and cooperative drafting. But the cheerful mood of handshaking and back-patting died a sudden death the following morning, once everyone in the Drafting Committee awoke to the realization that they had brazenly defied their mandate of following the Objectives Resolution. This was a charge which, as we opened by saying, they were right to fear, since the same accusation was parried about so frequently throughout the Constituent Assembly's three readings of the draft Constitution. The Drafting Committee got together in a huddle, for they were confident that they had followed the spirit of the Objectives Resolution in breaking the letter of it. On 10 February 1948, they devised one of the clumsiest solutions imaginable. The Drafting Committee decided to append a footnote to the Preamble!

The footnote, which was meant to justify other deviations by the Drafting Committee related to the contentious issue of sovereignty vis-à-vis the Commonwealth, and not only the addition of new clauses and concepts, would have been appraised by Queen Gertrude along the lines of her assessment of the play put on by her son, Hamlet: 'The lady doth protest too much, me thinks'; for, the footnote began:

> The Committee has followed the Objectives Resolution in drafting the Preamble.[10]

It evidently had not.

And in subsequent meetings of the Drafting Committee, from 11 February to 21 February 1948, Dr Ambedkar, with the backing of Constitutional Adviser B.N. Rau,[11] thought it was best for the committee to come clean. What exactly occurred in those meetings is lost to history, with neither transcripts nor minutes recorded. However, sometime between 11 and 21 February, the 'fraternity' clause was amended again. It finally read, on 21 February 1948, the exact same way that it would on 26 January 1950:

> Fraternity, assuring the dignity of the individual and the unity of the Nation.[12]

N. Madhava Rao did not attend the meetings on 11 and 13 February 1948, so it was only Dr Ambedkar and two others discussing the draft (Alladi Krishnaswami Ayyar and Maulavi Md Saadulla). Mysteriously, there was no mention of the Preamble in the extant minutes. Until we find the black box,[13] recording specifics from 11 to 21 February 1948, we will be left to speculate on the reasons for these later changes.

The line of explanation in standard commentary on the drafting of the Constitution is that the Drafting Committee opted for simplification in the preambular text, especially in cases where the preambular clauses were elaborated upon and given binding force in the body of the Constitution. From what we know of Dr Ambedkar, the true reasons were likely more pragmatic—concessional, yes, but also strategic and philosophical.

Need 'Never Greater than Now'

On 21 February 1948, Dr Ambedkar packed up the working draft Constitution created by the Drafting Committee since it first met on 30 August 1947. Sending the completed draft to the president of the Constituent Assembly, Dr Ambedkar enclosed an important cover note explaining the Drafting Committee's methods and decisions, and a clear and forthright confession of its departure from the Objectives Resolution, along with its justification. That note read in part:

> The committee has added a clause about fraternity in the Preamble although it does not occur in the Objectives Resolution. The committee felt that the need for fraternal concord and goodwill in India was never greater than now and that this particular aim of the new Constitution should be emphasized by special mention in the Preamble.
>
> In other respects the Committee has tried to embody in the Preamble the spirit and, as far as possible, the language of the Objectives Resolution.[14]

This was the right decision and would prove to be universally recognized as such. The 'fraternity' clause was met with enthusiasm across all the spectrums represented in the Constituent Assembly, and as the clear brainchild of Dr Ambedkar it certainly played a role—augmented by his formidable charisma, oratorial skill, dexterous wit and encyclopedic knowledge—in building upon his already enhanced reputation and profile within the Constituent Assembly itself.

Dr Ambedkar's note to the president of the Constituent Assembly mentioned that the need for fraternal concord was never greater than now, an obvious allusion to the ongoing tragedies in the wake of Partition. But there was another underlying discord in Dr Ambedkar's mind as he wrote this note: the contentious and divisive omnipresence of caste. And given the battery of assaults on Brahmanism and Brahmanical patriarchy that were inscribed into the body of the enclosed Constitution, as well as being unleashed in the form of the Hindu Code Bill, now being rewritten by Dr Ambedkar, 'the need for fraternal concord and goodwill in India was never greater than now'. For, as Dr Ambedkar would soon pen down in *Revolution and Counter-Revolution in Ancient India*, Brahmanism was divisive to the core:

> By the denial of education to the Shudras, by diverting the Kshatriyas to military pursuits, and the Vaishyas to trade and by reserving education to themselves, the Brahmins alone could become the educated class—free to misdirect and misguide the whole society. By converting Varna into Caste, they declared that mere birth was a real and final measure of the worth of a man. Caste and Graded Inequality made disunity and discord a matter of course.[15]

The long march towards the annihilation of caste and its inauguration through a radically egalitarian assault, by means of nascent constitutional law, on the ubiquitous and millennia-old social law of graded inequality was not going to be free of violence, bloodshed and tragedy. And so again, 'the need for fraternal concord and goodwill in India was never greater than now'.

Fraternity in Ambedkar's Thought

But 'now'—21 February 1948—was not the first time that Dr Ambedkar spoke of fraternity. While all of the available source documents that either formally or informally came to bear upon the form and content of the Constitution of India were silent on the concept of 'fraternity', it was of frequent and indeed continuously evolving usage in Dr Ambedkar's own writings and speeches.

The centrality of the idea of fraternity to Dr Ambedkar's thought cannot be overestimated. He not only appealed to it in the Drafting Committee and the Constituent Assembly Debates, or roughly the period from 1947–50, where Dr Ambedkar took recourse to 'fraternity', he made judicious use of the term even in *Annihilation of Caste* (1936)[16] and through essays like 'The Philosophy of Hinduism'[17] and the 'Hindu Social Order',[18] probably written during the period that he began working on the Hindu Code Bill (1947–51). It also appeared in books like *Riddles in Hinduism* (composed somewhere between 1951–53), a later important interview (on All India Radio in 1954) and a late speech on 'Buddha and Karl Marx' (an oblique reference, speaking of 'love and justice' in 1956),[19] right up to his final, posthumously published masterpiece, *The Buddha and His Dhamma* (written between 1953 and 1956, published in 1957 after his death).[20]

With such frequent use in so many different contexts, it is difficult to pin down one specific definition of the term that Dr Ambedkar consistently used over the twenty years that he took recourse to it. Its own meaning seemed to change, along with the synonyms that he employed while describing it. But in a very general way, there was a pattern to the evolution of the concept in his thought over the decades, which is broadly discernible and not too contentious. That is, Dr Ambedkar first thought of fraternity as a political concept, emerging most saliently from the French Revolution, with important social significance, one that he found sadly absent from Hindu society; this was his view pre-Preamble. Later, post-Preamble, Dr Ambedkar observed that what was absent from Hindu society was actually one of the central teachings of Buddhism, metta (metta is Pali, *maîtri* in Sanskrit). Thus, he began to see this ethico-spiritual concept as an indigenous and indeed superior formulation than the term 'fraternity', and sought to utilize it for both its social and political implications. In this account, the moment of the Preamble was the pivot from the earlier conception to the later one. This is important, because, as we shall see later, it was the continuously evolving conception of 'fraternity', as it was captured at one moment within the Preamble, that synthesized and harmonized the full breadth of Dr Ambedkar's multifaceted approach to society, politics and law.

The Morphology of Fraternity

Many other jurists, philosophers and historians have attempted to come up with a coherent account of the term 'fraternity' (or metta) in Dr Ambedkar's voluminous writings and speeches. One of India's finest contemporary philosophers, Pradeep P. Gokhale, has catalogued the most significant treatments of these terms ('fraternity' and 'metta', and also 'liberty' and 'equality') within Dr Ambedkar's writings and attempted to pin down the exact scope of their meaning for his political thought overall.

Dr Ambedkar's earliest major reference to what Gokhale called 'the trio of principles'[21] (liberty, equality and fraternity) can be found in *Annihilation of Caste*, where Dr Ambedkar referred to them as the foundations of an ideal society. He did not refer to Buddhism in this context; instead he chose to refer to the French Revolution. Thus, at this stage Dr Ambedkar was treating these principles as occasioned by the French Revolution. Even at a later stage, when he wrote 'The Hindu Social Order: Its Essential Principles', Dr Ambedkar discussed the principles in the context of the French Revolution. So, even here he did not refer to Buddhism as the source of these principles.

But in 1954, during an All India Radio interview, Dr Ambedkar seemed to have completely changed his point of view:

> My social philosophy may be said to be enshrined in three words: liberty, equality and fraternity. Let no one, however, say that I have borrowed my philosophy from the French Revolution. I have not. My philosophy has roots in religion

> and not in political science. I have derived them from the teachings of my master, the Buddha.[22]

Pradeep Gokhale has reasoned that when Dr Ambedkar said he derived his philosophy, which was enshrined in the three principles, from the teachings of the Buddha, his statement was not to be taken literally. Instead, it was to be interpreted in the context of the would-be Buddhist phase. What Gokhale aimed to show was that though Dr Ambedkar originally accepted these socio-political principles from the context of the French Revolution, he gradually reinterpreted them as ethico-religious principles. Thus, when Dr Ambedkar came to the conclusion that Buddhism was the ideal religion, towards the end of his life, he reappropriated this 'trio of principles' as being rooted in the Buddha's teaching, his dhamma.

Although the specificities of Gokhale's story may be contentious, and it should be pointed out that in his narrative there was no indication of a pivot in Dr Ambedkar's position occurring at the point of the Drafting Committee or the Constituent Assembly Debates, his reconstruction of Dr Ambedkar's 'trio of principles' teaches a very important lesson. That lesson is that we need to understand Dr Ambedkar's thought not as a static or constant viewpoint, but as a dynamic flow instead. I believe that his ideas evolved in accordance with new information that came in: new facts, momentous events, discovery of new literature. This was one of the virtues of his pragmatic philosophy that he learned from John Dewey.

The Influence of Deweyan Pragmatism

Indeed, Dewey's work, and even his words, were woven in throughout Dr Ambedkar's *Annihilation of Caste*, where he first spoke of fraternity at length:[23]

> I would not be surprised if some of you have grown weary listening to this tiresome tale of the sad effects which caste has produced. There is nothing new in it. I will therefore turn to the constructive side of the problem. What is your ideal society if you do not want caste is a question that is bound to be asked of you? If you ask me, my ideal would be a society based on Liberty, Equality and Fraternity. And why not? What objection can there be to Fraternity? I cannot imagine any. An ideal society should be mobile, should be full of channels for conveying a change taking place in one part to other parts. In an ideal society there should be many interests consciously communicated and shared. There should be varied and free points of contact with other modes of association. In other words, there must be social endosmosis. This is fraternity, which is only another name for democracy. Democracy is not merely a form of Government. It is primarily a mode of associated living, of conjoint communicated experience. It is essentially an attitude of respect and reverence towards fellow men.[24]

This passage has a great many ideas packed into it, Deweyan and otherwise. One of them is the surprising remark about fraternity, that it 'is only another name for democracy'. This then is a callback to a similar remark of his about justice; that it 'is simply another name for liberty, equality, and fraternity'.[25] Obviously, Dr Ambedkar had an organic view about how the political, social and juridical realms are related. And indeed the economic and the ethico-spiritual too, as his long-standing ideological battle on two simultaneous fronts attested—that is, one battle using Buddhism against the Hindu orthodoxy on the right; and the other using Buddhism against the Indian Marxists on the left.

Justice and democracy were imperilled by both of these defective ideologies according to him. The left one sacrificed political liberty for the sake of economic equality, and had the threat of totalitarianism constantly looming over it. The right one exploited freedom (political liberty) to sustain social inequality. We have seen Dr Ambedkar's entire life as a series of overlapping, complex and evolving, but perennial, struggles not just to overcome but to actually solve the dilemma of false alternatives on offer to India by the votaries of its left and right. This was exemplified through how he lived justly, personally working tirelessly in a democratic spirit. At least as long as he lived the principles of justice, he could sustain and preserve them, until the time came when this subjective way of being could be institutionalized. To institutionalize a subjective or personally practised ideal is to make it objective. To make Dr Ambedkar's subjective way of living justly an objective thing, it must take on legal, political and social actuality. As far as Dr Ambedkar saw it, it could be made objective through a democratic Constitution that proactively guaranteed both liberty and equality in equal measure.

Hence, Dr Ambedkar perceived at that time the need to devise a better alternative to the dominant form of freedom, which he characterized as non-inclusive Swaraj. This concept meant freedom from the external bondage of the British, but a freedom that afforded license for the internal bondage of the Dalit-bahujan and minority communities by an unfettered Hindu majority, which for millennia had been seeped in the ideology of Brahmanism through its vast philosophy and literature.

And hence, Dr Ambedkar also perceived the need to devise a better alternative to the towering leftist ideological critique of inequality. The leftist critique focused exclusively on class conflict. But for Dr Ambedkar, caste, not class, was the primordial conflict throughout India's long history of inequality, an inequality that was graded and thus largely immune to the revolutionary impulse as the leftist ideology understood it.

Fraternity as Goodwill

For all these antinomies, these impossible dilemmas—the failure of justice to be realized till date on Indian soil, the false or incomplete liberty on offer by the nationalist movement, the erroneous appraisal of the causes and cures of inequality by the leftists—the way through, the only way through, was by appealing to fraternity, that too in its more authentic understanding, as metta. Or pushing it even further, not just fraternity understood as metta, but—as Dr Ambedkar stated during an impromptu 1956 speech before a Buddhist gathering, just fifteen days before his death—metta understood as love, justice and goodwill. Dr Ambedkar's use of the word 'goodwill' in his 1956 speech is important; for, recall from 1948 that it was the urgent need for 'goodwill' that, according to Dr Ambedkar, justified the inclusion of the new 'fraternity' clause into the Preamble. In 1956, goodwill was supplemented with love.

But make no mistake, Dr Ambedkar was no beatnik, no Dharma Bum, no hippie—you need love, but love is *not* all you need. As logicians say, it is a necessary but not a sufficient condition. Sufficiency begins to be satisfied when we bring in justice, liberty, equality, dignity, nation, all taking objective form through institutionalization. Love (metta, fraternity) is what permits these institutions to flow and to function in the spirit of democracy. And this explains why Dr Ambedkar added 'fraternity' to the Preamble.

But that is only one part of the explanation.

The Incommensurability Problem

Dr Ambedkar was not the only political thinker who found himself struggling with the problems of reconciling the different demands of democratic principles like liberty and equality. The whole history of Western political philosophy has grappled with it, and a variety of solutions have been thrown up by a variety of authors, be it philosophers or statesmen.

Reconciling freedom and equality in particular has proven an intractable difficulty, as an increase in one seems to imply a decrease in the other, and yet both seem necessary in equal measure. There are of course factions who just come down in support of one over the other, such as libertarians, who champion liberty come what may, or hard-core egalitarians, who prioritize equality instead. But the greater tendency has been to attempt to overcome the zero-sum scenario, where one value can only be enhanced at the expense of the other. The seventeenth century thinker Thomas Hobbes, who gave us the *Leviathan*,[26] sought to suppress the conflicting demands of liberty and equality through the overwhelming might of the strong state, whose sovereign—gigantic and awesome like a leviathan—deployed the state machinery to quell all discord. But aside from this external solution, placing all responsibility outside of the governed, others proposed internal solutions as well. These internal solutions, where citizens themselves bear responsibility, have mainly been of two different types: affective (emotional, we could say) and cognitive (rational).

The well-known eighteenth-century economist Adam Smith, as well as his contemporary Scotsman David Hume (a name, alas, known only to philosophers), both developed theories of moral sentiments, offering affective ways of negotiating the treacherous waters of competing social, economic and political demands, like liberty and equality. On the other hand, notoriously difficult German philosopher Immanuel Kant and his inscrutable successor G.W.F. Hegel, who made Kant seem easy, attempted to resolve the apparent incommensurability of liberty and equality through the natural capacities of human reason.

The Solution of John Rawls

Finally, the most celebrated anglophone political theorist of the twentieth century, John Rawls, began thinking, in the year that Dr Ambedkar died, about how to reconcile the main traditions (cognitive and affective) and the main principles (liberty and equality) of Western parliamentary democracy. Yes, you read that right. This is philosophy after all.

His solution was to first seek a fusion of the cognitive and the affective, claiming that human nature was inherently endowed with two basic characteristics: to be rational (the cognitive capacity) and also to be reasonable (an affective tendency towards social cooperation and a sense of justice). The next step was to harmonize the essential institutions of parliamentary democracy in a way that optimized these dual inbuilt capacities of citizens, and to lay down structures of legal, political and social life that preconditioned the possibility of making justice more than subjective, but a real thing in the world; a justice 'assuring the dignity of the individual and the unity of the nation', to borrow the expression from Dr Ambedkar's preamble.

The reason for blending Dr Ambedkar's phraseology into the culmination of Rawls' project of attempting to reconcile the principles and institutions of constitutional democracy with the nature and capacities of the human being is to highlight something that very few political historians or political theorists recognize. That is, what the greatest academic philosopher of the United States was starting to wrestle with in 1956 in the arena of political theory was exactly what, in the very same year, the author of the 'fraternity' clause of India's preamble was wrestling with in political practice. There is of course a gross asymmetry here. The evaluation of Rawls' performance was undertaken through the precious processes of academic peer review; whereas

Dr Ambedkar's performance must be judged in the annals of social and political history. The latter, as we all know, was penned with an ink of blood, sweat and tears.

Nevertheless, by inheriting the political institutions of Western parliamentary democracy, India necessarily inherited the commensurability problems plaguing its foundational principles. Dr Ambedkar sought recourse to 'fraternity' in an effort to address the commensurability problem between liberty and equality. We see this in various writings of his where he depicted fraternity as the basic principle which sustains both equality and liberty:

> Without fraternity, liberty would destroy equality and equality would destroy liberty. If in Democracy liberty does not destroy equality and equality does not destroy liberty, it is because at the basis of both there is fraternity. Fraternity is therefore the root of Democracy.[27]

So much for the conceptual problem of reconciling the democratic principles, of conceptual commensurability. After all, there was not much at stake there other than to apprehend intellectually that it could be done. But what about the practical problems? Dr Ambedkar well understood that the conceptual problem was the easiest problem that he faced. Far more serious was the institutional problem. That is, harmonizing persons, given what they are, to the democratic institutions that embodied the constitutional principles. What he slowly discovered, and it took time, was that the commensurability problem existed only on one plane, whereas the practical problem entailed in the institutionalization of democratic principles existed at two interrelated planes simultaneously.

This slow but sure realization occurred at the point of pivot.

The Pivot

If we wanted to date the pivot with precision, it could be said to have begun on 6 February 1948, when the Preamble first saw the light of day, and endured until 27 September 1951, when Dr Ambedkar resigned as law minister, addressing the Parliament in a lucid and lengthy speech that gave the background and causes of his resignation. This period of pivot then includes Dr Ambedkar's 4 November 1948 motion in the Constituent Assembly, which launched the first reading of the draft Constitution by the Assembly, his 25 November 1949 speech in the Constituent Assembly that brought its third reading to a close and initiated the final vote and adoption of the Constitution the following day, and, as just mentioned, his 27 September 1951 speech regarding his resignation.

Each of these historic addresses included bone-chilling rhetorical devices, every bit as masterful as Martin Luther King's 1963 'I Have a Dream' speech. Arguably, they should be publicly read out, at least in part, every 26 January when we celebrate the achievements inherent to the Constitution. In the same way that King's dream for racial equality in the United States has yet to become a reality, we have failed to take note of Dr Ambedkar's consistently expressed warnings about institutional contradictions. These contradictions were adverted to by Dr Ambedkar in every speech that he made during the point of pivot.

Until we Indians resolve these contradictions, we must remain as attuned to them as we do to the glory and achievement of the Constitution itself. Preambular principles remain aspirational goals, not already-achieved ones. In order for these aspirations—like Martin Luther King's 'dream'—to become realities, it is essential for public servants and representatives of the government to practice 'constitutional morality', and the public at large (all citizens) to demonstrate 'public conscience'.

Constitutional Morality

On 4 November 1948, with the ink on the Preamble not yet dry, Dr Ambedkar introduced the Drafting Committee's new draft Constitution with his famous appeal for 'constitutional morality':

> While everybody recognizes the necessity of the diffusion of Constitutional morality for the peaceful working of a democratic Constitution, there are two things interconnected with it which are not, unfortunately, generally recognized. One is that the form of administration has a close connection with the form of the Constitution. The form of the administration must be appropriate to and in the same sense as the form of the Constitution. The other is that it is perfectly possible to pervert the Constitution, without changing its form by merely changing the form of the administration and to make it inconsistent and opposed to the spirit of the Constitution. It follows that it is only where people are saturated with Constitutional morality such as the one described by Grote the historian that one can take the risk of omitting from the Constitution details of administration and leaving it for the Legislature to prescribe them. The question is, can we presume such a diffusion of Constitutional morality? Constitutional morality is not a natural sentiment. It has to be cultivated. We must realize that our people have yet to learn it. Democracy in India is only a top-dressing on an Indian soil, which is essentially undemocratic.[28]

The trope to take note of is 'top-dressing on an Indian soil'. This was the articulation of an incommensurability between institutions—Parliament and bureaucracy in particular—and persons as social beings. And while the vast majority of commentary and celebratory evocation of Dr Ambedkar's notion of 'constitutional morality' that we find in newspapers, journal articles and books indicate that constitutional morality is something that we as Indians should aspire to, this was not what Dr Ambedkar was saying. He had discovered, in the Constituent Assembly, a new plane where the tension between an individual person and democratic institution did, and would continue long into the future, to play out: in the assemblies, legislatures, ministries and judiciaries of an independent and sovereign democratic republic. Constitutional morality was the call for public officials and public servants to transcend the values and principles that they had been imbrued with in Indian social life, and adopt the values and principles laid out before them ever-so succinctly in the Preamble.

What Dr Ambedkar called constitutional morality was what philosopher John Rawls referred to as the idea of 'public reason' in its stricter sense.[29]

Public Conscience

What about the rest of us who are not public officials? About this problem, Dr Ambedkar had already been thinking long and hard ever since *Annihilation of Caste*, where he first spoke of 'fraternity'. 'Public conscience' was the term that Dr Ambedkar employed to capture the ideas surrounding the individuals who constitute our social life more generally. By public conscience, he referred to 'conscience which becomes agitated at every wrong, no matter who is the sufferer' and 'leads an individual to join the struggle to remove that wrong'.[30] Public conscience was conditioned upon 'fellow feeling', the phrase that Dr Ambedkar had used to describe 'fraternity'.

In his essay on 'The Hindu Social Order', Dr Ambedkar had commented extensively on the contradictions not between liberty and equality as such, but between our espoused democratic principles ('top-dressing') and our actual social practices ('Indian soil'). Caste lay at the crux of this contradiction. The democratic principle we stand for is equality; but thanks to caste, the social principle we follow is graded inequality. The democratic principle we stand for is liberty; but thanks to caste, the social principle we follow is fixed occupation. Hence, Dr Ambedkar wrote:

> Caste has killed public spirit. Caste has destroyed the sense of public charity. Caste has made public opinion impossible. A Hindu's public is his caste. His responsibility is only to his caste.[31]

At work, then, are two overlapping contradictions, both about the incommensurability of our democratic institutions—championing liberty and equality—and our undemocratic social milieu, where caste dictates the practices opposite to our democratic principles. And for both of these, as well as for the prior purely conceptual problem of incommensurability, 'fraternity' must bear the manifold burdens; it does so at the level of the institutions themselves in the form of constitutional morality, and it does so at the purely social level in the form of public conscience.

A Life of Contradictions

With all of the burdens that fraternity must bear kept in mind, Dr Ambedkar's 25 November 1949 speech can be properly contextualized:

> We must make our political democracy a social democracy as well. Political democracy cannot last unless there lies at the base of it social democracy. What does social democracy mean? It means a way of life which recognizes liberty, equality and fraternity as the principles of life. These principles of liberty, equality and fraternity are not to be treated as separate items in a trinity. They form a union of trinity in the sense that to divorce one from the other is to defeat the very purpose of democracy. Liberty cannot be divorced from equality, equality cannot be divorced from liberty. Nor can liberty and equality be divorced from fraternity. Without equality, liberty would produce the supremacy of the few over the many. Equality without liberty would kill individual initiative. Without fraternity, liberty and equality could not become a natural course of things. It would require a constable to enforce them. We must begin by acknowledging the fact that there is complete absence of two things in Indian society. One of these is equality. On the social plane, we have in India a society based on the principle of graded inequality which means elevation for some and degradation for others. On the economic plane, we have a society in which there are some who have immense wealth as against many who live in abject poverty. On the 26th of January 1950, we are going to enter into a life of contradictions. In politics we will have equality and in social and economic life we will have inequality.[32]

It may seem that the speech has been cited at excessive length here. The truth is, there is so much more that should be reproduced from this magnificent text. In short, though, again, the trope to take note of is 'a life of contradictions'. We must tally that with 'top-dressing on an Indian soil' from the year before. Dr Ambedkar concluded the 'top-dressing' speech with another oft-cited zinger about man proving himself to be vile. He said that he found the Constitution to be workable and flexible, and 'strong enough to hold the country together . . . Indeed, if I may say so, if things go wrong under the new Constitution, the reason will not be that we had a bad Constitution. What we will have to say is that Man was vile'.[33] The contradiction, clearly, is between a workable Constitution and the Indian soil, which seeds a social ecosystem where inequality flourishes and man is at liberty for his vileness, rather than his virtues, to flourish.

The Hindu Code Bill

Still there was hope of resolving this contradiction, by means of fraternal concord, the cultivation of public conscience and constitutional morality. What changed, then, another year on? Did Dr Ambedkar give up on his decennial effort to resolve this contradiction?

> It may be said that my resignation is out of time and that if I was dissatisfied with the . . . treatment accorded to Backward Classes and the Scheduled Castes I should have gone earlier. The charge may sound as true. But I had reasons which held me back. In the first place, most of the time I have been a Member of the Cabinet, I have been busy with the framing of the Constitution. It absorbed all my attention till 26th January 1950 . . . In the second place, I thought it necessary to stay on, for the sake of the Hindu Code. In the opinion of some, it may be wrong for me to have held on for the sake of the Hindu Code. I took a different view. The Hindu Code was the greatest social reform measure ever undertaken by the legislature in this country. No law passed by the Indian Legislature in the past or likely to be passed in the future can be compared to it in

> point of its significance. To leave inequality between class and class, between sex and sex, which is the soul of Hindu Society untouched . . . is to make a farce of our Constitution and to build a palace on a dung heap.[34]

There's that trope again: 'a palace on a dung heap'. Tally it with 'a life of contradictions', 'top-dressing on an Indian soil' and not 'a bad Constitution' but that 'Man was vile'. Each one of them hit the same note, although with each passing year they were pitched an octave higher. Two years on, due to frustrations regarding the elections, regarding the continuing blockage of the Hindu Code Bill and other problems on both the political and personal front,[35] we see the note struck at a pitch so high that it shattered glass: Ambedkar unleashed his fiery remark in the Rajya Sabha in 1953 that he was a 'hack' and wrote the Constitution against his will; indeed, he would be willing to burn the Constitution.[36]

But the question that arises, when we look at all the tropes together, is: would the 1953 Ambedkar burn the Constitution because it was bad, or because man was vile? Whichever side you may be on, what is at least clear is that 'fraternity' was not able to perform all of the heavy lifting that Dr Ambedkar had hoped it would.

Fraternity and Religion

Fraternity is a concept of myriad virtues, and thus it was only natural that Dr Ambedkar had made so many demands of it. The history of political philosophy in the West had already been relying upon the qualities that fraternity possessed, whether in its own name or by others, to solve its conceptual dead ends or conundrums. It was an effective tool for them, thanks to a dual use capability, having both a cognitive side and an affective side.

Fraternity—with a genealogy commonly traced back to stories of Christ and the Pilgrims, and its residue of communitarian warmth and love—was a concept with a flavour entirely different from other political concepts. One could even feel this in the prepositions attached to these principle terms: liberty was often described as positive or negative, freedom *from* or freedom *to* and *for*; and equality was envisioned as *of* (opportunity) or *before* (the law). Fraternity, by contrast, was always *with*—no affront directed at you, nothing taken from you, just the cosy community fellow feeling of being *with*.

The Christian origins of this term, however, signalled a fundamental limitation that Dr Ambedkar only recognized through the pivot. Christianity, keeping to one side its theological flexibility as a tool to justify imperialism, had a long-standing and still-robust foundational equality: everyone is equal before God. While Dr Ambedkar held that what he called Brahmaism could have served India as an even stronger foundation for democratic equality than fraternity, unfortunately, Brahmaism was subverted by Brahmanism, which has graded inequality as its essence.

Brahmaism: Hinduism's Lost Opportunity

What was Brahmaism, according to Dr Ambedkar? It was the combination of three philosophical-theological doctrines from the *Chandogya Upanishad* and the *Brihadaranyaka Upanishad*.[37] These were *Sarvam Khalvidam Brahma*, *Aham Brahmasmi* and *Tattvamasi*.[38] Far more radical than the Abrahamic religions' notion of equality before God, this Brahmaist doctrine of 'everyone is God, I am God, and you are God' could have served as the foundation for an egalitarian India. But that was not the path the Hindu faithful took.

Either way, the premise that was beginning to reveal itself by looking at the features, virtues and failures of fraternity, and the lost opportunity of a radically egalitarian Hindu theology in Brahmaism, was that religious ideas, reinforced in sacerdotal practices, support (or undermine) political and juridical principles. As Dr Ambedkar put it:

> . . . wherein lie the roots of fraternity without which democracy is not possible? Beyond dispute, it has its origin in Religion.[39]

Liberty and equality, as constitutional essentials, will be undermined if they are not theologically supported. Thus, it is not enough for fraternity to function merely as a political principle; or even for it to operate socially as constitutional morality or public conscience. It must reveal its theological aspect too, as only with the support of its theology can individuals within society find the sufficient internal resource to undertake the ethical effort of putting political principles into personal practice.

And herein lies the rub. Hindu theology, married to caste, is inegalitarian and prohibits fellow feeling (untouchability) or love (outside of one's caste). And the theology behind fraternity is alien to the majority of Indians. What, then, is the way out?

Fraternity as Metta: The Buddhist Solution

We begin to see Dr Ambedkar's answer in his post-pivot essay titled 'Buddha and Karl Marx':

> Society has been aiming to lay a new foundation, summarized by the French revolution in three words: fraternity, liberty, and equality. The French Revolution was welcomed because of this slogan. It failed to produce equality. We welcomed the Russian

> Revolution because it aimed to produce equality. But it cannot be too much emphasized that in producing equality society cannot afford to sacrifice fraternity or liberty. Equality will be of no value without fraternity or liberty. It seems that the three can coexist only if one follows the way of the Buddha.[40]

The 'it seems' here speaks volumes. It shows that this was a revelation for Dr Ambedkar, something that took him time, trial and experience to apprehend. This also gave the proper context for understanding his bold claim in a 1954 radio interview, a part of which was cited earlier:

> My social philosophy may be said to be enshrined in three words: liberty, equality and fraternity. Let no one, however, say that I have borrowed my philosophy from the French Revolution. I have not. My philosophy has roots in religion and not in political science. I have derived them from the teachings of my master, the Buddha. In his philosophy, liberty and equality had a place; but he added that unlimited liberty destroyed equality, and absolute equality left no room for liberty. In his philosophy, law had a place only as a safeguard against the breaches of liberty or equality; but he did not believe that law can be a guarantee for breaches of liberty or equality. He gave the highest place to fraternity as the only real safeguard against the denial of liberty or equality—fraternity which was another name for brotherhood or humanity, which was again another name for religion.[41]

But what, then, were the teachings of Dr Ambedkar's master, as he said, or the way of the Buddha? This is a much larger question in answer to which Dr Ambedkar composed a much larger book, *The Buddha and His Dhamma*.[42] But for our purpose here, it will suffice to see one specific part of it; it is small but of enormous significance; it is the substitution of fraternity by metta. As Dr Ambedkar wrote:

> . . . what sustains equality and liberty is fellow feeling, what the French Revolutionists called fraternity. The word fraternity is not an adequate expression. The proper term is what the Buddha called Maitree.[43]

The inadequacy of fraternity was finally stated explicitly by Dr Ambedkar. He struggled against reaching this conclusion for nearly two decades, but his experiences from 6 February 1947 right up to that fateful day in 1953 when he spoke of burning the Constitution taught him that it had to be done. And it was cathartic. The step-by-step critique of the ineffectiveness of the Constitution to cope with the vileness of man receded. The piecemeal passage of the Hindu Code Bill legislation, as well as the passage of the Untouchability Offences Act, also helped. By 1955, Dr Ambedkar was heartily defending the Constitution in public once again.

Necessary and Also Sufficient

What fraternity could do, metta could do too. What fraternity could not do, metta could do that too. This was beautifully captured in some of the last words ever written by Dr Ambedkar. As you read them, you will find allusions to all of the various aspects that we have been discussing in this exploration through the backstory of fraternity in Dr Ambedkar's preamble: the logical dictum of necessary and sufficient; the cognitive function of fraternity; the affective function of fraternity; the transcendence of isolationism dictated by caste; the notion that love is all you need; the suggestiveness of the preposition 'with'.

The only thing that was missing from Dr Ambedkar's final account was the word 'fraternity' itself; for, in his last year of life he had finally fully sloughed it off. By understanding 'fraternity' to have really been 'metta' all along, Dr Ambedkar had finally cracked the code.

See if you can identify it too. This passage signals every cypher of fraternity's secret history:

> Love is not enough; what is required is Maitri. It is wider than love. It means fellowship not merely with human beings but with all living beings. It is not confined to human beings. Is not such Maitri necessary? What else can give to all living beings the same happiness which one seeks for one's own self, to keep the mind impartial, open to all, with affection for every one and hatred for none?[44]

5

Dignity: Not Bread but Honour

No past civilizational glories, no future superpower status, nothing redounds more to the true greatness of a nation than the dignity of every individual in it. Dr Ambedkar held this view, and the appearance of the term 'dignity' in the Preamble to our Constitution stemmed from this unique conviction.

Dr Ambedkar's conviction was unique in two different senses. First, as we shall see in the next chapter, it runs counter to most right-leaning ideologues, who regard the corporate body as the quintessential source of dignity—we know this story from the history of fascism—and it also runs counter to a great deal of leftist ideology, which tends to dismiss dignity as a bourgeois ruse, thereby opening the door to a great many occasions of degrading it—we know this story from the history of totalitarianism. Second, the uniqueness of Dr Ambedkar's conviction can be apprehended simply by the observation that the source documents, all the formal ones and most of the informal ones, are absolutely silent on it.

Neither the CWC Expert Committee 'declaration' of July 1946 nor Nehru's Objectives Resolution, which was based upon it, mentioned the term 'dignity'. B.N. Rau's preliminary draft Constitution did not mention it. It was absent from the 1930

Indian National Congress' 'Declaration of Purna Swaraj', as well as its Karachi Resolution in the ensuing year. In the case of the latter, it was quite ironic. For, as is apparent not only from many of the guarantees that it made, but especially from the constellation of events that were unfurling at the very moment that it was being drafted, the Karachi Resolution could have quite fruitfully deployed the concept, setting a proper precedent for the future Preamble:

> This Congress is of the opinion that in order to end the exploitation of the masses, political freedom must include real economic freedom of the starving millions. In order therefore, that the masses may appreciate what Swaraj as conceived by the Congress will mean to them, it is desirable to state the position of the Congress in a manner easily understood by them. The Congress therefore declares that any constitution that may be agreed to on its behalf, should include the following items, or should give the ability to the Swaraj Government to provide for them.
>
> 1. Fundamental rights of the people such as . . .
>
> iv. No disability to attach to any person of religion, caste or creed . . .
>
> vi. Equal rights to all citizens of access to and use of public roads, public wells and all other places of public resort . . .
>
> 3. A living wage for industrial workers, limited hours of labour, healthy conditions of work, protection against the economic consequences of old age, sickness, and unemployment . . .
>
> 4. Labour to be freed from serfdom or conditions bordering on serfdom . . .
>
> 6. Prohibition against employment of children of school going age in factories . . .[1]

The unstated reason behind all of these guarantees—why is it that we demand a living wage, free persons from serfdom, prohibit child labour—is of course to protect and promote the dignity of the person. Moreover, the Karachi Resolution was passed at the Indian National Congress' Karachi session in 1931, which was a momentous time. Gandhi had just been released from jail after the Salt Satyagraha. The Gandhi-Irwin pact was reached, terminating the Civil Disobedience Movement. And, only a week before the Karachi session, the British government had executed Bhagat Singh.[2] It is hard to imagine a better occasion than the Karachi Resolution to assert the inviolable dignity of every Indian; for, indignity, under British rule, was presumably a collective experience.

Or was it?

Autobiographical Experience

In Dr Ambedkar's autobiographical fragments curiously titled *Waiting for a Visa*, he recounted experiences from his youth that gradually awoke him to the indignities imposed upon him due to his prescribed social status in the Hindu social order:

> I knew that I was an untouchable and that untouchables were subjected to certain indignities and discriminations. For instance, I knew that in the school I could not sit in the midst of my class students according to my rank but that I was to sit in a corner by myself. I knew that in the school I was to have a separate piece of gunny cloth for me to squat on in the class room and the servant employed to clean the school would not touch the gunny cloth used by me.[3]

Dignity was not merely an abstract concept for Dr Ambedkar, forced since birth to suffer its degradation by the dictate of the

Hindu social order. Could this account for Dr Ambedkar's prolific use of the term (we find it more than 150 times in his writings and speeches), in stark contrast to its glaring absence from the archives of the national movement? Leftists seemed to have no use for 'dignity'. M.N. Roy's *Constitution of Free India: A Draft*,[4] of the Radical Democratic Party, as well as the Socialist Party of India's *Draft Constitution of the Indian Republic*,[5] carrying Jayprakash Narayan's foreword, both declined to mention it.

But to be fair, the concept did make a rare appearance in Shriman Narayan Agarwal's *The Gandhian Constitution of Free India*,[6] that included Gandhi's own foreword. Under the section of 'decentralization', there was a medley of Agarwal's and Gandhi's words:

> Ideals of Simplicity, Human Values and Sanctity of Labour are, in the last analysis, founded on non-violence, which is the bed-rock of Gandhian thought . . . 'Society based on non-violence can only consist of groups settled in villages in which voluntary co-operation is the condition of *dignified* and peaceful existence . . . The nearest approach to civilisation based upon non-violence is the erstwhile village republic of India' . . . Gandhiji, consequently, passionately pleads for a civilisation founded on 'Villagism'.[7]

About labour, here the expression 'sanctity of labour' was used. In other writings of Gandhi's, the term 'dignity' did in fact appear several times, in precisely the same context—as the 'dignity of labour'.

And let us not forget that a piece of Gandhi's justification for his haughty claim to speak on behalf of the untouchables, with a mandate even stronger than that of Dr Ambedkar's, was his belief that he too had been subject to analogous indignity on account of racial discrimination. As he put it in his own autobiography, *The Story of My Experiments with Truth*,[8] all Indians 'have become the untouchables of South Africa'.[9] Of course, we all know of the famous early episode of Gandhi being thrown out from the first-class carriage of a train in South Africa.

Although there is no question that Gandhi suffered colour prejudice routinely, he failed to realize that he was using a false analogy. The details surrounding Gandhi's own narration of the train episode undermined the analogy completely. For example, in the events that he described just prior to his observation, that he and all other Indians in South Africa were untouchables, Gandhi was seen interviewing, hiring and firing the white employees who worked under him; he had white guests living with him in his house; he was inter-dining with white South Africans; he talked about owning property and handling enormous sums of money; all of these and numerous other daily activities that he recounted would be inconceivable to the untouchables of Gandhi's era and were totally incongruous to their plight within the Hindu social order.

One may compare Gandhi's ejection from the first-class train carriage to scenes that Dr Ambedkar recounted from *Waiting for a Visa*, when the drivers of bullock carts and *tongawalla*s refused transport to him altogether. The differences did not exist in the simple fact that Gandhi had ready access to the third class instead, a tier of travel that he had elsewhere praised for its comfort on South African trains as compared to Indian ones. They existed, rather, in the fact that Gandhi enjoyed exit rights; he had access to a country where he would not be an untouchable. The untouchables of India enjoyed no such exit rights—their indignity was locked in, from the creation of man, as per the Rig Veda's *Purusha Sukta,*[10] until the Preamble to the Constitution.

For Dr Ambedkar, the irony was that he was alien in his own country, subject to every manner of inhospitality. Only a visa got

Dr Ambedkar out of this hostile land that was his homeland, so he could travel abroad, far from the dominion of Brahmanism, and only then enjoy the liberation of not being untouchable. For Dr Ambedkar, to suffer the injustice of the visible colour prejudice would be a luxury afforded by the visa out of India. This would take him away from the alienation and oppression sustained through the tyranny of invisible caste. Perhaps that was why his autobiographical writing is called *Waiting for a Visa*.

Back to the Village

We don't need to agree on those details or assessments to at least recognize the way that the falseness of Gandhi's analogy underlay the profound differences between Gandhi's estimation of the Indian village as ground zero for a 'civilisation based upon non-violence' and 'the condition of dignified and peaceful existence', versus Dr Ambedkar's polar opposite estimation that 'the village is a sink of localism, a den of ignorance, narrowmindedness and communalism'.[11] Far from being the sine qua non for achieving dignity, the village, according to Dr Ambedkar, represented how and where the indignities of caste were enforced and sanctified:[12]

> Indian villages represent a kind of colonialism of the Hindus designed to exploit the untouchables. The untouchables have no rights. They are there only to wait, serve and submit. They are there to do or to die. They have no rights because they are outside the village republic and they are outside the so-called republic because they are outside the Hindu fold.[13]

Dignity, for Dr Ambedkar, was precluded by caste. Brahmanism, with its principle of graded inequality, prescribed graded dignity—different status and rank for different castes. But even more than the concept of equality, the concept of dignity brooked no gradation; every gradation of dignity was degradation of dignity. Its absoluteness was its hallmark.

Not so for Gandhi, or at least for Dr Ambedkar's Gandhi. Dr Ambedkar argued that the social and moral consequences of caste separation espoused by Gandhi in his ideal theory of varna—about which we spoke when discussing 'liberty' versus 'freedom as Swaraj'—were degrading to those condemned hereditarily, in that ideal system, to serve the other varnas: 'It educates them into slaves and creates all the psychological complex which follows from a slave mentality . . . There is, on the one hand, tyranny, vanity, pride, arrogance, greed, selfishness' in the varnas, hereditarily entitled to service from others; 'and, on the other hand, insecurity, poverty, degradation, loss of liberty' as well as loss of self-reliance, loss of independence and loss of 'dignity and self-respect' for those condemned merely to serve. Dr Ambedkar brought to summation his appraisal of the social, political and psychological consequences of Gandhi's ideal theory of varna with these damning words:

> . . . democratic society cannot be indifferent to such consequences. But Gandhism does not mind these consequences in the least.[14]

Dignity in the Preamble

This pronounced correlation in Dr Ambedkar's mind between caste and its manifold deleterious effects on dignity was what accounted for the first iteration of 'dignity' in the Preamble. On 6 February 1948, the 'dignity' component of the 'fraternity' clause read:

> Fraternity, assuring the dignity of every individual without distinction of caste or creed.[15]

In the previous chapter, we chronicled the evolution and alteration of the 'fraternity' clause that included the 'dignity' component. For the reasons discussed there, we saw the gradual decoupling of fraternity (and thus dignity) from caste. Additionally, there was a slight alteration in the 'dignity' component by changing 'the dignity of every individual' to 'the dignity of the individual'; 'every' became 'the', which was simply more concise. Thus, by 21 February 1948 it read—and would remain so even on 26 January 1950—as:

> Fraternity, assuring the dignity of the individual and the unity of the Nation.[16]

But the original formulation, linking dignity and caste, unlocked the secret meaning of, and the ultimate necessity for using, the term 'dignity' for Dr Ambedkar.

The Constituent Assembly Debates

As mentioned in the first chapter, the draft Constitution that Dr Ambedkar, as the chairman of the Drafting Committee, had sent to the president of the Constituent Assembly, Rajendra Prasad, on 21 February 1948, was sent to all the members of the Constituent Assembly, asking them to submit their views by 22 March 1948. A number of amendments were suggested, including with reference to 'dignity'.

One noteworthy amendment came from B. Pattabhi Sitaramayya, who in that year was elected as the president of the Indian National Congress at the Jaipur session. Sitaramayya was a well-respected freedom fighter who had been in and out of jail for his role in the Home Rule Movement, the Salt Satyagraha, Gandhi's individual satyagraha and the Quit India Movement.

He was recognized as an authority on the history of the Indian National Congress, publishing a two-volume work called *History of the Indian National Congress.* He had also written a book titled *Indian Nationalism* as early as 1913.[17]

Sitaramayya's amendment read:

> That for the 'Fraternity' clause the following be substituted: 'Fraternity assuring unity of the Nation and the dignity of the individual'.[18]

The amendment appeared innocuous, but it did not suit Dr Ambedkar at all. He would not see individual dignity lose its pole position and take a back seat to the nation. Fortunately, he found allies in fellow Drafting Committee member K.M. Munshi as well as in Constitutional Adviser B.N. Rau. Munshi was a stalwart and had been a shoo-in for the future Drafting Committee since 1946, when he took part in drafting the CWC's 'declaration' as part of its Experts' Committee. In the Constituent Assembly, he held memberships in eleven committees, more than any other single member. His book *Pilgrimage to Freedom*[19] offers an insider's view of the thoughts circulating in the Drafting Committee at that time:

> The keynote of the Preamble was to emphasise the positive aspect of 'the unity of the Nation' as much as the 'dignity of the individual'. Dignity was a word of moral and spiritual import; it implied an obligation on the part of the Union to respect the personality of the citizen and to create conditions in which every citizen would be left free to find individual self-fulfillment.
>
> The incorporation of the phrase 'dignity of the individual', therefore, was an express rejection of the Hegelian theory on

> which modern totalitarianism is based; namely, that the State is a metaphysical entity, independent of and overshadowing the individual whose only aim was to secure its existence. It is also an explicit repudiation of the hereditary, social or feudal distinctions which we had inherited from the past.[20]

Did Someone Just Say *Hegel*? B.N. Rau Steps in

Such a philosophical explanation was music to Dr Ambedkar's ears, but the keen administrator's mind of Constitutional Adviser B.N. Rau knew better than to appeal to Hegelian metaphysics. In the process of completing his own draft preamble, on 30 May 1947, to the early original constitutional draft that he had been tasked with drawing up and presenting to the Drafting Committee as the basis for their labours, Rau had chanced upon the preamble of the 1937 Constitution of Ireland. After a visit to Ireland to discuss constitutional essentials, Rau incorporated its words into the declaratory part of his draft preamble. Rau's preamble had read:

> We, the People of India, seeking to promote the common good, do hereby through our chosen representatives Adopt, Enact and Give to ourselves this Constitution.[21]

This followed the declaratory part of the Irish Preamble, the only changes being the substitution of 'India' for 'Éire', and the addition of the words 'through our chosen representatives'. As we saw in the Introduction, much of the declaratory part of Rau's draft preamble was used for the declaratory part of the final constitutional Preamble. However, nothing from its descriptive part—there was anyway only the one line about the common good—was used.

As it turned out, the descriptive part of the Irish Preamble mentioned not only the common good and dignity, but the unity of the country as well:

> In the Name of the Most Holy Trinity, from Whom is all authority and to Whom, as our final end, all actions both of men and States must be referred, We, the people of Éire, Humbly acknowledging all our obligations to our Divine Lord, Jesus Christ, Who sustained our fathers through centuries of trial, Gratefully remembering their heroic and unremitting struggle to regain the rightful independence of our Nation, And seeking to promote the common good, with due observance of Prudence, Justice and Charity, so that the *dignity* and freedom *of the individual* may be assured, true social order attained, the *unity of our country* restored, and concord established with other nations, Do hereby adopt, enact, and give to ourselves this Constitution.[22]

The Preamble to the Irish Constitution read more like a liturgical prayer than a legal document, but we will come to that point later. For now, what is important is that B.N. Rau's recollection of the order of phrases in the Irish Preamble offered a simple solution to what might have otherwise become a serious problem. Rau perspicaciously supplemented Dr Ambedkar's firm conviction that we would not have unity in our nation until and unless the dignity of the individual was given priority, not by resorting to the metaphysical justification of K.M. Munshi, but by reducing this to a mere procedural issue. He mildly explained that the Drafting Committee decided to stand on the precedent set in the Irish Preamble.

Accordingly, the Constitutional Adviser prepared a long and sophisticated note to be circulated in the Constituent Assembly, which presented the main suggestions and amendments that had reached the Drafting Committee in response to the publication and dissemination of the draft Constitution in February 1948, and the decisions reached by the reconvened Drafting Committee (23–27 March 1948) as well as the Special Committee (10–11 April 1948) that had been assembled in order to scrutinize the draft Constitution in the light of all of the suggestions. In the note, Rau masterfully represented Dr Ambedkar's firm commitment toward the priority of dignity, skirting as much as possible the philosophy behind it:

> 3. This is a purely drafting amendment. It seeks to put the words 'unity of the Nation' first and then the words 'dignity of the individual' in the line commencing with the word 'Fraternity' in the Preamble. The reason for putting the dignity of the individual first was that unless the dignity of the individual is assured, the nation cannot be united. In the Preamble to the Irish Constitution, 'the dignity of the individual' comes before 'the unity of our country'. We may, therefore, retain the existing order of the phrase.[23]

One Word, Two Opposite Meanings

This was not the only occasion when the term 'dignity' was mentioned in the CAD. The word appeared during eight further debates, throughout the second reading of the draft Constitution. But the meaning of the word these later eight times was almost exactly the opposite of its meaning in the Preamble. Unlike in the first scuffle over the priority of individual dignity versus that of the nation, the predominant use of 'dignity' in the CAD was to denote its honorific and majestic sense, such as 'the dignity of his high office', or 'beneath the dignity of the esteemed judiciary', or to 'elevate the dignity of the Presidency', or 'the dignity of this august gathering'. In fact, when you rummage through the archives of India's Constitution in the making—to purloin the joyful title of one of Constitutional Adviser B.N. Rau's books[24]—the denotative meaning of the term 'dignity', almost universally, is in this sense as august, majestic and honorific. This was its preponderant meaning in all of Gandhi's collected works as well, with the sole exceptions of those mentioned above in relation to the village and to labour.

It was only Dr Ambedkar, in the Preamble as well as in his ample other writings, who systematically used its opposing, fundamentally egalitarian denotation as the intrinsic and inalienable worth to be equally recognized in and by each and every human person.

But how could one word even have two polar opposite dictionary definitions in the first place? How could 'dignity' simultaneously denote, in one usage, a rank of distinction, honour, exception, a higher value and estimation than others in a pyramid of hierarchy, and in another usage something inherent to any and every human life, equally shared by all?

To answer this question requires a glance back at the conceptual history of 'dignity', which morphed and mutated across four basic stages: first its pagan or pre-Christian origins in ancient Greece and Rome (along with some ready comparisons from ancient India); second, its subsequent appropriation in Catholic theology; third, its secularization through philosophy; and fourth, its universalization by revolutionary declarations (French and American) and ensuing assumption into the United Nations Charter in 1945, the Universal Declaration of Human Rights in 1948, with a domino effect on human rights conventions and fundamental rights articulation in constitutions around the world.

But tracing this morphology of 'dignity' does much more than satisfy the curiosity about its two inherently contradictory definitions. It also uncovers why all of Dr Ambedkar's contemporaries—either in the national movement, or in the revolutionary movements of the left—used the word only for its ranked and hierarchical denotation. Most important of all, it brings into the light the secret history of 'dignity' in Dr Ambedkar's preamble. We see how, where and why the egalitarian denotation of 'dignity' was of such conscious importance to Dr Ambedkar, from as far back as his 1930 Kalaram Temple Satyagraha, right up to and especially throughout the 1940s and 1950s.

Dignity As Distinction

Dignity understood as rank, special honour, can be traced all the way back to the origins of political thought in Greece, with ready comparisons from India. Not that hackneyed comparison of the Athenian golden age with Mauryan India in the era of Kautilya's *Arthashastra*, but much further back in the epic and religious literature preceding it, usually referred to as the archaic period in Greece and the Vedic and epic ages of India. This literature—in both Greece and India—was riddled with cosmological explanations about who ruled and why they were entitled to rule. Man's rule over man was of course associated with hierarchical domination, which is why all of us today prefer to think in terms of the rule of law instead.

But not in ancient Greece. The essence of the archaic Greek concept of rule was distinction; that is, rulers in this tradition established their legitimacy by hierarchically distinguishing themselves from those whom they ruled, by enhancing their prestige, glory, honour, reputation and the like. In some important ways, this was in contrast with the Vedic/epic conception of rule in India, with its emphasis on stewardship; that is, the Indian understanding locked the political ruler into a larger cosmology where his function was to guard, protect and sustain everything that he ruled. But still, this larger cosmology was infused with the hierarchy of varna, and later caste, according to which only certain varnas/caste were entitled to rule.[25] For both ancient Greece and ancient India, then, at least in the epic period, the prevailing conception of a person's worth or value depended upon ranks, distinctions and hierarchies that recognized the excellence of a few who naturally ruled, and the worthlessness of most, who served.

But it was not until the Romans that a proper name was given to this worth—*dignitas*. It was all the stored-up laurels and honours, wherein the worth of a person could be recognized and appreciated. This was when the majestic meaning of 'dignity' originated; a meaning that endured for centuries, adopted even by enlightened philosophers like Thomas Hobbes. Hobbes still defined 'dignity' (dignitas), as late as 1651, as the publicly recognized worth of a person.[26] But this was still not precisely the supporting reference for the ways that 'dignity' was bandied about in the Constituent Assembly Debates; as in, 'the dignity of high office', or 'beneath the dignity of the President', and so on. For that, we need to see the dizzier heights of 'pride, pomp and circumstance'—to borrow Othello's words—that would emerge through the rise of the Catholic Church.

Doubling Dignity

In the long and complex evolution of what is technically called the 'episcopal polity' of the Catholic Church, its whole hierarchy of government and administration, from the Pope at the top, down to the deacons at the bottom, there was somewhere along the way a 'dignitas', a selection to a rank higher than a priest. Considering the ornateness of the vestments even down to the very bottom, one is led to wonder how gilded, dazzlingly embroidered and spectacular the robes of 'dignitas' would have been. It is these robes, secularized, that continue rather ridiculously to fill our ceremonials to this day, as for instance worn by our judiciary, whose 'dignity' the Constituent Assembly vowed to defend. And it is these roles, secularized, that lie deep below our own 'episcopal polity', the intricate systems of protocol, from the special 'dignity of high offices' to the 'dignity of the Ambassador', that garnered attention in the Constituent Assembly Debates. These are magisterial offices of rank and their dignity gets preserved through dress and protocol befitting the hierarchy, status, the enhanced worth of persons up the pyramid and the decreased worth of those descending.

Thus, it is in and by institutions, and the way institutions structure persons hierarchically according to their worth within them, that we get the primordial meaning of 'dignity'. And yet, there was also something else, diametrically opposed, brewing within Catholic theology at exactly the same moment. Ironically, it was *theology* that the Church institutions purported to embody.

That man was made in the 'image of God', that all persons were equal in the eyes of God, were basic biblical teachings that could not be circumvented, however long and hard—as history readily attests—they tried. As the splendid Sistine Chapel at the Vatican depicts, God (the father) breathed his spirit into Adam, the ancestor of all men, who thus—irrespective of rank, status—carried within their very person some inherent resplendence. That God (the son) would condescend to incarnate, take human form, again establishes the worth inherent to the human form itself, its dignity.

This dignity, inherent in the person as such, was expressed in religious terms as the 'sanctity' of life. But, as with innumerable other concepts in the history of political thought, this theological term gradually secularized, and today we—from any (or even no) tradition of religious belief—freely use expressions like 'the sacredness of the person' or the 'sanctity of life'. We find precisely these expressions in universal declarations of human rights, meant to be universal and secular, not religious. More in line with expectations, we also find these expressions within the specific declarations of states that do or did identify themselves specifically as Catholic.

And with this observation we find ourselves back at the Preamble of the 1937 Irish Constitution, a text that read more like Catholic liturgy than secular, constitutional law.

> In the Name of the Most Holy Trinity . . . We, the people of Éire, Humbly acknowledging all our obligations to our Divine Lord, Jesus Christ . . . so that the dignity and freedom of the individual may be assured, true social order attained, the unity of our country restored . . .[27]

It was of course the purely secular sense of the term 'dignity' that made an appearance in the UN Charter or the Universal Declaration of Human Rights, which carried the term in its very first article:

> Article 1: All human beings are born free and equal in dignity and rights . . .[28]

And it was the purely secular usage of the term that made its way into the Preamble to the Indian Constitution—just as, most of us would agree, our judiciary are not regarded as wearing the robes of Catholic inquisitors, even if historically we could trace them back directly to those vestments.

But, for sure, this radically egalitarian conception of 'dignity' that had emerged in both theological and secular form could readily be deployed as an effective tool for highlighting the inegalitarian theology underlying Hindu social practices. And it is precisely in this vein that we see one of the primary uses of the concept of 'dignity' operating in Dr Ambedkar's writings:

> The Hindu has a Code of life, which is part of his religion. This Code of life gives him many privileges and heaps upon the Untouchable many indignities which are incompatible with the dignity and sanctity of human life. The Untouchables all over India are fighting against the indignities and injustices which the Hindus in the name of their religion have heaped upon them.[29]

The Dignity of Philosophers

On the constitutional and secular side, we find that the Constitution of the Federal Republic of Germany begins with one of the most profound and awe-inspiring expressions of the fundamental nature of human dignity:

> Article 1 [Human dignity]
> (1) Human dignity shall be inviolable. To respect and protect it shall be the duty of all state authority.
> (2) The German people therefore acknowledge inviolable and inalienable human rights as the basis of every community, of peace and of justice in the world.[30]

After Germany's role in spearheading the most systematic programme of utter contempt for human life and dignity in the history of the planet, new Germany's post-Second World War Constitution had to make the clearest and most pronounced statement with regard to human dignity's inviolability. But such a conception of human life was nothing new to the history of

German thought. Indeed, it was German philosopher Immanuel Kant who had already set up one of the primary formulae according to which we think about dignity today, and which the German Constitution was itself appealing to.

Obviously, we have no mandate here to muck around in Kant's moral and political philosophy, but there are a couple of its key features that we should draw attention to, and can do so rather simply. Kant's moral philosophy was centred around a sort of formal procedure for making judgements about right and wrong. In any and every given scenario of human experience, it was possible, inherently possible, because of the nature of the human person, to determine the moral course of action that a person should take—the right action followed from a determination of what was impartial, rational and thus universal. This moral imperative was categorical, the opposite of conditional. In conditionals, we evaluate consequences in relation to particular desires and goals, which means that these judgements only apply in particular cases, and cannot be universalized into an always-true maxim or principle. The categorical imperative, however, is impartial, and once reached is thus true for every human person, like a universal law.

Now, the most important way that the categorical imperative was formulated, according to Kant, was that we must never act in a way that treated a person, whether ourselves or others, merely as a means, but always as an end in itself. And the reason behind this was that the person had inherent, invaluable worth, what we refer to as dignity. Anything that we use as a means, by contrast, has a price; its worth or value can be negotiated, exchanged, bought and sold. But a person is priceless (hence it is morally reprehensible to buy or sell persons); or, again, as Kant put it, a person is an end in itself.

The impact of this philosophical formulation of 'dignity', as treating the person as an end in itself, was visible throughout all of Dr Ambedkar's writings. In fact, in essays such as 'The Hindu Social Order', Dr Ambedkar showed complete familiarity with both the Catholic doctrine of the sacredness of the person, as well as the philosophical idea of a person as an end in itself:

> Why must the individual be the end and not the means of all social purposes? Why should we sacrifice our most precious possessions and our lives to defend the rights of the human person? No better answer to this question can be found than what is given by Prof. Jacques Maritain: 'What do we mean precisely when we speak of the human person? . . . No matter how poor and crushed a person may be, he is a whole, and is a person subsistent in an independent manner. When we say that a man is a person is to say that in the depth of his being he is more a whole than a part and more independent than servile . . . It is this metaphysical mystery that religious thought designates when it says that the person is the image of God. The value of the person, his dignity and rights, belong to the order of things naturally sacred'. . .[31]

Testing Philosophy through Temple Entry

Dr Ambedkar made ready use of each of these sources of the idea of the inherent and inviolable dignity of the person, appreciating the social implications of both, in contrast to the dictates of Brahmanical theology and philosophy. As far back as 1930, Dr Ambedkar began leading temple-entry campaigns, justifying them on the basis of dignity. The way he articulated it at the time, he posed these campaigns as a challenge to the 'high caste Hindu mind', as to whether the Hindu mind could exhibit public conscience; whether it would be capable of grasping the fundamental and equal dignity of the human person. Gaining entry to the temple was not the goal; he did not really even desire to enter temples. The movement was for equality, the right to enter the temple if he and other so-called untouchables did wish to do so, as due recognition of their inherent dignity demands. As Dr Ambedkar said in front of the temple at the time:

> Entry into the Ram Temple . . . will not bring about any radical change in our life. But this is a test to judge . . . whether the Hindu mind is willing to accept the elevated aspirations of the new era that man must be treated as man; he must be given humanitarian rights; human dignity should be established . . . The main question is whether the high caste Hindus are going to consider these aspects and act accordingly.[32]

Tests such as these continuously yielded negative results. Dr Ambedkar was discernibly exasperated at the irrationality of it all. In speeches and written appeals framed in perfect philosophical logic, yet infused with passion and righteous indignation, Dr Ambedkar called out the contradictions built into the violence that was constantly being perpetrated against his community, that too when they were not asking for exclusive privileges but merely equal rights. Why should they suffer such violence? When so-called untouchables took out processions, they were attacked. To attack them for a procession made it seem as though their demand was for some special or exclusive privilege; as though only untouchables, and never caste Hindus, should be allowed to take out processions. The untouchables had no objection to caste Hindus doing the same; they only sought equal associational rights. If the untouchables wanted to wear gold or silver ornaments, they were attacked, as though they were threatening to take all the ornaments for themselves and leave the caste Hindus without any. But they merely wanted equal cultural rights. When the untouchables wanted to send their children to schools, they were attacked, as though they were against the education of caste-Hindu children, when all they wanted was equal educational rights. When the untouchables wanted to draw water from wells, they were beaten, as though their aim had been to prevent caste Hindus from having access to water, when all they wanted was basic, equal rights, in recognition of their dignity.

Dr Ambedkar laid it out clearly: whatever freedoms the untouchables were claiming were neither exclusive to them nor inconsistent with the rights of caste Hindus to an equal share of freedom. So what was it that was preventing the caste Hindus from being able to see the validity of these lawful and rational claims to basic equal rights? It was because their theology and philosophy, inscribed into the code of Hindu social life, recognized only rank, hierarchy, status, as some persons having worth and the rest being worthless, as hardly human—for that was, according to Dr Ambedkar, the very ideology of the Brahmanical tradition and its ideology of caste:

> The acts and omissions [of caste Hindus against Untouchables] are not mere inequities; they are not mere indignities. They are gross instances of man's inhumanity to man. For a doctor not to treat a patient because the patient is an Untouchable, for a body of Hindu villages to burn the houses of the Untouchables, to throw human excreta in their well — if these are not acts of inhumanity, I wonder what can be?[33]

From Philosophy into Law

As we saw, philosophers like Kant aimed to offer a rational justification for human dignity, so that one need not rely upon the theological justifications of the Catholic Church. The Church, anyway, had been subject to a new era of challenges in the various forms of Protestantism sweeping Europe in the seventeenth century (the period following the treaty of Westphalia of 1648, for instance, and the emergence of a new paradigm of 'rights talk' launching with the English Bill of Rights of 1689). This new language of rights crescendoed in the revolutionary periods of the eighteenth century, with the American Declaration of Independence in 1776, its Constitution of 1787, and its Bill of Rights in 1791, and of course the French Revolution and the Declaration of the Rights of Man and Citizen from 1789.

Through all of these documents came the common catchphrases of current human rights discourse: 'We hold these truths to be self-evident, that all men are created equal, that they are endowed by their Creator with certain unalienable Rights, that among these are Life, Liberty and the pursuit of Happiness' (United States Declaration of Independence, 1776). However, the revolutionary rights period of the eighteenth century was a time of liberal nationalism. That meant that their view on rights was that they were anchored in a people, a nation, who were free to govern themselves and to do so under a free and fair system of self-rule. This is in contrast with our prevailing idea of rights today. We see rights as human rights, not just the rights of citizens; these rights accrue to all persons as persons, outside and irrespective of their belonging to a nation or country. It is a cosmopolitan conception, transnational and global, because it is anchored in individual dignity rather than in belonging to a nation or state.

That means that it is much more within the era of 1945–48 where our idea of human rights really crystallizes, as visible from the Universal Declaration of Human Rights [UDHR]. The UDHR was being drafted and debated at the very time that Dr Ambedkar was composing *States and Minorities*, his first effort to formulate a constitution for free India. Jacques Maritain, the

French professor whom Dr Ambedkar had cited in the quote earlier (where he praised his explanation of the person and of the sources of personal dignity), was the one spearheading the UDHR effort, on behalf of UNESCO, to find philosophical common ground from major traditions around the world, in order to build consensus on the universality of the rights being framed. It might nicely tie up a loose thread from the Introduction if we recall here the name of a certain Humayun Kabir, who back in 1946 had been a member of the Experts' Committee that drafted the 'declaration' that would ultimately be reborn as Nehru's Objectives Resolution. I had there described Kabir as a public intellectual and the compiler of Maulana Azad's well-known autobiography *India Wins Freedom*. He was also the author of a book on Immanuel Kant. Moreover, Kabir was an adviser to this very same Jacques Maritain (while he was at UNESCO), who consulted Kabir regarding India's heritage of human rights during the drafting of the UDHR in the mid-1940s.

The Kantian notion of the philosophical ground for dignity—the individual as an end in itself—was fully integrated into the UDHR, just as it would later be into the German Constitution. What is fascinating is that it was also integrated into Dr Ambedkar's own political philosophy. The Kantian formula for the dignity of the person is the first of the four basic premises upon which, according to Dr Ambedkar, democracy rests.[34] In *States and Minorities*, he wrote:

> Political Democracy rests on four premises which may be set out in the following terms:
>
> (i) The individual is an end in himself.
>
> (ii) That the individual has certain inalienable rights which must be guaranteed to him by the Constitution.

(iii) That the individual shall not be required to relinquish any of his constitutional rights as a condition precedent to the receipt of a privilege.

(iv) That the State shall not delegate powers to private persons to govern others.[35]

The following year, as we know very well by now, the 'dignity' clause appeared in Dr Ambedkar's preamble. This obscure philosophical background was a crucial part of the secret history of that appearance.

The other part of that secret history was unravelled by way of documenting the context in which the term 'dignity' first manifested in Dr Ambedkar's preamble on 6 February 1948. Again, it had been with specific reference to caste. The clause read: 'assuring the dignity of every individual without distinction of caste or creed'.[36] Let's now return to the context of caste in order to tease out further hidden connections within Dr Ambedkar's preamble. This is especially important since the explicit ligature of dignity and caste was erased by the time of its final version. Though erased, the palimpsest of caste remained legible below the later drafting surfaces of the 'dignity' clause.

Castes of Mind

While battling the Gandhian claim that a dignified life in India could only be achieved in his ideal village, Dr Ambedkar raised an important issue that we are yet to explore, for it was not historical, theological, philosophical, legal or political, but essentially psychological. Recall from his critique of Gandhi, what Dr Ambedkar accused caste of doing to the mind of the outcastes:

> It educates them into slaves and creates the psychological complex which follows from a slave mentality . . . [loss of] 'dignity and self-respect'.[37]

The psychology of graded inequality, graded dignity, was often on Dr Ambedkar's mind. At one point, he suggested that the hierarchical principle inherent to caste was 'responsible for producing a social psychology which is noteworthy'. This social psychology referred to the social and psychological effects of caste on all castes, not just outcastes. He continued: 'In the first place, it produces a spirit of rivalry among the different castes for dignity. Secondly, it produces an ascending scale of hatred and descending scale of contempt'.[38] How can we possibly assure the unity of our nation if the social psychology of caste generates constant hatred and contempt? As we observed in the previous chapter, it was precisely this conundrum that called out for fraternity, or, later in Dr Ambedkar's view, for metta. It was thus no accident that the 'dignity' component of the Preamble found its place nestled within the 'fraternity' clause.

But let us go back to one side of this social psychology that Dr Ambedkar kept pointing to. That is, the psychological effects specific to those at the bottom of the hierarchies built into caste. Those psychological consequences that Dr Ambedkar claimed resulted from Gandhianism, he also argued in several other places, were a natural consequence of Brahmanism, especially for those outside of its fold:

> Brahmanical philosophy . . . [is] hostile to those who are outside its fold, . . . is inimical to their aspirations. [It] does not favour any advance in their education, promotion to high office, and disfavours every movement calculated to raise their dignity and their self-respect.[39]

From the vantage point of psychology, this bond between dignity and self-respect is important. Dr Ambedkar repeated it often, applying it in a variety of ways. For example, while laying the foundation stone for Milind College in Aurangabad, he said about the scheduled castes:

> The problem . . . is to remove from them that inferiority complex which has stunted their growth and made them slaves to others, to create in them the consciousness of the significance of their lives for themselves and for the country, of which they have been cruelly robbed by the existing social order.[40]

Autobiographical Experience, Again

At the beginning of this chapter we looked at autobiographical expression in relation to how a particular person's experiences may have contributed to his or her conception of dignity. We delved a bit into Gandhi's 1927 autobiography, *The Story of My Experiments with Truth*, as well as Dr Ambedkar's unfinished *Waiting for a Visa* (circa 1937). Now, towards the end of the chapter, we should pick up this trail again. The reason is that Dr Ambedkar's story, as well as his persistent reiteration of the psychological dimensions of caste, the intertwining of dignity and self-respect, would prove in later years to become a recurring theme throughout Dalit autobiography as a genre of its own.

There is no doubt, for example, that self-respect is one of the most recurring motifs in Eknath Awad's powerful autobiography *Strike a Blow to Change the World*,[41] which is heavily infused with reflections on the psychology of caste and the psychology of violence. And although Awad did not know it, in this respect, his life story shared a great deal in common with the life and writings of Frantz Fanon, a psychiatrist and major voice for the decolonization of Algeria, just as it did with Dr Ambedkar. But we must keep in mind that Fanon's and Dr Ambedkar's views on violence were starkly different.

Fanon's masterpiece, *The Wretched of the Earth* (1961),[42] was based on the necessity of violence for decolonization, and this seemed to resonate well with Awad's experiences. According to Fanon, violence righteously exercised by the oppressed had an emancipatory and cathartic power that allowed a colonized (read: caste-oppressed) subject to physically and psychologically liberate himself or herself. It allowed him or her to recreate themselves with a new, positive identity grounded in essential equality, ultimately laying the ground of self-respect.

Awad's book, right along these lines, was peppered with episodes of sacrifices that had to be made towards the crucial end of self-respect. For example:

> When the Dalit begins to discover selfhood and self-respect, she begins to speak out. When she speaks out, there's always a backlash and atrocities happen . . . For four wounds inflicted, only one may be returned, but even this change is very significant.[43]

Or again:

> At every festival or village event, the Mangs would play the *haalki* and *sanai* . . . The Mangs were not paid for their Mangbaajaa . . . And so, the bonfire of [a] village's musical instruments was set alight. When those beautiful *shehnai*s were burning, I felt bad but it was the self-respect that I could see generated in the Mangs through these flames that was of prime importance.[44]

In a certain sense, Awad's autobiography functioned as a guide for achieving self-respect. The term 'self-respect' itself appeared dozens of times throughout the book, and always within the most poignant of events. For example, in passages describing families suffering from hunger but refusing to eat carrion; in numerous descriptions of the coerced shaving of the heads of institutionalized religious Mang beggars (the *potraj*); and always whenever the question of education arose.

Indeed, Awad even saw his long years of development work and social activism as ultimately geared towards helping Dalits attain this immaterial, but priceless value:

> It is not possible to solve the problem of untouchability by providing the Dalit with food and building a few cement houses for them. It is much more important to awaken their sense of self-respect.[45]

Another, early and famous autobiography, called *Baluta*, by activist, poet and writer Daya Pawar, confirmed precisely all of these same motifs. Pawar recorded how the Ambedkarites would go from village to village 'urging the Mahars . . . to refuse demeaning labour, to live with self-respect'.[46] Interestingly, throughout Pawar's book, Dr Ambedkar himself took form as the perfect incarnation of self-respect.

> As long as Babasaheb was alive, he was a vital force in politics . . . 'Maharki is slavery. We won't do this work!' was the slogan of self-respect that resounded in our world. We now had the power and the courage to bring down mountains.[47]

Part of this was because, as Pawar pointed out, Dalits everywhere were inspired by the Mahad agitation that Dr Ambedkar had led—the great Dalit revolt for dignity and self-respect. Another big component was of course his role in shaping the egalitarian

Constitution.[48] Behind the term 'dignity' that appeared in Dr Ambedkar's preamble, the Dalits could hear echoes of Dr Ambedkar's many rousing speeches, like the one at the Kalaram Temple, or those at the Mahad water tank, where Dr Ambedkar so defiantly slaked his thirst.[49]

Photograph by Sundar Lal, copyright © Buddhist Society of India (BSI), courtesy of BSI Delhi state president Shanti Swaroop Baudh.

Not Bread but Honour

While Dr Ambedkar eschewed violence, there was no question that Awad and Dr Ambedkar met with one voice on the crucial importance of awakening self-respect, an idea confirmed by numerous Dalit activists and authors, such as Daya Pawar. Dr Ambedkar summed up this conception of dignity and self-respect beautifully in an essay condemning the patronizing attitude that Gandhi and certain other leaders of the nationalist movement had with regard to the untouchables. In it, Dr Ambedkar pointed out that the impoverishment of the untouchables, which they had been forced to endure for centuries, was of less consequence than the 'insult and indignity' that it had been their misfortune to bear:

> Is social amelioration the be all and end-all of Swaraj? Speaking for the servile classes, I have no doubt that what they expect to happen in a sovereign and free India is a complete destruction of Brahmanism as a philosophy of life and as a social order. If I may say so, the servile classes do not care for social amelioration. The want and poverty which has been their lot is nothing to them as compared to the insult and indignity which they have to bear as a result of the vicious social order. Not bread but honour is what they want.[50]

6

Nation: The Future of a Delusion

On 6 February 1948, the first iteration of Dr Ambedkar's preamble appeared, but the term 'nation' did not. It eventually found its place at the end of the 'fraternity' clause, which at first read:

> Fraternity, assuring the dignity of every individual without distinction of caste or creed.[1]

The two key terms that did feature in the first iteration—'fraternity' and 'dignity'—were characteristic and indeed essential to Dr Ambedkar's thought and writings, but they did not feature elsewhere with much frequency. They were absent from the various kinds of official source documents that were incorporated into the final Constitution, and they were absent from the unofficial documents and writings that in other ways proved influential on the ideas and phrasing of the final Constitution. They were even generally absent from rivals to the primary source documents, such as the alternative constitutions propagated by M.N. Roy, Jayprakash Narayan or Shriman Narayan Agarwal.

I emphasize this point precisely because the opposite was true for the term 'nation'.

This term was absent from Dr Ambedkar's original preamble on 6 February 1948, but concessionally included on 9 February 1948, when it first made its appearance:

> Fraternity, without distinction of caste, class or creed, so as to assure the dignity of every individual and the unity of the Nation.[2]

But what first appeared only reluctantly in Dr Ambedkar's preamble was a term that featured ubiquitously throughout the archives of the nationalist movement, and throughout all the sources—official and unofficial—that contributed towards India's Constitution. Every document above made ample use of it. 'Nation' (with permutations such as 'nationhood' or 'nationalism') was in that era as fundamental a concept as space or time. It was the organizing principle according to which all the motley and disparate and chance events over the last seventy years could be made sense of, retrospectively arranged, justified, venerated. As far as the members of the Constituent Assembly were concerned, and surely also so many others beyond these nascent institutions of India's independence, it was precisely the 'Nation' that they were constituting; the Constitution was a means to *that* end.

In the meetings of the Drafting Committee subsequent to 9 February 1948, the clause wherein 'Nation' found its place was finalized. By 21 February 1948, the clause read exactly as it would on 26 January 1950:

> Fraternity, assuring the dignity of the individual and the unity of the Nation.[3]

And this is how it would remain until the 42nd Amendment to the Constitution (1976/77), when 'integrity' was added; after which it read, '. . . and the unity and integrity of the Nation'. The idea of using the term 'integrity' had a strong precedent from thirty years earlier, as Nehru's Objectives Resolution had itself employed the term. And the other two words added by the 42nd Amendment—'secular' and 'socialist'—were also prime candidates for inclusion in the 26 January 1950 Preamble, as the Constituent Assembly had heatedly and repeatedly debated the terms.

Constituting the Nation or the State?

And indeed, when understood from the perspective of the Constituent Assembly itself—that what they were constituting was the *nation*, with the Constitution being the means to that end—then the frequent recurrence of flashpoint concepts within the Constituent Assembly Debates (CAD) make a great deal of sense. The leftists did not wish to relent on the demand to include 'socialist' and 'secular' into the Preamble—not to mention into the main structure and articles—and various factions of nationalists enjoyed every opportunity available to bemoan the absence of Gandhian principles, or the absence of an invocation to a godhead.

These debates were heated because they were treating the inherently hot subject of the nation and its being. It was metaphysical, not just political.

Dr Ambedkar, however, saw things far more coolly. For him, it was a Constitution that he was drafting, not the 'Nation'. To ascribe the term 'Nation' to the India of that moment was a delusion at best, and dangerously short-sighted: 'in believing that we are a nation, we are cherishing a great delusion. How can people divided into several thousands of castes be a nation?'[4] What we needed was a Constitution first and foremost, as the basis for the state. Whether that state would eventually become something like a nation remained to be seen. At this moment, it was just the future of an illusion. Any substantial sense of nationhood for India would never be achieved until a basic set of minimum conditions were fulfilled in order to prepare the ground for it.

As we saw in the previous chapter, assuring the dignity of the individual was one such basic condition. Hence Dr Ambedkar and the Drafting Committee, in response to the recommendation to amend the Preamble to read 'assuring unity of the Nation and the dignity of the individual', declined to accept the amendment, explaining that 'unless the dignity of the individual is assured, the nation cannot be united'.[5]

And what good is a nation without unity?

The Constituent Assembly Debates

Three speeches that Dr Ambedkar gave within the Constituent Assembly provide panoramic perspective on his sense of the tremendous task facing the Assembly, and on the priority of a good, workable and widely legitimated Constitution as the sine qua non of any future Indian nation. The first he gave very early, on 17 December 1946, speaking in response to the motion to adopt the 'Resolution Regarding Aims and Objectives' (that is, Nehru's Objectives Resolution), before the Drafting Committee had even been assembled. At that moment, Dr Ambedkar had no idea what a central role he would later be called upon to play. The second speech he gave on 4 November 1948, when for the first time he introduced the Drafting Committee's new draft Constitution to the Constituent Assembly, thereby inaugurating the first reading. The third was towards the end of the entire process, on 25 November 1949. Here Dr Ambedkar made his famous final speech leading into the Assembly's vote to adopt the Constitution the next day, thus bringing the third reading to a close.

17 December 1946

Biographers of Dr Ambedkar have vividly brought to life the events of 17 December 1946, because many people regard the undeniable perfection of Dr Ambedkar's completely extempore speech—which opened with, 'your invitation has come to me as a surprise . . . I have come without any preparation whatsoever'—to be the moment that sealed his destiny to be chosen as, and become, the chief architect of the Constitution of India. As one member of the Constituent Assembly who witnessed the events that day described it: 'His speech was so statesmanlike, so devoid of bitterness and so earnestly challenging that the whole of the Assembly listened to it in rapt silence. The speech was greeted with tremendous ovation and he was smothered with congratulations in the lobby.'[6]

At its heart, the speech was about unity. Unity, Dr Ambedkar implored the Constituent Assembly, was absolutely essential 'when deciding the destinies of nations'. 'I know today we are divided . . . We are a group of warring camps and I . . . confess that I am probably one of the leaders of such a camp . . . . With all our castes and creeds, I have not the slightest hesitation that we shall in some form be a united people.'[7]

The verbatim transcripts of the Constituent Assembly, which we are lucky to have, mark how Dr Ambedkar's speech was punctuated by cheers and thunderous applause. This applause was as unexpected by Dr Ambedkar as was the call to speak. The Assembly itself had no expectations from this notorious gadfly, who had just published the chargesheet, *What Congress and Gandhi Have Done to the Untouchables*.[8] It was into the vacuum of this three-fold unexpectedness that Dr Ambedkar sent out blasts of fresh air with his sincerity, erudition, oratorial mastery, overall command and yet what could be called a Buddhist repose.

> So far as the ultimate goal is concerned, I think none of us need have any apprehensions. None of us need have any doubt. Our difficulty is not about the ultimate future. Our difficulty is how to make the heterogeneous mass that we have today take a decision in common and march on the cooperative way which leads us to unity . . . It would be an act of greatest statesmanship for the majority party even to make a concession to the prejudices of people who are not prepared to march together and it is for that, that I propose to make this appeal. Let us leave aside slogans, let us even make a concession to the prejudices of our opponents, bring them in, so that they may willingly join with us on marching upon that road, which as I said, if we walk long enough, must necessarily lead us to unity . . . Let us prove by our conduct that if this Assembly has arrogated to itself governing powers it is prepared to exercise them with wisdom. That is the only way by which we can carry with us all sections of the country. There is no other way that can lead us to unity.[9]

The unity that Dr Ambedkar was championing was political and not metaphysical. That is, political unity permits us to establish a basic structure of the state where liberty and equality may set the parameters for our otherwise wide freedom with respect to metaphysical beliefs—including Advaita Vedanta, for example, which posits a metaphysical unity. Dr Ambedkar's preference for the state over nation derived from this. The reverse process of using the assumed content of the nation—such as its cherished literature, its majority religion, its primary language, the values of its dominant community—to dictate the basic structure of the state would be imprudent and unwise, in addition to unjust. According to Dr Ambedkar's way of thinking, the state, as a political consensus emerging from the unifying points of rival interests and factions and differences, would be able to accommodate a variety of metaphysical beliefs, and (who knows?) might one day even give rise to something like the 'Nation'. But a state conceived as the institutional construct of a Nation, on the contrary, inherited the metaphysical dogmas, religious beliefs and practices only of the dominant voices in that nation, which could so easily slip from democracy into theocracy, fascism and totalitarianism.

In this light, we can understand one aspect of the different representations in the statuary of Dr Ambedkar and Gandhi that we find around India today: while we may occasionally find Gandhi holding the *Gita*, the prized literature of the dominant conception of the nation at the moment of the Constituent Assembly, Dr Ambedkar always held the Constitution. Dr Ambedkar did not believe that the function of the Constituent Assembly was to draft the nation's Constitution; its function was to draft the Constitution of India as a sovereign and independent democratic state. A just, principled and unifying document that could lay the foundation for a nation to come.

4 November 1948

Hence Dr Ambedkar's 4 November 1948 speech, when he introduced the Drafting Committee's draft Constitution into the Constituent Assembly, famously warning that 'Democracy in India is only a top-dressing on an Indian soil, which is essentially undemocratic', and that 'If things go wrong under the new Constitution, the reason will not be that we had a bad Constitution. What we will have to say is that Man was vile.' It was not to be the undemocratic, vile values of some metaphysical entity like 'Nation' that was to dictate the structure, content and operations of the Constitution, but the Constitution that was to elevate the thought and practices of the people of India towards unity, in the spirit of a fellow feeling that could make a future nation possible. Towards this end, Dr Ambedkar stated that he found the Constitution to be workable and flexible, and 'strong enough to hold the country together'.[10]

With this in mind, we can see why Dr Ambedkar spent time in his speech defending the absence of 'ancient Indian polity' in the draft Constitution, and its lack of Gandhian principles. To succumb to these demands would be tantamount to accepting some preconceived idea of 'Nation'—irrespective of how that idea excluded the literature and culture, beliefs and practices, of so many citizens of India—as the basic structure of the State. It is fascinating that a year later, in his speech to the Constituent Assembly, Dr Ambedkar was able to prove this point with specific details. For, according to the nationalists (based on their false historiography which biased their idea of 'Nation'), the draft Constitution included nothing from ancient Indian polity. However, Dr Ambedkar—in line with his emerging revisionist account of Indian history that would eventually get formulated as *Revolution and Counter-Revolution in Ancient India*[11]— stated the exact opposite in his later speech, proving that the false pretences of the nation were dangerous for how we thought about the state:

> It is not that India did not know what is Democracy. There was a time when India was studded with republics . . . It is not that India did not know Parliaments or Parliamentary Procedure. A study of the Buddhist Bhikshu Sanghas discloses that not only there were Parliaments—for the Sanghas were nothing but Parliaments—but the Sanghas knew and observed all the rules of Parliamentary Procedure known to modern times . . . rules regarding Motions, Resolutions, Quorum, Whip, Counting of Votes . . . This democratic system India lost.[12]

But back to the implications of Dr Ambedkar's press for unity. His call for unity also allowed us to understand his advocacy in this speech for a unitary rather than a federal state, a firm position of Dr Ambedkar's going back at least to 1939, when he published *Federation Versus Freedom*,[13] defending the principles of unity and union over federation. The state should be a union, and the unity afforded by its institutional basic structure may ground, in the future, something like a nation to truly form. Thus, Dr Ambedkar was proposing a 'dual polity', taking the best practices from both unitary and federal systems: 'The Draft Constitution has sought to forge means and methods whereby India will have Federation and at the same time will have uniformity in all basic matters which are essential to maintain the unity of the country.'[14]

But the basic structure of state institutions, howsoever arranged to maximize justice, would mean little if it would be undermined by an administration whose heart remained devoted to the pre-democratic ideology that permeated so much of Indian social life: 'it is perfectly possible to pervert the Constitution' if its administration is 'inconsistent and opposed to the spirit of the Constitution'. Hence the demand for constitutional morality.

> Can we presume such a diffusion of Constitutional morality? Constitutional morality is not a natural sentiment. It has to be cultivated. We must realize that our people have yet to learn it. Democracy in India is only a top-dressing on an Indian soil, which is essentially undemocratic.[15]

To apply this into the context of 'Nation', the so-called nation that Dr Ambedkar's contemporaries were so fervently championing was essentially undemocratic. And although the heat and passion built into the nation and nationalism has been useful whenever it could be harnessed for revolutionary struggles towards freedom and independence, unless that passion were doused with the colder principles of justice—like *equal* liberty and *individual* dignity—the hot hegemony of the exclusive 'Nation' will never give way to the cooler logic of the inclusive state.

25 November 1949

These ideas from the beginning of the Constituent Assembly, before the existence of the Drafting Committee, and from the middle of the Constituent Assembly, when the Drafting Committee had completed its draft of the Constitution and introduced it for the first reading, were eloquently expressed by Dr Ambedkar when the Constituent Assembly was drawing to a close, at the end of the third reading. This was Dr Ambedkar's historic and rightly cherished speech of 25 November 1949, where he advocated a way of life which recognized liberty, equality and fraternity as its principles, warning us that with the adoption of the Constitution we were entering into a life of contradictions, with political equality assured, but social and economic inequality rampant.

The contradiction can be understood in terms of the tension between the state and the nation; that is, between a workable Constitution and an Indian nationalist ideology where inequality was allowed to flourish and man was free to be vile. It was not the old, inegalitarian nation that characterized the spirit of the Constitution; it was the spirit of the Constitution that could recast what we understand by 'nation' and what we valued in it, bestowing upon it a new dignity as the synergistic repository of every individual's dignity who collectively constituted that future nation. This could only come through unity, which relied upon fraternity: 'fraternity means a sense of common brotherhood of all Indians—of Indians being one people. It is the principle which gives unity and solidarity to social life.'[16]

If we can put the Constitution first, there remains hope for resolving the life of contradictions by means of fraternal concord, practised at both the social and the personal levels, with the cultivation of a public conscience and the practice of constitutional morality. There will be no nation without unity, and we will never achieve this unity and become a nation unless we forsake the iniquities of caste, and substitute caste separation with constitutional morality and public conscience. On another occasion, speaking on 'a subject of the greatest importance to this nation', Dr Ambedkar defined 'public conscience' as 'conscience which becomes agitated at every wrong, no matter who is the sufferer, and it means that everybody, whether he suffers that particular wrong or not, is prepared to join him in order to get him relieved'.[17] Thus, public conscience and constitutional morality transcend the separatist logic of caste and lay a ground for unity that can seed a nation. Or, to put it into the powerful language of Dr Ambedkar's 25 November 1949 speech before the Constituent Assembly, caste is anti-national:

> I remember the days when politically-minded Indians resented the expression 'the people of India'. They preferred the expression 'the Indian nation'. I am of the opinion that in believing that we are a nation, we are cherishing a great delusion. How can people divided into several thousands of castes be a nation? The sooner we realize that we are not as yet a nation in the social and psychological sense of the word, the better for us. For then only we shall realize the necessity of becoming a nation and seriously think of ways and means of realizing the goal. The realization of this goal is going to be very difficult . . . In India there are castes. The castes are anti-national. In the first place because they bring about separation in social life. They are anti-national also because they generate

jealousy and antipathy between caste and caste. But we must overcome all these difficulties if we wish to become a nation in reality. For fraternity can be a fact only when there is a nation. Without fraternity, equality and liberty will be no deeper than coats of paint.[18]

Competing Visions of the Nation

Within the Constituent Assembly there were numerous rival conceptions of what constituted the nation, and the source documents as well as the alternative constitutional drafts being churned out envisioned it differently. The one thing they all shared was usage of the term. Hence the irony that Dr Ambedkar had originally chosen to exclude it altogether from the Preamble.

The ubiquity of the term 'nation' permeated all varieties of documents, official and unofficial, formal and informal, non-fiction and fiction, throughout the Constituent Assembly years. And while it was mostly the competing visions within the Indian National Congress (from Gandhian to Nehruvian to the far more rightward leaning and Brahmanical options), rather than the rival visions outside of it that horizoned the way 'nation' would be bandied about in the CAD, it is still important to recognize that a great many variations and alternatives were on offer at the time.

Rabindranath Tagore's ambivalence regarding nationalism and the nation had much in common with Dr Ambedkar. Tagore anticipated perspicaciously way back in 1916 through the narrative of his novel *Ghare Baire*[19] what Dr Ambedkar would systematically deduce thirty years later in *States and Minorities*:

> Unfortunately for the minorities in India, Indian Nationalism has developed a new doctrine which may be called the Divine

> Right of the Majority to rule the minorities according to the wishes of the majority. Any claim for the sharing of power by the minority is called communalism while the monopolizing of the whole power by the majority is called Nationalism.[20]

Tagore delivered a series of lectures, both in India and abroad, on the topic of the nation and nationalism. In them, he condemned the 'organizing selfishness of nationalism' and stated that it was a concept alien to India's past: 'India never had a real sense of nationalism.'[21] People often refer to Tagore's vision as a cosmopolitan alternative to nationalism, but it is difficult to determine what Tagore himself would have made of that ascription.

The ascription of 'internationalist' to the many Marxists, and even socialists, present within and around the Constituent Assembly is less troublesome, as internationalism—as opposed to nationalism—was built into the very platform of their parties. As strange as it may seem, there were actually a great number of overlapping concerns for the Marxists and Dr Ambedkar regarding the hegemonic idea of the nation. It was, on the one hand, a perennial commitment to the labouring class, the toiling masses, and on the other hand, a foreboding sense of creeping fascism in India arising out of the hegemonic idea of 'Nation', which prompted Dr Ambedkar again and again to try to find common cause with the left.

Two-Nation Theory

One of the most salient and current conceptions of the nation was that of the two-nation theory, championed by the Muslim League. In his 1940 presidential address to the Muslim League session at Lahore, Muhammad Ali Jinnah gave new currency to a century-old idea: 'India cannot be assumed today to be a unitarian and homogenous nation, but on the contrary, there are two nations in the main—the Hindus and the Muslims.'[22]

Dr Ambedkar took up the two-nation theory for scrutiny in his *Pakistan, or the Partition of India*. In the process he gave this definition of the nation:

> What is a nation? Tomes have been written on the subject . . . but the core . . . can be set down in a few words. Nationality is a social feeling. It is a feeling of a corporate sentiment of oneness which makes those who are charged with it feel that they are kith and kin. This national feeling is a double-edged feeling. It is at once a feeling of fellowship for one's own kith and kin and an anti-fellowship feeling for those who are not one's own kith and kin. It is a feeling of 'consciousness of kind' which on the one hand binds together those who have it, so strongly that it overrides all differences arising out of economic conflicts or social gradations and, on the other, severs them from those who are not of their kind. It is a longing not to belong to any other group. This is the essence of what is called a nationality and national feeling.[23]

It was this very double-edged nature of the idea of the nation that underlay Dr Ambedkar's apprehensions. The 'fellowship' that it engendered was welcome, especially as it 'overrides' conflicts arising out of 'economic conflicts or social gradations' (that is, class and caste), but this came at a hefty price—exclusion of other groups, an 'anti-fellowship feeling' towards others. Therein lay the grave danger of the non-inclusive nation as the basis for the state.

Gandhi's *Hind Swaraj*

This danger, of insiders versus outsiders, friends versus enemies, had an authoritative precedent in Gandhi's *Hind Swaraj*,[24] a true milestone text within the history of the Indian national movement. This was especially ironic given that Gandhi was the most passionate and vocal opponent of the two-nation theory that, at least conceptually, had parallels to all the binaries that Gandhi employed.

A long-winding and paradoxical story emerged from the various publications of Gandhi's *Hind Swaraj*; first in 1909 in Gujarati, then in 1910 in English, but abroad, and then later, in 1919, an Indian edition in English appeared. In the book, Gandhi developed a series of oppositions between what he called 'Western civilization' and 'Indian civilization'. Western civilization was irreligious and displayed 'the tendency . . . to propagate immorality'. Indian civilization, on the contrary, had 'the tendency to elevate the moral being'. Western civilization was 'satanic'; it was the 'Kingdom of Satan' dominated by the 'God of War'. In contrast, Indian civilization was the 'Kingdom of God'; it was ruled by the 'God of Love'. For these reasons, India was 'fitter to teach others than to learn from others'.[25]

In India, as elsewhere, hearkening back to a pre-modern golden age had been a frequent trait of nationalist thought. Gandhi evoked the 'ancient civilization of India which . . . represents the best the world has ever seen'. 'So understanding and so believing, it behoves every lover of India to cling to the old Indian civilisation even as a child clings to its mother's breast.'[26]

Gandhi eased up on many of these ideas as his thought and practice matured. But the 1919 Indian edition appeared with no alteration of these dichotomies, and no added refinement. As late as the CAD, Gandhi was referencing *Hind Swaraj* in his exchanges with Nehru regarding how the Constitution of India should be framed.

This valorization of ancient India, particularly its Brahmanical literature culminating in Advaita Vedanta, had a number of later permutations in other thinkers, practitioners and even statesmen (S. Radhakrishnan being a ready example). Some were quirky, such as the articulation by Shradhananda Sanyasi of the Arya Samaj: 'national self-realization and virile existence is impossible without Swaraj. I, as a Sanyasi, should devote the rest of my life to this sacred cause—the cause of sexual purity and true national unity'.[27] And some would prove to metastasize into the cause of Gandhi's own death.

Hindutva

Vinayak Damodar Savarkar's *Hindutva* was penned from inside his Ratnagari prison cell in 1921,[28] immediately upon the heels of the Indian English edition of Gandhi's *Hind Swaraj* (1919). It was clear that Savarkar had read it; his own text lay out a striking theory of Indian nationhood anchored in the glories of Hindu ethos and the wonder of its civilizational history.[29] This romance of the nation soon found an even more systematic expression in M.S. Golwalkar's powerful manifesto, *We: Our Nationhood Defined* (1939).[30] Due to Golwalkar's praise of the Nazi effort to maintain its racial purity and territorial integrity, the writing was later disavowed by the Rashtriya Swayamsevak Sangh (RSS), of which Golwalkar was the second Sarsanghchalak and its longest-serving leader.

In the classical RSS view emerging from writings such as those of Savarkar and Golwalkar, the nation was defined by five essentials:

> (1) blood (race, ethnicity); (2) soil (territory), captured in the term *Hindustan*; (3) language (Sanskrit as the sacred language and Hindi as the national language); (4) Religion, Hinduism, obviously; and, (5) culture (or shared history).[31]

Paradoxically, these five essentials were characterized with very similar traits that were present even in the key rival ideology of Gandhi. In both sets of work, we find cultural essentialism, the claim of an exclusivist or unique spirituality, exceptional moralism and an anti-modernism in the hankering for a golden past.

For Dr Ambedkar, what was fundamentally troubling about this idea of the nation was how it held a state hostage to its metaphysical and dubious historiographical and philosophical assumptions. What if a person residing within the borders of the Indian state was not Advaitan, or was an animist, atheist, Anglo-Indian, Christian, tribal, Muslim, and so on? There was only a stiflingly narrow conception of a state that could arise from such a reactionary conception of the nation. That a Constitution must be designed to found a state and not to incarnate a Nation became apparent upon analysis of the essentials of the RSS's idea of nation. Blood or race was disqualified if we wished to retain within the Indian state the numerous and variegated ethnicities throughout the Indian subcontinent; soil, or territory was disqualified by the very act of Partition, which rested on arbitrary man-made borders rather than the natural borders of mountains and seas; language was disqualified if we wished to retain south India in our Indian state; religion was disqualified because the subcontinent was home to nearly every religion known to humankind; and, culture or shared history was inherently problematic, since no one knew where to rightfully draw these lines.

As Dr Ambedkar summed it up:

> The point is that nationality is not primarily a matter of geography, culture or language . . . The nation is not a physical thing in which certain objective characteristics, such as commonality of language, race, territory, persists. Nation on

the contrary is a spiritual reality binding people into a deep comradeship.[32]

Nation As Future Promise, Not Past Delusion

If the many members of the Constituent Assembly were thinking along the lines of giving the nation a state, via the Constitution, Dr Ambedkar's line was more akin to giving this now-independent subcontinent—its borders having been drawn where they were—a Constitution, thereby making it a state, which was the necessary condition for allowing a nation, a just nation, eventually to emerge. This future orientation for the nation was in contrast to the many romantic projections of the nation through its glorious past. As far as Dr Ambedkar saw, a just nation would mean so many more future glories for every Indian, inclusively, to claim a share in.

Dr Ambedkar, therefore, had always been wary of the idea of the nation and nationalism, which was hearkening back to a contrived past, sacrificing the many possibilities of the future. Even as far back as when Dr Ambedkar was serving on the Bombay Legislative Council around 1930, he could be found warning his colleagues about preferring the glories of the past to the principles of the future:

> I do not think that we need to bring in historians here; we ought to be wary of historians. In these days when you are striving for bringing about a national spirit, in these days when you are striving for bringing about a common nationality and a common sense of Indian citizenship, in my opinion we ought to do nothing which will nullify and which will dilute that sense.[33]

From the 1930s right up to his Constituent Assembly speeches, Dr Ambedkar could be found challenging the obsession of Hindu nationalists to fixate on the past, be it the fixation on reviving the literature and philosophy of Brahmanism, or the romantic idealization of the Indian village. In *Annihilation of Caste*, he wrote, 'the Hindus must consider whether they must not cease to worship the past as supplying its ideals':

> The Hindus must consider whether they should conserve the whole of their social heritage or select what is helpful and transmit to future generations only that much and no more. Prof. John Dewey, who was my teacher and to whom I owe so much, has said: 'Every society gets encumbered with what is trivial, with dead wood from the past, and with what is positively perverse . . . As a society becomes more enlightened, it realizes that it is responsible not to conserve and transmit the whole of its existing achievements, but only such as make for a better future society'.[34]

Pragmatic Futures

Dr Ambedkar's evocation of John Dewey was a hint about the pragmatic approach that he took with regard to the idea of the nation. He could welcome the idea of the nation as long as its best practices of promoting fellowship and belonging were kept as the centre. But, as he said, nationalism was a double-edged sentiment. Thus, the sharpness of its 'anti-fellowship edge' must be dulled; otherwise, the cost of nation comes at too dear a price for the state to pay. Towards the end of Dr Ambedkar's life, as we saw in an earlier chapter, he set out on a mission to spread the Buddha's message of metta—complementing its inherent qualities for its own sake, metta also had the further virtue of dulling the sharp edge of nationalist sentiment.

Dr Ambedkar's pragmatic approach was clearly at work throughout the meetings of the Drafting Committee subsequent to 6 February 1948, as the clause wherein 'Nation' would find its place was finalized. By 21 February 1948, the clause read exactly as it would on 26 January 1950:

> Fraternity, assuring the dignity of the individual and the unity of the Nation.[35]

But Dr Ambedkar's concession of accommodating the term 'Nation' was conditional upon two things. First, as the clause itself showed, it must be clear that it was fraternity that assured the unity of the nation and not some romantic sense of a Nation that was delusionally believed to offer us fraternity. Second, as the Drafting Committee's unanimous rejection of the amendment to place 'Nation' prior to 'dignity of the individual' evidenced, it must be abundantly clear to all that 'unless the dignity of the individual is assured, the nation cannot be united'.[36]

Dr Ambedkar's preamble, the Preamble to the Constitution of India, makes these claims axiomatic. In the process, the Preamble espouses exactly what Dr Ambedkar long maintained. First, that true national pride must derive not merely from the glories of the past, but by unlocking the glories that the future holds. This is a future where the state enforces the dignity of every individual, which may be achieved by all of its officials practicing constitutional morality. This is a future when, in fellowship, every violation of any individual's dignity sounds the alarm of our public conscience.

At that future point, our 'life of contradictions', which began on 26 January 1950, ceases and the Indian nation truly begins.

Epilogue

> Once upon a time a man went on a sea voyage and returned to his village after a long time, and people asked him what was the greatest wonder that he had seen. He said the greatest wonder that he had experienced was that he had returned home. So far as this Constitution is concerned, the greatest wonder is that we have finished it.
>
> —Naziruddin Ahmad to the Constituent Assembly, 17 November 1949

Naziruddin Ahmad, who had accused Dr Ambedkar of drafting the Constitution in secret, was nevertheless struck with a certain sense of wonder upon its completion. But dismissive of the Drafting Committee's two years of labour, Ahmad regarded its adoption as its sole redeeming feature. Dr Ambedkar, dismissive of Ahmad, thanked by name every member of the Constituent Assembly who had rebelled against him . . . however he didn't include Ahmad.

Dr Ambedkar was grateful for their opposition because it forced him to think deeply about the underlying meaning of clauses, instead of just hammering out the draft: 'But for them, I would not have had the opportunity which I got for expounding the principles underlying the Constitution, which was more important than the mere mechanical work of passing the Constitution.'[1] The ideas and principles behind a clause can be more important than the mere mechanics of the clause itself.

The Greatest Wonder

The 'greatest wonder', as Ahmad called it, is not that the Preamble was finished. It is that we still don't know who wrote it. Who authored the Preamble to the Constitution of India? The answer to that question is, at the very least, book-length. Each of the four most common responses—Jawaharlal Nehru, B.N. Rau, the Drafting Committee as a whole, or B.R. Ambedkar alone—arose from a lack of information, misinformation, or even disinformation, which falsely provided each answer the cover of plausibility. A basic understanding of the anatomy of any preamble informs us that the very question itself is problematic.

Preambles have distinctive parts. These include the severable *invocative, declaratory, descriptive* and *objective* portions.

As we know, the Indian Preamble lacks an invocative part (that is, the portion invoking help or guidance, usually from God). At first blush, this would seem to simplify things for us. It is one less part to be troubled by about its authorship. But unfortunately, the opposite is the case. The CAD are full of demands for inclusion of an invocative part, but certain members of the Drafting Committee, above all Dr Ambedkar, strongly resisted. What this tells us is that determining the precise authorship of the Preamble does not just entail answering who wrote the words, but also answering who ultimately decided which words would be left out.

What a mess! Let's try something simpler.

Who wrote the declaratory part of the Preamble to the Constitution of India? Now, here it seems that a definite answer could be provided. After all, we learned in Chapter 5 that the declaratory part of the Preamble (that is, the part that declares the authority behind the Constitution) was the one and only portion taken from the preamble of the preliminary draft Constitution prepared by Constitutional Adviser B.N. Rau. It follows then that Rau was the author of the declaratory part of the Preamble to the Constitution of India.

No, it doesn't, and he isn't.

Remember that Rau had sourced the declaratory part of his preliminary draft preamble word for word from the Irish Constitution of 1937, only substituting 'India' for 'Éire'. When we use the word 'author', we surely do not mean to say scribe.

Word-for-word sourcing was also a problem that plagued Jawaharlal Nehru's Objectives Resolution. While we have seen throughout the book that a fair portion of the Objectives Resolution got taken up for use in both the objective part (that is, the part that reads, 'sovereign, democratic, republic') as well as in the descriptive part (the part with all the basic principles), we also learned in the Introduction that Nehru himself sourced the Objectives Resolution from an earlier 'declaration' that was collectively drafted.

Well, perhaps therein lies the solution. The answer could be option three, collective drafting. It certainly does seem like an easy way out of this conundrum. But it is false.

Two members of the Drafting Committee—T.T. Krishnamachari and K.M. Munshi—both said that this was not what actually occurred, offering reasons and evidence. The deeply mysterious minutes of the Drafting Committee meetings between 11 and 21 February 1948, with portions missing and lost to history, reveal that only two other members joined Dr Ambedkar for the final revisions of the Preamble. All this lends credence to both Krishnamachari's and Munshi's perspectives.

Moreover, as we learned in Chapters 4 and 5, there were two terms introduced in the draft preamble—'fraternity' and 'dignity'—that were in no way collective at all, but just came right out of the blue. Come to think of it, when we study the minutes of the Drafting Committee, it was not just a few stray and sundry words that came from out of the blue, but a fully-written text of eighty words:

> We, the people of India, having solemnly resolved to constitute India into a sovereign independent state, and to secure to, or promote among, all its citizens: Justice, social, economic and political; Liberty of thought, expression, belief, faith, worship, vocation, association and action; Equality of status, and of opportunity; and, Fraternity assuring the dignity of every individual without distinction of caste or creed, in our Constituent Assembly this . . . of . . . (day of May, 1948 AD), do hereby adopt, enact and give to ourselves this Constitution.[2]

This fully written text became the official working draft as of 6 February 1948, and all evidence indicates that it could have appeared from nowhere other than Dr Ambedkar's shirt pocket.

All right then, so can we just settle on the fourth option as the correct answer: the author of the Preamble to the Indian Constitution was Dr Ambedkar?

Yes.

But also no. The very nature of logic requires that inasmuch as some of the aspects of the first three options are partially true, the fourth option has to be partially false. For example, it was not Dr Ambedkar alone who ensured that the Preamble would not include an invocative part, though you can be sure that he must have fought tooth and nail against the proposed invocation to 'the Father of our Nation, Mahatma Gandhi, [who] led the Nation from slavery'. And again, Dr Ambedkar was happy enough just to adopt the declaratory part that B.N. Rau proposed. The objective part, which we did not explore in this book, was extremely contentious, and although many members of the Constituent Assembly accused Dr Ambedkar of writing it in just any way that he was in a mood to, the fact is that it is almost entirely based upon the Objectives Resolution.

And that brings us, finally, to the descriptive part, the epitome of any preamble, and certainly the heart of ours. As we have seen in Chapters 4 and 5, the authorship of two of the primary terms of the descriptive part—'fraternity' and 'dignity'—can only be attributed to Dr Ambedkar. In Chapters 1 and 3, we learnt that two other primary terms of the descriptive part—'justice' and 'equality'—are sourced directly from the Objectives Resolution. And we saw in Chapters 2 and 6 that two other primary terms of the descriptive part—'liberty' and 'nation'—were ubiquitous throughout the source documents that informed the drafting process. So where does that leave us in terms of authorship?

The Preamble As Dr Ambedkar's

As Dr Ambedkar suggested in his closing address to the Constituent Assembly, it was not the mere mechanics of the clauses that gave them their meaning, but the principles underlying them. In this book, we have seen this play out in at least two main ways, and a few minor ways as well.

The first main way is that the meaning of every term from the descriptive part of the Preamble that we scrutinized was imbrued by the experiences and imbued by the unrivalled erudition of Dr Ambedkar, irrespective of that term's genesis within his mind or outside of it. All of the preambular concepts had a particular meaning for Dr Ambedkar, and a meaning particular to Dr Ambedkar, as evident from seeking out their provenance in his writings and praxis. Throughout the pages of this book we continuously dug through archaeological layers to excavate the underlying practices and principles that informed the later-sedimented meanings of the preambular terms. Some of these were secret meanings that they held for Dr Ambedkar, and these meanings and resonances were also shared by many of his fellow travellers.

The second main way is different, yet related. The unprecedented terms that Dr Ambedkar introduced served to inflect the meaning of the terms that he himself did not. From Dr Ambedkar's freshly written 6 February 1948 draft of eighty words right through to the finally, albeit mysteriously, negotiated version of 21 February 1948, an entirely new conceptual economy emerged among and between all of the concepts. Their meanings would in this way get recast to harmonize with the fundamental principles that Dr Ambedkar had sought to declaim. For instance, although the inclusion of the term 'nation' originally hearkened back to nationalist conceptions, both mainstream as well as right-leaning, the asserted priority of 'dignity' over 'nation' would reorient that term to better refract Dr Ambedkar's own unique understanding of nationhood through it. We can no longer properly think about the pre-existing terms (justice, liberty, equality and nation) without sensing that their centre of gravity shifted by the introduction of the new ones (fraternity and dignity).

Both of these main ways of seeing the Preamble were accessed by hacking in to its secret history, both the untold backstory of its mysterious and secretive drafting process, as well as the unknown genealogy of its concepts in Dr Ambedkar's life story and his enormous corpus of work. What this special access allowed us to understand was not just that the Preamble to the Indian Constitution was distinctively Dr Ambedkar's preamble, but also how and why the Preamble is his, authoritatively so.

Making Ambedkar's Preamble Our Own

The era of history that culminated on 26 January 1950 was one within which the makers of the newly emerging Indian Republic, such as Dr B.R. Ambedkar, were obsessively preoccupied with giving us, the people of India, our freedom and dignity. Today, some seventy years later, it often strikes us that the preservers of the republic are equally preoccupied with taking many of these away. During the process of this reversal, our enthusiasm for the Preamble has clearly dulled. It would seem as if the Preamble did not declare our most fundamental aspirations as a democratic state, but only some utopian impossibility for a listless nation.

The occasion of celebrating seventy-five years of the Republic of India affords the opportunity to reawaken our commitment to the promise that Dr Ambedkar had so carefully coded into his Preamble. Dr Ambedkar's story was the story of Ambedkar's preamble. By making his story our own, his struggle and his lifelong quest for justice, we can make his preamble our own too. Right now.

I hope this book helps in some way to spark that renewed passion for the Preamble.

Appendix 1

CHRONOLOGY OF EVENTS

1927	Dr B.R. Ambedkar's march to Mahad to drink water from the public well
1927	Dr Ambedkar publicly burns the *Manusmriti*
1927	Dr Ambedkar appointed as MLA of Bombay Province for a term of five years (renewed in 1932 for another five years)
29 May 1928	Dr Ambedkar submits a statement before the Simon Commission explicating the nature of constitutional democracy and highlighting the plight of untouchables
1929	Call for complete independence or *purna* Swaraj at Indian National Congress' Lahore session against offer of dominion status forwarded by the British government
26 January 1930	Indian National Congress' declaration of Purna Swaraj - M.K. Gandhi publishes in an article: 'Today is the day to proclaim that we will not be satisfied with dominion status; we want purna Swaraj, or complete independence.' 26 January celebrated as Purna Swaraj Diwas

1930	Dr Ambedkar delivers opening address at the 1930 Round Table Conference in London, despite the Congress boycott, on the dilemmas of freedom or Swaraj for 'depressed classes'
1930	Dr Ambedkar's Kalaram Temple Satyagraha
March 1931	Karachi Resolution 1931 of Indian National Congress' Karachi session
1931	Dr Ambedkar's clash with Gandhi at the Second Round Table Conference in London, inaugurates lifelong debate
1932	Communal Award that Dr Ambedkar fought hard for at the Round Table Conference granted
24 September 1932	Gandhi's fast-unto-death forced Dr Ambedkar into signing the Poona Pact
1935	Government of India Act, 1935
1935	Dr Ambedkar makes public vow at Yeola that although he was born a Hindu, he would not die a Hindu
1935–36	Dr Ambedkar writes unfinished autobiographical story, *Waiting for a Visa*
1936	Dr Ambedkar publishes 'Annihilation of Caste', a speech he was not permitted to deliver
August 1936	Dr Ambedkar forms the Independent Labour Party
1937	The salutation 'Jai Bhim!' coined by an MLA of the Independent Labour Party from Kamptee (Nagpur), Babu L.N. Hardas
1939	M.S. Golwalkar writes manifesto, *We: Our Nationhood Defined*
1939	Dr Ambedkar publishes *Federation versus Freedom*
1940	Muhammad Ali Jinnah speaks of two nation theory at his presidential address to the Muslim League session at Lahore
1944	M.N. Roy's *Constitution of Free India: A Draft* published under the auspices of the Radical Democratic Party

1945	Assumption of 'dignity' into the United Nations Charter
1945	Dr Ambedkar writes *Pakistan, or the Partition of India* as well as *What Congress and Gandhi Have Done to the Untouchables*
1946	*The Gandhian Constitution of Free India* published by Shriman Narayan Agarwal, with a foreword by Gandhi
1946	Dr Ambedkar writes *Who Were the Shudras?*
16 May 1946	Cabinet Mission and Viceroy recommendations regarding the future Constitution of India
22 July 1946	'Declaration' of the Expert's Committee tasked by the Congress Working Committee with preparing material for the future Constituent Assembly, outlining the objectives of the CA With Jawaharlal Nehru as chairman, Asaf Ali, K.M. Munshi (later a member of Drafting Committee), N. Gopalaswami Ayyangar (later a member of Drafting Committee), K.T. Shah, and Humayun Kabir
13 December 1946	Jawaharlal Nehru moves revised 'Declaration' in the Constituent Assembly as a 'Resolution Regarding Aims and Objectives'
17 December 1946	Dr Ambedkar gives an extempore speech on unity, speaking in response to the motion to adopt Nehru's Objectives Resolution
22 January 1947	Objectives Resolution unanimously approved and adopted
15 March 1947	Dr Ambedkar submits *States and Minorities* to the Constituent Assembly's Advisory Committee on Fundamental Rights, Minorities and Tribal and Excluded Areas, chaired by Vallabhbhai Patel. 'Proposed Preamble' appears in Dr Ambedkar's *States and Minorities*

30 May 1947	Admission of Memorandum on the Union Constitution by Constitutional Adviser B.N. Rau Preamble: - We, the people of India, seeking to promote the common good, do hereby, through our chosen representatives, enact, adopt and give to ourselves this Constitution.
3 June 1947	Prime Minister Attlee announces Mountbatten Plan fixing the terms of Partition
30 June 1947	Union Constitution Committee of the Constituent Assembly provisionally accepts the draft preamble prepared by B.N. Rau
18 July 1947	Nehru tells Constituent Assembly: It is proposed to constitute a Drafting Committee which will produce a formal draft for the consideration of the next session of the Constituent Assembly . . . The Preamble . . . ha[s] been dealt with in the Objectives Resolution . . . and the final Constitution will have to incorporate parts . . . That Objectives Resolution will have to undergo some modification . . . but the basic principles . . . will remain . . .
15 August 1947	India declares Independence - Partition of India and Indian Independence Act, 1947. Nehru becomes Prime Minister of India. Tryst with destiny speech
August 1947	Dr Ambedkar joins the Nehru cabinet as law minister
29 August 1947	Drafting Committee for India's Constitution appointed through a resolution of the Constituent Assembly with the task to scrutinize the draft of the text of the Constitution of India prepared by the Constitutional Adviser, giving effect to the decisions already taken in the Assembly and including all matters which are ancillary thereto or which have to be provided in such a Constitution, and to submit to the Assembly for consideration the text of the draft Constitution as revised by the committee

30 August 1947	Drafting Committee meets for the first time. Dr Ambedkar elected chairman
October 1947	Drafting Committee begins scrutinizing the draft Constitution prepared by B.N. Rau, the Constitutional Adviser, who sat in on Drafting Committee meetings
1948	Assumption of 'dignity' into the Universal Declaration of Human Rights
6 February 1948	Consideration of the Preamble of the draft Constitution examined by the Drafting Committee With Dr Ambedkar as chair, Alladi Krishnaswami Ayyar; Maulavi Md Saadulla; and, N. Madhava Rao. B.N. Rau also present, but not a member
9 February 1948	Committee meets again (same people as previous meeting) to debate on the draft of Dr Ambedkar's preamble. Words 'class' and 'unity of the nation' added
10 February 1948	Sparsely attended committee meeting again takes up the preamble. No changes were made to the text itself, but it was decided to append a footnote to the preamble, that clarifies that 'the Committee has followed the Objectives Resolution in drafting the Preamble'
11–21 February 1948	'Fraternity' clause amended again, but neither transcripts nor minutes recorded. Further changes made to the draft preamble, mostly deletions of terms for simplification

21 February 1948	Draft Constitution prepared by the committee forwarded by Dr Ambedkar to the president of the Constituent Assembly, Rajendra Prasad. The final form sent to the Constituent Assembly read: WE, THE PEOPLE OF INDIA, having solemnly resolved to constitute India into a SOVEREIGN DEMOCRATIC REPUBLIC and to secure to all its citizens: JUSTICE, social, economic and political; LIBERTY of thought, expression, belief, faith, and worship; EQUALITY of status and of opportunity; and to promote among them all FRATERNITY assuring the dignity of the individual and the unity of the nation . . . (This 21 February 1948 version turns out to be the final version adopted nearly two years later on 26 January 1950)
26 February 1948	Draft Constitution published widely for public consideration
22 March 1948	Deadline by which all the members of the Constituent Assembly asked to submit their views *~ An amendment came from B. Pattabhi Sitaramayya, elected Indian National Congress president at the Jaipur session, for the 'Fraternity' clause asking for the sequence of 'unity of the Nation' and 'dignity of the individual' to be swapped*
23–27 March 1948	Drafting Committee reconvenes
March 1948	Socialist Party of India prepares its own draft Constitution, entitled *Draft Constitution of the Indian Republic*, with a foreword by Jayprakash Narayan
10–11 April 1948	Special Committee assembles to scrutinize the draft Constitution in the light of all the suggestions. The committee declines to consider the Preamble, passing responsibility to the Constituent Assembly instead

18–20 October 1948	Drafting Committee meets again to assess all of the new submissions and decisions of the Special Committee
4 November 1948	Week-long first reading of the draft Constitution (inaugurated by Dr Ambedkar through a motion for its consideration in the Constituent Assembly) to debate the broader framework and principles of the draft Dr Ambedkar's famous appeal for 'constitutional morality'
6 November 1948	Constituent Assembly member Thakur Das Bhargava, one of the contrarian 'rebels', expresses gratitude to Dr Ambedkar for having added the word 'fraternity' to the Preamble
15 November 1948	Second reading, scrutiny of the once-again amended draft Constitution begins and continues until 17 October 1949 It is opened with discussion on the Preamble; but then postponed to be taken up only at the end of discussion on the draft
1948	Dr Ambedkar marries Dr Sharada Kabir
1948	Dr Ambedkar writes Preface for Laxmi Narasu's *The Essence of Buddhism*
28 August 1949	The snail and the whip cartoon by Shankar published in *Shankar's Weekly*
17 October 1949	Close of second reading, Preamble taken up for debate - J.B. Kripalani, confidant of Gandhi and chairman of the Sub-Committee on Fundamental Rights, speaks at length on the draft preamble, making remarks specifically about the 'liberty' clause, namely that these freedoms can only be guaranteed on the basis of non-violence - J.B. Kripalani commends the Preamble for inclusion of the fraternity clause with its spiritually uplifting morality during the Constituent Assembly of India Debates (Proceedings)

17 November 1949	Third reading of the Constitution commences—members expected to give their comments on overall structure of the Constitution. Members again express dissatisfaction that Gandhiji's concepts were excluded
25 November 1949	Dr Ambedkar makes his famous final speech leading into the Assembly's final vote to adopt the Constitution the next day, bringing the third reading to a close
26 November 1949	Adoption of the Constitution, with the date within text of Preamble: WE, THE PEOPLE OF INDIA . . . IN OUR CONSTITUENT ASSEMBLY this twenty-sixth day of November, 1949, HEREBY ADOPT, ENACT AND GIVE TO OURSELVES THIS CONSTITUTION Celebrated as Constitution Day
26 January 1950	The Constitution of India comes into full force as the basic law for the sovereign democratic Republic of India, abrogating the Government of India Act, 1935. Celebrated as Republic Day
1951	First amendment to the Constitution (concerning equality)
1947–51	Dr Ambedkar works on Hindu Code Bill
27 September 1951	Dr Ambedkar resigns as law minister from the cabinet with the failure of the Hindu Code Bill, which in his resignation speech he called 'the greatest social reform measure ever undertaken by the legislature in this country'
1951	Dr Ambedkar begins drafting specific chapter plans for a magisterial history of India, *Revolution and Counter-Revolution in Ancient India*, which remained unfinished at the time of his death
1951–53	Dr Ambedkar probably composes *Riddles in Hinduism*
January 1952	Dr Ambedkar defeated in his bid for MP by N.S. Kajrolkar of Congress

June 1952	Dr Ambedkar invited by Columbia University to receive honorary doctorate
1953	Dr Ambedkar remarks in Rajya Sabha: 'I was a hack. What I was asked to do, I did much against my will'. It is believed that he also said that he would burn the Constitution.
1953	Dr Ambedkar starts on *The Buddha and His Dhamma* (published in 1957 after his death)
1954–56	Hindu Code Bill is passed piecemeal
1954	Dr Ambedkar's interview to All India Radio saying that his social philosophy is enshrined in three words: liberty, equality and fraternity, with roots in religion derived from the teachings of the Buddha, and not the French Revolution
1955	Untouchability Offences Act adopted
1955	Ambedkar states that 'the Constitution which has been given to this country is a wonderful document' and defends the Constitution in public once again
1955	Ambedkar's BBC radio interview about Gandhi
1956	Speech on 'Buddha or Karl Marx'
1956	Dr Ambedkar's impromptu speech—not fraternity as metta, but metta understood as love, justice, and goodwill
June 1956	Dr Ambedkar refers to his book *Revolution and Counter-Revolution* by name, and calls it urgent
14 October 1956	Dr Ambedkar converts to Buddhism
6 December 1956	Dr Ambedkar passes away
1976	42nd Amendment to the Constitution of India. Three terms added to the Preamble: 'secular', 'socialist' and 'integrity'

Appendix 2
A Snapshot of the Draft Preambles

'DECLARATION' OF THE EXPERTS' COMMITTEE, 22 JULY 1946

This Constituent Assembly declares its firm and solemn resolve to proclaim India as an Independent Sovereign Republic and to draw up for her future governance a Constitution wherein the territories that now comprise British India, the territories that now form the Indian States, and such other territories and parts of India as are outside British India and the States and are willing to be constituted into the Independent Sovereign India, shall be a Union of them all; and the said territories, either with their present boundaries or with such others as may be determined by the Constituent Assembly and thereafter according to the Law of the Constitution, shall possess and retain the status of autonomous units, together with residuary powers, and exercise all powers and functions of government and administration, save and except those that are assigned to and vested in the Union, and save and except such powers and functions as are inherent in the Union by virtue of the sovereignty of the Union; and wherein all power and authority of the Sovereign Independent India, its constituent parts and organs of government, are derived from the people; and wherein shall be guaranteed to all the people of India by law and secured to them by declared social objectives and purposes, economic organization and administrative machinery

(a) justice, social, economic and political;
(b) equality of status, of opportunity, and before the law;
(c) freedom of thought, belief, vocation, association and action, subject to law and public morality;

and wherein adequate safeguards shall be provided for minorities, backward areas, and classes; and whereby shall be maintained the integrity of the territory of the Republic and its sovereign rights on land, sea, and air according to Justice and the law of civilised nations, and this ancient land attains its rightful and honoured place in the world and makes its full and willing contribution to the promotion of world peace and the welfare of mankind.

NEHRU'S OBJECTIVES RESOLUTION (13 DECEMBER 1946) ADOPTED 22 JANUARY 1947

(1) This Constituent Assembly declares its firm and solemn resolve to proclaim India as an Independent Sovereign Republic and to draw up for her future governance a Constitution;
(2) WHEREIN the territories that now comprise British India, the territories that now form the Indian States, and such other parts of India as are outside British India and the States as well as such other territories as are willing to be constituted into the Independent Sovereign India, shall be a Union of them all; and
(3) WHEREIN the said territories, whether with their present boundaries or with such others as may be determined by the Constituent Assembly and thereafter according to the Law of the

Constitution, shall possess and retain the status of autonomous Units, together with residuary powers, and exercise all powers and functions of government and administration, save and except such powers and functions as are vested in or assigned to the Union, or as are inherent or implied in the Union or resulting therefrom; and

(4) WHEREIN all power and authority of the Sovereign Independent India, its constituent parts and organs of government, are derived from the people; and

(5) WHEREIN shall be guaranteed and secured to all the people of India justice, social, economic and political; equality of status, of opportunity, and before the law; freedom of thought, expression, belief, faith, worship, vocation, association and action, subject to law and public morality; and

(6) WHEREIN adequate safeguards shall be provided for minorities, backward and tribal areas, and depressed and other backward classes; and

(7) WHEREBY shall be maintained the integrity of the territory of the Republic and its sovereign rights on land, sea, and air according to Justice and the law of civilised nations, and

(8) This ancient land attains its rightful and honoured place in the world and make its full and willing contribution to the promotion of world peace and the welfare of mankind.

B.R. AMBEDKAR, 'PROPOSED PREAMBLE', *STATES AND MINORITIES* (15 MARCH 1947)

Dr Ambedkar published a *Memorandum on the Safeguards for the Scheduled Castes submitted to the Constituent Assembly on behalf of the All India Scheduled Castes Federation*. Dr Ambedkar sketched the framework of a Constitution, dubbed *Constitution for the United States of India*. This Constitution began with a 'Proposed Preamble', which read:

We the people of the territories of British India distributed into administrative units called Provinces and Centrally Administered Areas and of the territories of the Indian States with a view to form a more perfect union of these territories do—

ordain that the Provinces and the Centrally Administered Areas (to be hereafter designated as States) and the Indian States shall be joined together into a Body Politic for Legislative, Executive and Administrative purposes under the style *The United States of India* and that the union so formed shall be indissoluble
and that with a view:

(i) To secure the blessings both of self-government and good government throughout the United States of India to ourselves and to out posterity,
(ii) To maintain the right of every subject to life, liberty and pursuit of happiness and to free speech and free exercise of religion,
(iii) To remove social, political and economic inequality by providing better opportunities to the submerged classes,
(iv) To make it possible for every subject to enjoy freedom from want and freedom from fear, and
(v) To provide against internal disorder and external aggression,

establish this Constitution for the United States of India.

B.N. RAU'S PREAMBLE, 30 MAY 1947

We, the people of India, seeking to promote the common good, do hereby, through our chosen representatives, enact, adopt and give to ourselves this Constitution.

DR AMBEDKAR'S PREAMBLE, 6 FEBRUARY 1948

06 February 1948 MINUTES: 'Preamble: It was decided that for the [B.N. Rau] Preamble, the Preamble . . . should be substituted':

> We, the people of India, having solemnly resolved to constitute India into a sovereign independent state, and to secure to, or promote among, all its citizens: Justice, social, economic and political; Liberty of thought, expression, belief, faith, worship, vocation, association and action; Equality of status, and of opportunity; and, Fraternity assuring the dignity of every individual without distinction of caste or creed . . . do hereby adopt, enact and give to ourselves this Constitution.

SOURCES:

- From the 'Declaration' (22 July 1946) we have freedom of thought, belief, vocation, association, and action,
- Freedoms introduced by the Objectives Resolution, expression, faith, and worship.
- From both we have the 'solemn resolve', the 'sovereign independent', the 'Justice, social, economic and political', and the 'Equality of status, and of opportunity'.
- From B.N. Rau's draft, there is the 'We, the people of India', and the 'adopt, enact and give to ourselves this Constitution'.
- Dr Ambedkar added terms that could not have been anticipated: fraternity, dignity, caste.

AMENDED DRAFT PREAMBLE, 9 FEBRUARY 1948

> We, the people of India, having solemnly resolved to constitute India into a sovereign independent state, and to

secure to all its citizens: Justice, social, economic and political; Liberty of thought, expression, belief, faith, worship, vocation, association and action; Equality of status, and of opportunity; and to promote among all its citizens, Fraternity, without distinction of caste, class or creed, so as to assure the dignity of every individual and the unity of the nation . . .

PREAMBLE 10 FEBRUARY 1948

No changes were made to the text itself, but it was decided to append a footnote to the Preamble, that clarifies that 'the Committee has followed the Objectives Resolution in drafting the Preamble'.

FINAL DRAFT, 21 FEBRUARY 1948

WE, THE PEOPLE OF INDIA, having solemnly resolved to constitute India into a SOVEREIGN DEMOCRATIC REPUBLIC and to secure to all its citizens: JUSTICE, social, economic and political; LIBERTY of thought, expression, belief, faith, and worship; EQUALITY of status and of opportunity; and to promote among them all FRATERNITY assuring the dignity of the individual and the unity of the nation . . .

PREAMBLE, 26 NOVEMBER 1949

WE, THE PEOPLE OF INDIA . . . IN OUR CONSTITUENT ASSEMBLY this 26th day of November, 1949, do HEREBY ADOPT, ENACT AND GIVE TO OURSELVES THIS CONSTITUTION.

Notes

Preface: Anatomy of a Secret

1. 'Constituent Assembly of India Debates (Proceedings): Volume XI', https://www.constitutionofindia.net/constitution_assembly_debates/volume/11/1949-11-17.
2. Ibid.
3. https://www.constitutionofindia.net/constitution_assembly_debates/volume/11/1949-11-25.
4. Loksabha Secretariat, *Constituent Assembly Debates*, vol. VII (Delhi, 1999), p. 262.
5. Loksabha Secretariat, p. 291.
6. Loksabha Secretariat, p. 416.
7. Nehru Memorial Museum and Library's Oral History Project, https://nehruportal.nic.in/shri-t-t-krishnamachari-0.
8. Loksabha Secretariat, p. 231.
9. B.R. Ambedkar, *Dr. Babasaheb Ambedkar: Writings and Speeches*, vol. 15 (Bombay: Education Department, Government of Maharashtra, 1997), p. 976.
10. K.C. Markandan, *The Preamble: Key to the Mind of the Makers of the Indian Constitution* (Delhi: National, 1984), pp. 56–7.

Introduction: A Tale of Four Preambles

1. Narendra Chapalgaonker, *Mahatma Gandhi and the Indian Constitution* (London: Routledge, 2016), p. 35.
2. Ibid.

3. The snail and the whip, *Shankar's Weekly*, 28 August 1949, Shankar. The cartoon controversy erupted in 2012, when Dalit activists discovered that the image was being used in Class XI NCERT textbooks. If you take the context away, what you are presented with is a Brahmin whipping a Dalit, which is offensive at a basic level. Further layers of context complicate the offense. The full history of the controversy regarding this cartoon can be found in *No Laughing Matter: The Ambedkar Cartoons 1932–1956*, edited and selected by Unmati Shyam Sundar (New Delhi: Navayana, 2019), pp. 224–25. The book also cites Dr Ambedkar's own response to accusations of delays in Constitution drafting:

   '[A]t one stage it was being said that the Assembly had taken too long a time to finish its work, that it was going on leisurely and wasting public money. It was said to be a case of Nero fiddling while Rome was burning. Is there any justification for this complaint?' He followed this up with the number of years taken up to finish the constitutions of United States, South Africa, Australia and Canada, and also the number of variant ideological views that were allowed to be tabled and considered through the 2,473 amendments read in the house. 'If the Drafting Committee was drifting, it was never without mastery over situation. It was not merely angling with the off-chance of catching a fish. It was searching in known waters to find the fish it was after. To be in search of something better is not the same as drifting.'
4. B. Shiva Rao, ed., *The Framing of India's Constitution, Select Documents*, vol. III (Bombay: N.M. Tripathi, 1968), pp. 329–30.
5. Ibid., pp. 334–35.
6. *Constituent Assembly Debates, Official Report, Book 1* (New Delhi: Lok Sabha Secretariat), p. 63.
7. Ambedkar, *Dr. Babasaheb Ambedkar: Writings and Speeches*, vol. 13 (Bombay: Education Department, Government of Maharashtra, 1994), p. 9.
8. *Constituent Assembly Debates, Official Report*, p. 65.
9. Ambedkar, *Memorandum on the Safeguards for the Scheduled Castes submitted to the Constituent Assembly on behalf of the All*

India Scheduled Castes Federation (1947), in *BAWS*, vol. 1 (1979), p. 381ff.

10. Ibid.
11. Ibid.
12. Suraj Yengde, *Caste Matters* (New Delhi: Penguin Random House, 2019), pp. 79–80.
13. Anand Teltumbde, *Republic of Caste: Thinking Equality in the Time of Neoliberal Hindutva* (New Delhi: Navayana, 2018), pp. 24–25.
14. It is worth mentioning that some of these ideas overlap with those of Raja Dhale and the Dalit Panther Movement. Both the conspiratorial view and the Panther view(s) challenge Ambedkarites' reluctance to circumvent constitutional means as the 'grammar of anarchy'; however, the Panther views were not necessarily conspiratorial.
15. See Yengde and Teltumbde, *The Radical in Ambedkar: Critical Reflections* (Delhi: Penguin Random House, 2018), pp. xi–xviii.
16. Niraja Jayal, *Citizenship and Its Discontents: An Indian History* (Delhi: Orient BlackSwan, 2015), p. 153.
17. For a complete biography of Dr Ambedkar, covering all of his myriad trials and triumphs, see: Aakash Singh Rathore, *B.R. Ambedkar: A Definitive Biography* (Macmillan, forthcoming in 2021).
18. B. Shiva Rao, *Volume III*, p. 4.
19. K.C. Markandan, *The Preamble*, p. 38.
20. Ibid., p. 39.
21. B. Shiva Rao, *Volume III*, p. 4.
22. *Constituent Assembly Debates* (New Delhi: Lok Sabha Secretariat).
23. https://nehruportal.nic.in/shri-t-t-krishnamachari-0.
24. K.M. Munshi, *Indian Constitutional Documents: Pilgrimage to Freedom*, 1902–1950 (Bombay: Bharatiya Vidya Bhavan, 1967), pp. 182–85, and regarding B.N. Rau, see p. 116ff.
25. B. Shiva Rao, *Volume III*, p. 481.
26. Ibid., p. 484.
27. As confirmed by Drafting Committee member K.M. Munshi, who frequently mentions that Ambedkar's appointment as Law Minister gave him final authority. See: *Indian Constitutional Documents: Pilgrimage to Freedom, 1902–1950*, pp. 185, 202ff.
28. B. Shiva Rao, *Volume III*, p. 489.
29. Ibid., p. 510.

30. The deletion of the term 'caste' calls for explanation. Taken up in Chapter 5 of this book.
31. B. Shiva Rao, *Volume III*, pp. 517–18.
32. Ibid., p. 750.

Chapter 1. Justice: The Story of B.R. Ambedkar

1. B. Shiva Rao, *The Framing of India's Constitution*, vol. IV, pp. 408–09.
2. *Constituent Assembly Debates, Volume 1*, https://www.constitutionofindia.net/constitution_assembly_debates/volume/1/1946-12-19.
3. K.C. Markandan, *The Preamble*, p. xx.
4. Narendra Chapalgaonker, *Mahatma Gandhi and the Indian Constitution* (New Delhi: Routledge, 2016), p. 89.
5. Ambedkar, *Dr. Babasaheb Ambedkar: Writings and Speeches*, vol. 3 (Bombay: Education Department, Government of Maharashtra, 1987), p. 25.
6. See, for example, the multi-volume collection of essays on Dr Ambedkar's idea of justice: Aakash Singh Rathore, ed., *B.R. Ambedkar: The Quest for Justice* (Oxford University Press, 2020).
7. Editions of each of these texts are available in *Dr. Babasaheb Ambedkar Writings and Speeches* [BAWS], in seventeen volumes.
8. Editions available in BAWS.
9. Gail Omvedt, *Ambedkar: Towards an Enlightened India* (Delhi: Penguin India, 2008).
10. Arun Shourie, *Worshipping False Gods* (Delhi: HarperCollins, 2012).
11. The title 'Young Bhim' is taken from the childhood stories of B.R. Ambedkar dramatized into a storybook for children by Devyani Khobragade (Delhi: Juggernaut, forthcoming).
12. See Aakash Singh Rathore, *A Philosophy of Autobiography: Body & Text* (Delhi: Routledge, 2019).
13. I rely here on Scott R. Stroud's pioneering work, which painstakingly details Dr Ambedkar's debt to Dewey. Among Stroud's many important writings, see for example, 'What Did Bhimrao Ambedkar Learn from John Dewey's *Democracy and Education*?' *The Pluralist*, 12 (2), 2017, pp. 78–103.

14. *Columbia Alumni News*, 19 December 1930, p. 12, available in Stroud, and also Zelliot and elsewhere.
15. Eleanor Zelliot, *Ambedkar's World* (New Delhi: Navayana, 2013), p. 69.
16. Nanak Chand Rattu, *Last Few Years of Dr. Ambedkar* (New Delhi: Amrit Publishing House, 1997), p. 35.
17. Much of this section relies upon Chapter 9, 'Gandhi and Ambedkar', of my earlier book *Indian Political Theory: Laying the Groundwork for Svaraj* (London: Routledge, 2017).
18. B.R. Ambedkar, BBC Interview, 1955, https://www.youtube.com/watch?v=omGcgEstVIE.
19. Upendra Baxi, 'Justice as Emancipation: The Legacy of Babasaheb Ambedkar', in Upendra Baxi and Bhikhu Parekh eds., *Crisis and Change in Contemporary India* (New Delhi: Sage, 1995), pp. 123–24.
20. Ramachandra Guha, 'Gandhi's Ambedkar', in Aakash Singh and Silika Mohapatra eds., *Indian Political Thought: A Reader* (London: Routledge, 2010), p. 33.
21. Even the historiography of the Poona Pact is complicated. See Karthik Raja, 'Foregrounding Social Justice in Indian Historiography: Interrogating the Poona Pact' in Aakash Singh Rathore ed., *B.R. Ambedkar: The Quest for Justice, Volume II: Social Justice* (Delhi: Oxford University Press, 2020), Chapter 11.
22. Round Table India, 'Dr. Ambedkar Remembers the Poona Pact in an Interview on BBC' (2012), http://roundtableindia.co.in/index.php?option=com_content&view=article&id=3797:dr-ambedkar-remembers-the-poona-pact-in-an-interview-on-the-bbc-&catid=116:dr-ambedkar&Itemid=128.
23. M.K. Gandhi, *Collected Works of Mahatma Gandhi* (1958–94), vol. 84, p. 272, www.gandhiserve.org/cwmg/VOL084.PDF.
24. Editions of each of these texts are available in BAWS.
25. *Constituent Assembly Debates: Official Report, Volume 7: 04 November to 08 January 1949, Issues 1–11*, p.1.
26. *Constituent Assembly Debates*, Book 3, p. 39.
27. Ibid., p. 212.
28. M.K. Gandhi, *Hind Swaraj and Other Writings*, edited by Anthony Parel, (Cambridge: Cambridge University Press, 1997), pp. 149–56
29. Pyarelal, *Mahatma Gandhi on Human Settlements* (Ahmedabad: Navajivan, 1977), p. 21.

30. Bidyut Chakrabarty, *Confluence of Thought: Mahatma Gandhi and Martin Luther King Jr.* (New York: Oxford University Press, 2006), p. 44.
31. Ibid.
32. Harold G. Coward, *Indian Critiques of Gandhi*, SUNY series in Religious Studies, (New York: State University of New York Press, 2003).
33. http://www.questforequity.org/about.html.
34. Available in BAWS.
35. E. Newbigin, 'B.R. Ambedkar's Code Bill: Caste, Marriage and Postcolonial Indian Citizenship', in *The Hindu Family and the Emergence of Modern India: Law, Citizenship and Community* (Cambridge Studies in Indian History and Society), (Cambridge: Cambridge University Press, 2013), pp. 162–96.
36. For more on Dr Ambedkar's views on women's emancipation, see Sunaina Arya, 'Ambedkar as a Feminist' in Aakash Singh Rathore ed., *B.R. Ambedkar: The Quest for Justice, Volume IV: Gender and Racial Justice* (Delhi: Oxford University Press, 2020), Chapter 4.
37. Available in BAWS.
38. B.R. Ambedkar, *The Buddha and His Dhamma: A Critical Edition*, edited, introduced and annotated by Aakash Singh Rathore and Ajay Verma (New Delhi: Oxford University Press, 2011).
39. Sangharakshita, *Ambedkar and Buddhism* (London: Windhorse Publications, 1986), p. 20.

Chapter 2. Liberty: Swaraj Is Whose Birthright?

1. *Constituent Assembly Debates.*
2. B. Shiva Rao, *Volume III*, pp. 334–35.
3. Ibid.
4. Ibid., pp. 517–18.
5. Freedom of association, however, has a more ignominious backstory. As the constitutional adviser explained: 'The reason for omitting "association" was that it would have seemed odd to stress so prominently freedom of association at a time when certain associations dangerous to the State were being banned' (B. Shiva Rao, *Volume IV*, p. 5). The association being hinted at is the RSS,

whom we have to thank for the inability of the Constituent Assembly to underscore the freedom of association in the Constitution.

6. Dr Ambedkar's own use of the term 'liberty' is interesting, but will not be the focus of the present chapter. We might merely mention here three works where the term is specifically addressed. One is in *Annihilation of Caste* (Chapter 2 in *BAWS*, vol. 1, 1979). There, Dr Ambedkar suggests that the concept of *liberty* implies a right to life and limb, a right to property, and a right to choose one's profession. In the *Philosophy of Hinduism*, Dr Ambedkar challenges the idea that liberty is primordial, showing instead that it is dependent upon preconditions such as social equality, economic security, and knowledge. The third is the early manuscript, *The Hindu Social Order* (Chapter 2 and 3 in *BAWS*, vol. 3, 1987), where Dr Ambedkar classifies liberty into civil liberty and political liberty.
7. *Constituent Assembly Debates: Official Report, Volume 10* (17 October 1949), p. 452.
8. As per Drafting Committee member K.M. Munshi's description from his memoirs. K.M. Munshi, *Indian Constitutional Documents: Pilgrimage to Freedom*, 1902–50, p. 183.
9. *Constituent Assembly Debates: Official Report, Volume 7: 04 November to 08 January 1949, Issues 1–11*, p. 1.
10. Gurpreet Mahajan, *India: Political Ideas and the Making of a Democratic Discourse* (New York: Zed Books, 2013), p. 41.
11. See Ananya Vajpeyi's *Righteous Republic: The Political Foundations of Modern India* (Cambridge, MA: Harvard University Press, 2012).
12. Gurpreet Mahajan, *India*, p. 42.
13. In his editorial in the *Bahishkrut Bharat* (29 July 1927), cited in Dhananjay Keer, *Dr. Ambedkar, Life and Mission* (Bombay: Popular Prakashan, 1962), p. 81.
14. This and the following six sections of the chapter have been drawn from my book *Indian Political Theory: Laying the Groundwork for Svaraj* (London: Routledge, 2017), Chapter 9.
15. These are Gandhi's words, as discussed further below. Dr Ambedkar himself fully characterized the situation thus: 'The British have an empire. So have the Hindus. For is not Hinduism a form of imperialism and are not the Untouchables a subject race, owing their

allegiance and their servitude to their Hindu Master?' Ambedkar, *BAWS*, vol. 9, (1991), p. 429.

16. In the *Young India* of 29 December 1920, quoted in Ambedkar, *BAWS*, vol. 9. (1991), p. 37.
17. Gandhi, cited in B.R. Ambedkar, *BAWS*, vol. 5 (1989), p. 315. Also see M.K. Gandhi, *Collected Works of Mahatma Gandhi* (1958–94), vol. 53, p. 318, www.gandhiserve.org/cwmg/VOL084.PDF.
18. Gandhi, cited in Ambedkar, *BAWS*, vol. 5 (1989), p. 318.
19. Ambedkar, *BAWS*, vol. 9 (1991), p. 20.
20. Ibid. p. 22.
21. Ambedkar, *BAWS*, vol. 5, (1989), p. 299.
22. Ambedkar, *BAWS*, vol. 5, pp. 307–09.
23. Ambedkar, *BAWS*, vol. 2, (1982), pp. 503–06.
24. *Young India*, cited in Ambedkar, *BAWS*, vol. 9 (1991), pp. 36–37.
25. Ambedkar, *BAWS*, vol. 17, part 3 (2003), p. 443.
26. Ibid., p. 64.
27. Ambedkar, *BAWS*, vol. 5, p. 314.
28. Ibid., pp. 299–300.
29. Ambedkar, *BAWS*, vol. 8 (1990), p. 154.
30. Ambedkar, *BAWS*, vol. 9, pp. 290–91.
31. Ambedkar, BAWS, vol. 1 (1979), p. 40.
32. Ambedkar, *BAWS*, vol. 10 (1991), p. 496.
33. Ambedkar, *BAWS*, vol. 9, p. 312.
34. Ambedkar, *BAWS*, vol. 17, part 3, p. 366.
35. Ambedkar, *BAWS*, vol. 9, p. 209.
36. *Young India*, cited in Ambedkar, *BAWS*, vol. 5, pp. 474–75.
37. Ambedkar, *BAWS*, vol. 10, p. 154.
38. Ibid., p. 135.
39. Ibid., p. 145.
40. Ambedkar, *BAWS*, vol. 5, p. 306.
41. *Selected Works of Dr. BR Ambedkar*, p. 1891, https://drambedkarbooks.files.wordpress.com/2009/03/selected-work-of-dr-b-r-ambedkar.pdf.
42. Ibid., p. 1892.
43. Ambedkar, *BAWS*, vol. 7 (1990).

44. Ibid., unnumbered dedication prior to title page.
45. Ibid., vol. 7, p. 12.
46. Ibid., p. 14.
47. Ibid., p. 13.
48. Ibid.
49. *Selected Works of Dr. BR Ambedkar*, Wordpress.com, p. 1841.
50. Ambedkar, *BAWS*, vol. 7, p. 15.
51. Ambedkar, *BAWS*, vol. 17, part 3, p. 304.
52. *Selected Works of Dr. BR Ambedkar*, p. 1981.
53. Ambedkar, *BAWS*, vol. 10, p. 41.
54. When Gandhi came to know that Chambar activist P. Rajbhoj was working in the HSS, Gandhi wrote him a letter asking him to desist. Gandhi emphasized that the HSS was meant for savarnas who repented of discrimination against Harijans. (Letter from Gandhi to Rajbhoj, dated 31 August 1934, M.K. Gandhi, *Collected Works of Mahatma Gandhi*, vol. 58, 1974, p. 383).
55. Ambedkar, *BAWS*, vol. 9, p. 212.
56. Ibid.
57. According to Dhananjay Keer, *Dr. Ambedkar, Life and Mission*, p. 274.
58. Pokala Laxmi Narasu, *The Essence of Buddhism* (New Delhi and Chennai: Asian Educational Services, 1912).
59. Ambedkar, *BAWS*, vol. 17, part 3, pp. 87–88.

Chapter 3. Equality: The Constitution as Revolution

1. B. Shiva Rao, *Volume III*, pp. 517–18.
2. Ibid., pp. 334–35.
3. Ibid.
4. Friedrich Engels and Karl Marx, *Revolution and Counter-Revolution in Germany*, edited by Eleanor Marx Aveling (New York: Swan Sonnenschein & Co., 1896).
5. M.N. Roy, *Revolution and Counter-Revolution in China* (Kolkata: Renaissance Publishers, 1946).
6. Ambedkar, *BAWS*, vol. 3, p. 267.
7. Dr Ambedkar cooperated with leftist parties throughout his long career; even as late as the 1952 elections, he led his Scheduled Castes Federation (SCF) into an alliance with the Praja Socialist Party.

8. 'Materialism' in *Selected Works of M.N. Roy, Volume IV: 1932–1936*, edited by Sibnarayan Ray (New Delhi: Oxford University Press, 1997), p. 326.
9. B.R. Ambedkar, *Buddhist Revolution and Counter Revolution in Ancient India*, edited by D.C. Ahir (Delhi: Buddhist World Press, 1996), p. 67.
10. The varna system prior to *Manusmriti* did not claim that one had his or her place by birth into a varna, but was based more on the characteristics, accomplishments and attributes of the person. In other words, an ignorant Brahmin would have been an oxymoron in the varna system, because ignorance precludes one from belonging to the Brahmin varna. But the *Manusmriti* changed all this and made varna hereditary. Thus, varna became caste, when one's place was determined by birth, when status and occupation became hereditary. Hence, the possibility of an ignorant Brahmin arises, and hence, the *Manusmriti* obsessively looks after that category by enforcing graded inequality: 'A Brahmin, whether learned or ignorant, is a powerful divinity, even as fire is a powerful divinity'. (B.R. Ambedkar, *Buddhist Revolution and Counter Revolution in Ancient India*, edited by D.C. Ahir, p. 99).
11. Sunaina Arya and Aakash Singh Rathore eds, *Dalit Feminist Theory—A Reader* (Delhi: Routledge, 2019).
12. B.R. Ambedkar, BAWS, vol. 1, p. 14.
13. Ibid., p. 9.
14. E. Newbigin, 'B. R. Ambedkar's Code Bill: Caste, Marriage and Postcolonial Indian Citizenship', in *The Hindu Family and the Emergence of Modern India: Law, Citizenship and Community*, pp. 162–96.
15. Ambedkar, *BAWS*, vol. 3, pp. 465–66.
16. Werner Keller, *The Bible as History* (London: Hodder and Stoughton, 1955).
17. Ambedkar, *BAWS*, vol. 3, p. 267
18. B.R. Ambedkar, *The Buddha and His Dhamma: A Critical Edition*, edited, introduced and annotated by Aakash Singh Rathore and Ajay Verma.
19. Ibid., *Preface.*
20. Mark Siderits, *Buddhism as Philosophy: An Introduction* (London: Ashgate, 2007), p. 17.

21. Alexander Syrkin, 'On the Beginning of Sutta Pitaka (The Brahmajala Sutta)', in S.N. Eisenstadt, et al. eds., *Orthodoxy, Heterodoxy and Dissent in India* (New York: Mouton publishing, 1984), p. 69.
22. Ambedkar, *BAWS*, vol. 3, p. 186.
23. Rhys Davids, *Dialogues of the Buddha*, translated from the Páli of the *Dìgha Nikáya Sutta* no. 5 by T.W. Rhys Davids (London: Páli Text Society, 1899).
24. Rhys Davids, *Dialogues of the Buddha*, in the series Sacred Books of the Buddhists, translated from the Páli of the *Dìgha Nikáya Sutta* no. 5.
25. Ambedkar, *BAWS*, vol. 3, p. 222.
26. Ibid., p. 229.
27. Peter Harvey, *An Introduction to Buddhism: Teachings, History and Practices* (Cambridge: Cambridge University Press, 2013), p. 194.
28. Ambedkar cites Haraprasad Shastri, *Mahamahopadhyaya Haraprasad Sastri Memorial Volume*, Narendra Nath Law ed., in *BAWS*, vol. 3, p. 235, footnote 1.
29. Ambedkar, *BAWS*, vol. 3, p. 235.
30. Smith's 1924 text, p. 336, is cited in Ambedkar, *BAWS*, vol. 3, p. 237.
31. Romila Thapar, *A History of India, Volume One* (New Delhi: Penguin, 1957).
32. Upinder Singh, *Political Violence in Ancient India* (Cambridge, MA: Harvard University Press, 2017).
33. Peter Robb, *A History of India* (New York: Palgrave Macmillan, 2002).
34. Edward Gibbon, *Decline and Fall of the Roman Empire* (Hertfordshire: Wordsworth Classics, 1998).
35. G.W.F. Hegel, *The Philosophy of History*, translated by J. Sibree (New York: Cosimo Classics, 2007).
36. See Aakash Singh Rathore and Rimina Mohapatra, *Hegel's India: A Reinterpretation, with Texts* (Delhi: Oxford University Press, 2018).

Chapter 4. Fraternity: Affection for Everyone, Hatred for None

1. Thakur Das Bhargava, 6 November 1948, *Constituent Assembly of India Debates (Proceedings)*, vol. VII.

2. 17 October 1949, *Constituent Assembly of India Debates (Proceedings)*, vol. X.
3. Shriman Narayan Agarwal, *The Gandhian Constitution of Free India*, foreword by M.K. Gandhi (Allahabad: Kitabistan, 1946).
4. *Draft Constitution of the Indian Republic*, foreword by Jayprakash Narayan (Socialist Party [India], 1948).
5. Draft Constitution of the Republic of India (Socialist Party, 1948), Remarks, https://www.constitutionofindia.net/historical_constitutions/draft_constitution_of_the_republic_of_india__socialist_party__1948__1st%20January%201948.
6. The Preamble of the Socialists' Constitution incorporated many clauses from the Objectives Resolution and itself looks similar to the final Preamble to the Indian Constitution, except that it has no 'fraternity' clause! It read: 'We, the people of India, having solemnly resolved to form a Sovereign Democratic Republic and to establish Democratic Socialist Order, wherein social justice will prevail and all citizens will lead comfortable, free and cultured life, and enjoy equality of status and opportunity and liberty of thought, expression, faith and worship, do hereby, through our chosen representatives assembled in the Constituent Assembly, adopt, enact, and give to ourselves this Constitution', https://www.constitutionofindia.net/historical_constitutions/draft_constitution_of_the_republic_of_india__socialist_party__1948__1st%20January%201948
7. Even Dr Ambedkar's own 'Proposed Preamble' from his *States and Minorities* did not mention it; however, as we shall soon see, the term appeared throughout Dr Ambedkar's writings from the 1930s to 1950s.
8. B. Shiva Rao, *Volume III*, p. 484.
9. Ibid., p. 489.
10. Ibid., p. 491.
11. As evidenced in an elaborate note that Rau later circulated to the members of the Constituent Assembly, citing Dr Ambedkar. See K.C. Markandan, *The Preamble*, p. 44.
12. B. Shiva Rao, *Volume III*, p. 491.
13. As we shall discuss in the next chapter, we do have the testimony of one of the Drafting Committee members, who in his autobiography

comments on related clauses; see K.M. Munshi, *Indian Constitutional Documents: Pilgrimage to Freedom*, 1902–1950. But even this 'inside view' is limited for the specific period in question; for, unless he appeared in the undocumented meetings between 13 and 21 February, Munshi was not in attendance.

14. B. Shiva Rao, *Volume III*, p. 510.
15. B.R. Ambedkar, *Buddhist Revolution and Counter Revolution in Ancient India*, edited by D.C. Ahir, p. 147.
16. Ambedkar, *Annihilation of Caste*, Chapter 2 in BAWS, vol. 1.
17. Ambedkar, 'The Philosophy of Hinduism', Chapter 1 in *BAWS*, vol. 3.
18. Ambedkar, 'Hindu Social Order', Chapters 2 and 3 in *BAWS*, vol. 3.
19. Ambedkar, 'Buddha and Karl Marx', Chapter 18 in *BAWS*, vol. 3.
20. B.R. Ambedkar, *The Buddha and His Dhamma: A Critical Edition*, edited, introduced and annotated by Aakash Singh Rathore and Ajay Verma.
21. Pradeep Gokhale, 'Ambedkar on the Trio of Principles' in *B.R. Ambedkar: The Quest for Justice* (Five-volume box set), vol. 1, *Political Justice*, edited by Aakash Singh Rathore (Delhi: Oxford University Press, 2020).
22. Ambedkar, 'Buddha and Karl Marx' (an address to All India Radio, 1954), Chapter 18 in *BAWS*, vol. 3.
23. Scott R. Stroud, 'Pragmatism and the Pursuit of Social Justice in India: Bhimrao Ambedkar and the Rhetoric of Religious Reorientation', *Rhetoric Society Quarterly*, vol. 46, no. 1, (2016) pp. 5–27, DOI: 10.1080/02773945.2015.1104717, https://www.tandfonline.com/doi/pdf/10.1080/02773945.2015.1104717?needAccess=true.
24. Ambedkar, *Annihilation of Caste*, pp. 30–31.
25. Ambedkar, *BAWS*, vol. 3, p. 25.
26. Thomas Hobbes, *Leviathan* (Baltimore: Penguin Books, 1968).
27. Ambedkar, *Riddles in Hinduism: An Exposition to Enlighten the Masses*, in *BAWS*, vol. 4, p. 283. Also see B.R. Ambedkar, *Riddles in Hinduism: The Annotated Critical Selection*, Introduced by Kancha Illaiah (New Delhi: Navayana, 2016).
28. *Constituent Assembly Debates: Official Report, Volume 7: 04 November to 08 January 1949, Issues 1–11*, p. 38. Also see Ambedkar, *BAWS*, vol. 17, part 1.

29. John Rawls, *The Law of Peoples: With, the Idea of Public Reason Revisited* (Cambridge, MA: Harvard University Press, 2001).
30. Smit Panchbai, *B.R. Ambedkar: Conditions Precedent for the Successful Working of Democracy* (Nagpur: Buddha Nagar, 1976), p. 3.
31. Ambedkar, *BAWS*, vol. 3, pp. 95–115.
32. 25 November 1949 (third reading), *Constituent Assembly of India Debates (Proceedings), Volume XI*.
33. 4 November 1948 speech, *Constituent Assembly of India Debates (Proceedings), Volume XI*.
34. Dr Ambedkar, 27 September 1951, *Constituent Assembly of India Debates (Proceedings), Volume IX*. Also see Ambedkar, *BAWS*, vol. 15, p. 784.
35. For details, see Aakash Singh Rathore, *B.R. Ambedkar: A Biography* (HarperCollins, forthcoming).
36. Suraj Yengde, *Caste Matters*, pp. 79–80.
37. Som Raj Gupta, Śaṅkarācārya, *The Word Speaks to the Faustian Man: Bṛhada-raṇyaka Upaniṣad*, vol. 5 (Delhi: Motilal Banarasidass Publishers, 2008).
38. Ambedkar, *Riddles in Hinduism: The Annotated Critical Selection*, pp. 173–77.
39. Ambedkar, *Riddles in Hinduism: An Exposition to Enlighten the Masses*, *BAWS*, vol. 4, p. 284.
40. Ambedkar, *BAWS*, vol. 3, p. 462.
41. Ambedkar, 'Buddha and Karl Marx', audio.
42. B.R. Ambedkar, *The Buddha and His Dhamma: A Critical Edition*, edited, introduced and annotated by Aakash Singh Rathore and Ajay Verma.
43. Ambedkar, *Riddles in Hinduism: An Exposition to Enlighten the Masses*, *BAWS*, vol. 4, p. 284.
44. B.R. Ambedkar, *The Buddha and His Dhamma: A Critical Edition*, edited, introduced and annotated by Aakash Singh Rathore and Ajay Verma, p. 129.

Chapter 5. Dignity: Not Bread but Honour

1. 'Karachi Resolution (1931)', https://www.constitutionofindia.net/historical_constitutions/karachi_resolution__1931__1st%20January%201931.

2. https://www.constitutionofindia.net/historical_constitutions/karachi_resolution__1931__1st%20January%201931.
3. B.R. Ambedkar, *Waiting for a Visa* (circa 1937), Chapter 1 of Part V, in *Dr. Babasaheb Ambedkar: Writings and Speeches*, vol. 12, p. 670.
4. M.N. Roy, *Constitution of Free India: A Draft* (Radical Democratic Party [India], 1944).
5. *Draft Constitution of the Indian Republic*, foreword by Jayprakash Narayan (Socialist Party [India], 1948).
6. Shriman Narayan Agarwal, *The Gandhian Constitution of Free India*, foreword by M. K. Gandhi.
7. Ibid., p. 58, https://www.constitutionofindia.net/historical_constitutions/gandhian_constitution_for_free_india__shriman_narayan_agarwal__1946__2nd%20April%201945#_ednref73.
8. M.K. Gandhi, *Autobiography: The Story of My Experiments with Truth* (Boston: Beacon Press, 2015).
9. M.K. Gandhi, *Autobiography*, p. 264.
10. 'The Brahman was his mouth, of both his arms was the Rājanya made. His thighs became the Vaiśya, from his feet the Śūdra was produced'. Hymn 90, the Purusha Sukta, https://sacred-texts.com/hin/rigveda/rv10090.htm.
11. *Constituent Assembly Debates*, Book no. 3, p. 39.
12. It is precisely this ghetto that serves as the setting for Baburao Bagul's short stories (*When I Hid My Caste: Stories*, translated by Jerry Pinto, New Delhi: Speaking Tiger, 2018) that puncture the myth of the romantic village ideal, plainly revealing that such an ideal could only be envisioned by myopic eyes engaged in privileged seeing. But Bagul's fiction is not only free of romanticizing tradition; it is equally free of romanticizing dissent. Of course, many of Bagul's characters are engaged in defying the social roles thrust upon them, and some of them are triumphant (the second story, entitled Bohada—about 'the village Mahar' who irrepressibly asserts himself and ends up dominating a village festival, to the awe and astonishment of everyone—is probably the best example). But for the most part, such revolutions end tragically (the eighth story, Revolt—about a brilliant boy forced to give up his studies to inherit his father's job of cleaning dry toilets with his bare hands—may be the most agonizing example). Bagul's stories thereby dramatize the lesson of all social

reform movements: it takes more than a solitary individual, no matter how gifted, to overturn a hydra-headed system of oppression.

13. Ambedkar, 'Outside the Fold', in *The Essential Writings of B.R. Ambedkar*, edited by Valerian Rodrigues (New Delhi: Oxford University Press, 2002), p. 331.
14. Ambedkar, *What Congress and Gandhi Have Done to the Untouchables, BAWS*, vol. 9, p. 285.
15. B. Shiva Rao, *Volume III*, p. 484.
16. Ibid., p. 491.
17. B. Pattabhi Sitaramayya, *Indian Nationalism* (Masulipatam: Kistna Swadeshi Press, 1913), https://www.inc.in/en/leadership/past-party-president/b-pattabhi-sitaramayyaa.
18. B. Shiva Rao, *Volume IV*, p. 5.
19. K.M. Munshi, *Indian Constitutional Documents: Pilgrimage to Freedom*, 1902–1950.
20. Ibid., pp. 193–94.
21. K. C. Markandan, *The Preamble*, p. 33.
22. My own emphasis. D.D. Basu, *Commentary on the Constitution of India: Being a Comparative Treatise on the Universal Principles of Justice and Constitutional Government with Special Reference to the Organic Instrument of India, Volume 1* (Calcutta: S.C. Sarkar, 1961), p. 64.
23. B. Shiva Rao, *Volume IV*, p. 5.
24. B.N. Rau, *India: India's Constitution in the Making* (Calcutta: Orient Longmans, 1960).
25. Stuart Gray, *A Defense of Rule: Origins of Political Thought in Greece and India* (New York: Oxford University Press, 2017).
26. Thomas Hobbes, *Leviathan or The Matter, Forme, & Power of a Common-wealth: Ecclesiasticall and Civill* (London: 1951), I.10.
27. D.D. Basu, *Commentary on the Constitution of India*, p. 64.
28. 'Universal Declaration of Human Rights', Article 1, https://www.un.org/en/universal-declaration-human-rights/.
29. Ambedkar, *States and Minorities*, Chapter 10 in *BAWS*, vol. 1, pp. 425–26, Part II-Clause 2.
30. 'Basic Law', *The Constitution of the Federal Republic of Germany*, https://www.bundesregierung.de/breg-en/chancellor/basic-law-470510.

31. Ambedkar, 'Hindu Social Order: Its Essential Principles', in *BAWS*, vol. 3, pp. 95–96.
32. Ambedkar, *BAWS*, vol. 17, part 1, p. 182.
33. Ambedkar, *Hindus and Want of Public Conscience*, Chapter 9 in *BAWS*, vol. 5, p. 89.
34. Some good work has been done teasing out Kantian elements in Ambedkar's thought. See, for example, Bansidhar Deep, 'B.R. Ambedkar's Philosophy of Religion' in Aakash Singh Rathore ed., *B.R. Ambedkar: The Quest for Justice, Volume V: Religious and Cultural Justice* (Delhi: Oxford University Press, 2020), Chapter 6.
35. Ambedkar, *States and Minorities*, *BAWS*, vol. 1, p. 409.
36. B. Shiva Rao, *Volume III*, p.484.
37. Ambedkar, *What Congress and Gandhi Have Done to the Untouchables*, *BAWS*, vol. 9, p. 285.
38. Ambedkar, 'The Philosophy of Hinduism', in *BAWS*, vol. 3, p. 48.
39. Ambedkar, *What Congress and Gandhi Have Done to the Untouchables*, in *BAWS*, vol. 9 pp. 235–26.
40. Dhananjay Keer, *Dr. Ambedkar, Life and Mission*, p. 557.
41. Eknath Awad, *Strike a Blow to Change the World*, translated by Jerry Pinto (New Delhi: Speaking Tiger, 2018).
42. Frantz Fanon, *The Wretched of the Earth*, translated by Richard Philcox (New York: Grove Press, 2004).
43. Eknath Awad, *Strike a Blow*, p. 209.
44. Ibid., pp. 182–83.
45. Ibid., p. 118.
46. Daya Pawar, *Baluta*, translated by Jerry Pinto (New Delhi: Speaking Tiger, 2015), p. 95.
47. Ibid., p. 253.
48. Ibid., p. 133.
49. The Municipal Board of Mahad, Maharashtra, passed an order to open the public water tank of Mahad city to all communities in 1926. Prior to this, the untouchables were not allowed to use water from the Mahad tank. This order was opposed by so-called 'high caste' Hindus and in response, Ambedkar called for a satyagraha of ten thousand untouchables to support the decision of the Municipal Board, at Mahad on March 20, 1927. They marched to the tank and asserted

their right to drink and take water from it. It came to be known as Mahad Satyagraha and was the first such collective protest of untouchables led by Ambedkar. Now, March 20 is observed as Social Empowerment day in India every year to commemorate the Mahad Satyagraha. A full account of these events and their significance is painstakingly documented in Anand Teltumbde's *Mahad: The Making of the First Dalit Revolt* (Delhi: Aakar, 2016).

50. Ambedkar, *What Congress and Gandhi Have Done to the Untouchables, BAWS*, vol. 9, pp. 212–13.

Chapter 6. Nation: The Future of a Delusion

1. B. Shiva Rao, *Volume III*, p. 484.
2. Ibid., p. 489.
3. Ibid., p. 491.
4. 25 November 1949, *Constituent Assembly of India Debates (Proceedings)-Volume XI.*
5. B. Shiva Rao, *Volume IV*, p. 5.
6. N.V. Gadgil, *Dr. Ambedkar and Democracy*, edited by Christopher Jaffrelot and Narender Kumar (Delhi: Oxford University Press, 2018), p.125.
7. Ibid.
8. B.R. Ambedkar, *What Congress and Gandhi Have Done to the Untouchables.*
9. 17 December 1946, *Constituent Assembly Debates (Proceedings)-Volume I*, p. 38.
10. *Constituent Assembly Debates: Official Report, Volume 7: 04 November to 08 January 1949, Issues 1–11*, p. 38.
11. Ambedkar, *Buddhist Revolution and Counter Revolution in Ancient India*, edited by D.C. Ahir.
12. 25 November 1949, *Constituent Assembly of India Debates (Proceedings)-Volume XI.*
13. Ambedkar, *Federation versus Freedom*, Chapter 8 in *BAWS*, vol. 1.
14. 9 November 1948, *Constituent Assembly of India Debates (Proceedings)-Volume VII.*

15. *Constituent Assembly Debates: Official Report, Volume 7: 04 November to 08 January 1949, Issues 1–11*, p. 38.
16. 25 November 1949, *Constituent Assembly of India Debates (Proceedings)-Volume XI.*
17. Christopher Jaffrelot and Narender Kumar, eds., *Dr. Ambedkar and Democracy*, p. 228.
18. 25 November 1949, *Constituent Assembly of India Debates (Proceedings)-Volume XI.*
19. Rabindranath Tagore, *Ghare Baire*, http://www.gutenberg.org/ebooks/7166.
20. Ambedkar, *States and Minorities*, Chapter 10 in *BAWS*, vol. 1, p. 427.
21. Rabindranath Tagore, *Nationalism,* https://archive.org/details/nationalism00tagorich.
22. Cited in Ambedkar, *Pakistan, or the Partition of India: The Indian Political What's What!* (1945), *BAWS*, vol. 8, p. 142.
23. Ibid., p. 31.
24. M.K. Gandhi, *Hind Swaraj and Other Writings*, edited by Anthony Parel, (Cambridge: Cambridge University Press, 1997).
25. M.K. Gandhi, *Hind Swaraj and Other Writings*, p. 1.
26. Ibid., p. 71.
27. Shradhananda Sanyasi, cited in Ambedkar, *BAWS*, vol. 5, p. 306.
28. V.D. Sawarkar, *Hindutva: Who is a Hindu* (Bombay: Hindi Sahitya Sadan, 2012).
29. Vaibhav Purandare, *Savarkar: The True Story of the Father of Hindutva* (Delhi: Juggernaut, 2019), p. 177.
30. M.S. Gowalkar, *We or Our Nationhood Defined* (Nagpur: Bharat Prakashan, 1944).
31. Ibid.
32. Sukhadeo Thorat, in *Dr. Ambedkar and Democracy*, p. xviii
33. Ambedkar, cited in Christopher Jaffrelot and Narender Kumar, eds., p. 57
34. Ambedkar, *Annihilation of Caste*, Chapter 2 in *BAWS*, vol. 1, p. 79.
35. B. Shiva Rao, *Volume III*, p.491.
36. Rao, *Volume IV*, p. 5.

Epilogue

1. *Constituent Assembly of India Debates (Proceedings)-Volume XI*, https://www.constitutionofindia.net/constitution_assembly_debates/volume/11/1949-11-25?paragraph_number=325%2C326%2C328%2C290%2C329%2C292.
2. B. Shiva Rao, *Volume III*, p. 484.

Bibliography

Agarwal, Shriman Narayan, *The Gandhian Constitution of Free India*, foreword by M.K. Gandhi. Allahabad: Kitabistan, 1946, https://www.constitutionofindia.net/historical_constitutions/gandhian_constitution_for_free_india__shriman_narayan_agarwal__1946__2nd%20April%201945#_ednref73.

Ahir, D.C., *Dr. Ambedkar's Vision of Dhamma: An Assessment.* New Delhi: B.R. Publishing, 1998.

Ahir, D.C, *Buddhism and Ambedkar.* New Delhi: B.R. Publishing, 2004.

Ahir, D.C., ed., *Selected Speeches of Dr. B.R. Ambedkar (1927–1956).* New Delhi: Blumoon Books, 1997.

Aloysius, G., *Nationalism without a Nation in India.* New Delhi: B.R. Publishing Corporation, 1997.

Aloysius, G., *Religion as Emacipatory Identity.* New Delhi: New Age International, 1998.

Ambedkar, B.R., *Annihilation of Caste* (1936), Chapter 2 in *Dr. Babasaheb Ambedkar: Writings and Speeches* (BAWS), vol. 1 (1979).

Ambedkar, B.R., *Autobiographical Notes.* Pondicherry: Navayana, 2003.

Ambedkar, B.R., *Bahishkrut Bharat* (29 July 1927), cited in Dhananjay Keer, *Dr Ambedkar, Life and Mission.* Bombay: Popular Prakashan, 1962.

Ambedkar, B.R., *BAWS*, vol. 10, October 1991.

Ambedkar, B.R., *BAWS,* vol. 13, 1994.

Ambedkar, B.R., *BAWS,* vol. 15, 1997.

Ambedkar, B.R., *BAWS*, vol. 17, part 3, 2003.

Ambedkar, B.R., BBC Interview, 1955, https://www.youtube.com/watch?v=omGcgEstVIE.

Ambedkar, B.R., *Buddha and Karl Marx* (an address to All India Radio, 1954), Chapter 18 in B.R. Ambedkar, B.R., *BAWS*, vol. 3, April 1987.

Ambedkar, B.R., *Buddhist Revolution and Counter Revolution in Ancient India*, edited by D.C. Ahir. Delhi: Buddhist World Press, 1996.

Ambedkar, B.R., BAWS. Bombay: Education Department, Government of Maharashtra.

Ambedkar, B.R., *Federation versus Freedom*, Chapter 8 in *BAWS*, vol. 1, 1979.

Ambedkar, B.R., *Hindu Social Order*, Chapters 2 and 3 in *BAWS*, vol. 3, April 1987.

Ambedkar, B.R., *Hindus and Want of Public Conscience*, Chapter 9 in *BAWS*, vol. 5, 1989.

Ambedkar, B.R., *Memorandum on the Safeguards for the Scheduled Castes submitted to the Constituent Assembly on behalf of the All India Scheduled Castes Federation*, 1947.

Ambedkar, B.R., *Pakistan, or the Partition of India: The Indian Political What's What!*, 1945; *BAWS*, vol. 8, 1990.

Ambedkar, B.R., *Riddles of Hinduism: An Exposition to Enlighten the Masses*, *BAWS*, vol. 4, October 1987.

Ambedkar, B.R., *Riddles of Hinduism: The Annotated Critical Selection*, introduced by Kancha Illaiah. New Delhi: Navayana, 2016.

Ambedkar, B.R., *The Buddha and His Dhamma*, *BAWS*, vol. 11, 1992.

Ambedkar, B.R., *The Buddha and His Dhamma: A Critical Edition*, edited, introduced and annotated by Aakash Singh Rathore and Ajay Verma. New Delhi: Oxford University Press, 2011.

Ambedkar, B.R., *The Philosophy of Hinduism*, Chapter 1 in *BAWS*, vol. 3, April 1987.

Ambedkar, B.R., *Waiting for a Visa* (circa 1937), Chapter 1 of Part V, in *BAWS*, vol. 12, 1993.

Ambedkar, B.R., *What Congress and Gandhi Have Done to the Untouchables*, *BAWS*, vol. 9, January 1991.

Ambedkar, B.R., *Conditions Precedent for the Successful Working of Democracy*. Nagpur: Panchbai, 1976.

Ambedkar, B.R., *Selected Works of Dr BR Ambedkar*, https://drambedkarbooks.files.wordpress.com/2009/03/selected-work-of-dr-b-r-ambedkar.pdf.

Awad, Eknath, *Strike a Blow to Change the World*, translated by Jerry Pinto. New Delhi: Speaking Tiger, 2018.

B. Pattabhi Sitaramayya, *Indian Nationalism.* Masulipatam: Kistna Swadeshi Press, 1913, https://www.inc.in/en/leadership/past-party-president/b-pattabhi-sitaramayyaa.

Basu, D.D., *Commentary on the Constitution of India: Being a Comparative Treatise on the Universal Principles of Justice and Constitutional Government with Special Reference to the Organic Instrument of India, Volume 1.* Calcutta: S.C. Sarkar, 1961.

Baxi, Upendra, 'Justice as Emancipation: The Legacy of Babasaheb Ambedkar', in Upendra Baxi and Bhikhu Parekh (eds.), *Crisis and Change in Contemporary India.* New Delhi: Sage, 1995.

Baxi, Upendra, 'Emancipation as Justice: Legacy and Vision of Dr. Ambedkar' in K.C. Yadav, ed., *From Periphery to Center Stage, Ambedkar, Ambedkarism & Dalit Future.* New Delhi: Manohar, 2000.

Chakrabarty, Bidyut, *Confluence of Thought: Mahatma Gandhi and Martin Luther King Jr.* New York: Oxford University Press, 2006.

Chakrabarty, Bidyut, *The Socio-Political Ideas of B.R. Ambedkar.* London: Routledge, 2019.

Chakrabarty, Bidyut, *India's Constitutional Identity.* London: Routledge, 2019.

Chapalgaonker, Narendra, *Mahatma Gandhi and the Indian Constitution.* New Delhi: Routledge, 2016.

Chatterjee, Partha, 'Anderson's Utopia', *Diacritics, vol.* 29, no. 4, Grounds of Comparison: Around the Work of Benedict Anderson, Winter, 1999, pp. 128–34.

Chatterjee, Partha, 'Beyond the Nation or Within', *Social Text,* no. 56, Autumn, 1998, pp. 57–69.

Chatterjee, Partha, *Nationalist Thought and the Colonial World* in Partha Chatterjee, *The Partha Chatterjee Omnibus.* New Delhi: Oxford University Press, 1999.

Chowdhuri, Satyyabarata Rai, *Leftist Movements in India, 1917–1947.* Calcutta: Minerva Associates, 1977.

Constituent Assembly Debates, (set of five books). Lok Sabha Secretariat: Government of India, 2014.

Constituent Assembly Debates, Official Report, Book 1. New Delhi: Lok Sabha Secretariat, Government of India, 2014.

Constituent Assembly Debates: Official Report, Volume 10, 17 October 1949.

Constituent Assembly Debates: Official Report, Volume 7: 04 November to 08 January 1949, Issues 1–11. Lok Sabha Secretariat: Government of India, 2014.

Contursi, Janet A., 'Militant Hindus and Buddhist Dalits: Hegemony and Resistance in an Indian Slum', *American Ethnologist,* vol. 16, no. 3, August 1989, pp. 442–557.

Coward, Harold G., *Indian Critiques of Gandhi* (SUNY series in Religious Studies). New York: State University of New York Press, 2003.

Davids, Rhys, *Dialogues of the Buddha*, in the series Sacred Books of the Buddhists, translated from the Páli of the *Dìgha Nikáya Sutta* numbers 3 and 5 by T.W. Rhys Davids. London: Páli Text Society, 1899.

Dewey, John, *Democracy and Education: An Introduction to the Philosophy of Education.* New York: The MacMillan Company, 1921.

Dirks, Nicholas B., *Castes of Mind: Colonialism and the Making of Modern India.* Princeton: Princeton University Press, 2001.

Draft Constitution of the Indian Republic, foreword by Jayprakash Narayan (Socialist Party India, 1948).

Draft Constitution of the Republic of India (Socialist Party, 1948), remarks, https://www.constitutionofindia.net/historical_constitutions/draft_constitution_of_the_republic_of_india__socialist_party__1948__1st%20January%201948.

Eleanor Zelliot, 'The American Experience of Dr. B.R. Ambedkar (1977)' in Eleanor Zelliot, *From Untouchable to Dalit: Essays on the Ambedkar Movement.* New Delhi. Manohar, 1996.

Engels, Friedrich, *The Origins of the Family, Private Property and the State.* London: Lawrence and Wishart, 1972.

Engels, Friedrich and Karl Marx, *Revolution and Counter-Revolution in Germany*, edited by Eleanor Marx Aveling. New York: Swan Sonnenschein & Co., 1896.

Fanon, Frantz, *The Wretched of the Earth*, translated from French (1961) by Richard Philcox, preface by Jean-Paul Sartre, foreword by Homi K. Bhabha. New York: Grove Press, 2004.

Feuer, Lewis S., ed., *Marx and Engles: Basic Writings on Politics and Philosophy*. New York: Anchor Books, 1959.

Gandhi, M.K., 'A Vindication of Caste by Mahatma Gandhi' in 'Annihilation of Caste With a Reply to Mahatma Gandhi (1936)', *Ambedkar.org*, 2006 / Dr. B.R. Ambedkar, Dalit E-Forum, http://www.ambedkar.org, 1 April 2008.

Gandhi, M.K., 'Ambedkar's Indictment–II (1936)', in *The Collected Works of Mahatma Gandhi,* vol. LXIII. Ahmedabad: Navajivan Trust, 1963.

Gandhi, M.K., 'Hind Swaraj or Indian Home Rule (1908)', in *The Collected Works of Mahatma Gandhi,* vol. X. Ahmedabad: Navajivan Trust, 1963.

Gandhi, M.K., 'Letter to B.R. Ambedkar (1933)', in Aravinda Malagatti, et al, ed., *What Gandhi Says about Ambedkar.* Mysore: Prasaranga, 2000.

Gandhi, M.K., 'Letter to M.A. Jinnah (1944)' in Aravinda Malagatti, et al, ed., *What Gandhi Says about Ambedkar.* Mysore: Prasaranga, 2000.

Gandhi, M.K., *Autobiography: The Story of My Experiments with Truth.* Boston: Beacon Press, 2015.

Gandhi, M.K., *Collected Works of Mahatma Gandhi* (1958–94), vol. 84, p. 272, www.gandhiserve.org/cwmg/VOL084.PDF.

Gandhi, M.K., *Hind Swaraj and Other Writings,* edited by Anthony Parel. Cambridge: Cambridge University Press, 1997.

Ganguly, Debjani, 'Buddha, Bhakti and Superstition: A Post-Secular Reading of Dalit Conversion,' *Postcolonial Studies,* vol. 7, no. 1, 2004, pp. 49–62.

Ganguly, Debjani, *Caste, Colonialism and Counter-Modernity: Notes on the Postcolonial Hermeneutics of Caste.* New York: Routledge, 2005.

Garfield, Jay L., trans. and commentary, *The Fundamental Wisdom of the Middle Way: Nāgārjuna's Mūlamadhyamakakārikā.* New York: Oxford University Press, 1995.

Geetha, V. and S.V. Rajadurai, *Towards a Non-Brahmin Millenium: From Iyothee Thass to Periyar.* Calcutta: Samya, 1998.

Gibbon, Edward, *Decline and Fall of the Roman Empire*. Hertfordshire: Wordsworth Classics, 1998.

Goldman, Robert P., 'Transsexualism, Gender, and Anxiety in Traditional India', *Journal of the American Oriental Society*, vol. 113, no. 3, July–September 1993, pp. 374–401.

Gowalkar, M.S., *We or Our Nationhood Defined*. Nagpur: Bharat Prakashan, 1944.

Gray, Stuart, *A Defense of Rule: Origins of Political Thought in Greece and India*. New York: Oxford University Press, 2017.

Gupta, Som Raj, Śaṅkarācārya, *The Word Speaks to the Faustian Man: Bṛhada-raṇyaka Upaniṣad*, vol. 5. Delhi: Motilal Banarasidass Publishers, 2008.

Guru, Gopal, 'The Man who Thought Differently: An Inquiry into the Political Thinking of Dr. Ambedkar', in K.C. Yadav, ed., *From Periphery to Centre Stage: Ambedkar, Ambedkarism and Dalit Future*. New Delhi: Manohar, 2000.

Hay, Stephen, 'The Making of a Late-Victorian Hindu: M. K. Gandhi in London, 1888–1891', *Victorian Studies*, vol. 33, no. 1, 1989, pp. 75–98.

Hegel, G.W.F., *The Philosophy of History*, translated by J. Sibree. New York: Cosimo Classics, 2007.

Hobbes, Thomas, *Leviathan or The Matter, Forme, & Power of a Common-wealth: Ecclesiasticall and Civill*. St. Pauls Church Yard: London, 1951.

Jaffrelot, Christophe, *Dr. Ambedkar and Untouchability: Analyzing and Fighting Caste*. Delhi: Permanent Black, 2005.

Jaffrelot, Christopher and Narender Kumar, eds., *Dr Ambedkar and Democracy*. Delhi: Oxford University Press, 2019.

Jatava, D.R., *The Critics of Dr. Ambedkar*. Jaipur: Surabhi Publications, 1997.

Jayal, Niraja, *Citizenship and Its Discontents: An Indian History*. Delhi: Orient BlackSwan, 2015.

Jodhka, Surinder S., 'Nation and Village: Images of Rural India in Gandhi, Nehru and Ambedkar', *Economic and Political Weekly*, vol. 37, no. 32, 2002, pp. 3343–54.

Junghare, Indira Y., 'Dr. Ambedkar: The Hero of the Untouchables, Ex-Untouchables of India', *Asian Folklore Studies*, vol. 47, no. 1, 1988, pp. 93–121.

Kadam, K.N., *Dr. Babasahed Ambedkar and the Significance of his Movement.* Bombay: Popular Prakashan, 1991.

Kasbe, Raosaheb, 'The Ambedkarian Ideology: A Perspective' in K.C. Yadav, ed., *From Periphery to Center Stage, Ambedkar, Ambedkarism & Dalit Future.* New Delhi: Manohar, 2000.

Keer, Dhananjay, *Dr. Ambedkar: Life and Mission.* Bombay: Popular Prakashan, 1954.

Keller, Werner, *The Bible as History.* London: Hodder and Stoughton, 1955.

Mahajan, Gurpreet, *India: Political Ideas and the Making of a Democratic Discourse.* New York: Zed Books, 2013.

Markandan, K.C., *The Preamble: Key to the Mind of the Makers of the Indian Constitution.* Delhi: National, 1984.

Mookerjee, Satkari, *The Buddhist Philosophy of Universal Flux.* Delhi, Motilal Banarsidass, 2017.

Munshi, K.M., *Indian Constitutional Documents: Pilgrimage to Freedom,* 1902–1950. Bombay: Bharatiya Vidya Bhavan, 1967.

Narasu, Pokala Laxmi, *The Essence of Buddhism.* New Delhi and Chennai: Asian Educational Services, 1912.

Newbigin, E., 'B.R. Ambedkar's Code Bill: Caste, Marriage and Postcolonial Indian Citizenship', in *The Hindu Family and the Emergence of Modern India: Law, Citizenship and Community (Cambridge Studies in Indian History and Society).* Cambridge: Cambridge University Press, 2013.

Omvedt, Gail, 'Ambedkar as a Human Rights Leader', Ambedkar.org, 15 April 2002 / Commentary, Dalit E-Forum, http://ambedkar.org/gail/AmbedkarAs.htm, 1 April 2008.

Omvedt, Gail, 'Undoing the Bondage: Dr. Ambedkar's Theory of Dalit Liberation' in K. C Yadav, ed., *From Periphery to Centre Stage: Ambedkar, Ambedkarism and Dalit Future.* New Delhi: Manohar, 2000.

Omvedt, Gail, *Ambedkar: Towards an Enlightened India.* New Delhi: Penguin, 2004.

Omvedt, Gail, *Dalit Visions: The Anti-Caste Movement and the Construction of an Indian Identity.* New Delhi: Orient Longman Private Limited, 2006.

Omvedt, Gail, *Dalits and the Democratic Revolution: Dr. Ambedkar and the Dalit Movement in Colonial India.* London: Sage Publications, 1994.

Pawar, Daya, *Baluta*, translated by Jerry Pinto. New Delhi: Speaking Tiger, 2015.

Purandare, Vaibhav, *Savarkar: The True Story of the Father of Hindutva*. Delhi: Juggernaut, 2019.

Pyarelal (Nayyar) 'The Epic Fast (1932)' in Homer A. Jack, ed., *The Gandhi Reader: A Source Book*. Bloomington: Indiana University Press, 1956.

Pyarelal, *Mahatma Gandhi on Human Settlements*. Ahmedabad: Navajivan, 1977.

Queen, Christopher S. and Sallie B. King, *Engaged Buddhism: Buddhist Liberation movements in Asia*. Albany: State University of New York, 1996.

Rabindranath Tagore, *Nationalism*, https://archive.org/details/nationalism00tagorich.

Rajagopalachari, C., *Ambedkar Refuted*. Bombay: Hind Kitabs, 1946.

Rau, B.N., *India: India's Constitution in the Making*. Calcutta: Orient Longman, 1960.

Rao, B. Shiva, ed., *The Framing of India's Constitution, Select Documents, Volume III*. Bombay: N.M. Tripathi, 1968.

Rathore, Aakash Singh and Silika Mohapatra, eds., *Indian Political Thought: A Reader*. London: Routledge, 2010.

Rathore, Aakash Singh, *A Philosophy of Autobiography: Body & Text*. New York: Routledge, 2019.

Rathore, Aakash Singh, ed., *B.R. Ambedkar: The Quest for Justice* (five volumes). Oxford University Press, 2020.

Rathore, Aakash Singh, *Indian Political Theory: Laying the Groundwork for Svaraj*. New York: Routledge, 2017.

Rathore, Aakash Singh, *B.R. Ambedkar: A Biography*. HarperCollins, forthcoming in 2022.

Rathore, Aakash Singh and Rimina Mohapatra, *Hegel's India: A Reinterpretation, with Texts*. Oxford University Press, 2017

Rathore, Aakash Singh and Ajay Verma, *B.R. Ambedkar's The Buddha and His Dhamma: A Critical Edition*. Oxford University Press, 2011.

Rathore, Aakash Singh and Sunaina Arya, *Dalit Feminist Theory: A Reader*. Routledge, 2019.

Rathore, Aakash Singh and Ashis Nandy, *Vision for a Nation: Paths and Perspectives*. Penguin, 2019.

Rattu, Nanak Chand, *Last Few Years of Dr. Ambedkar*. New Delhi: Amrit Publishing House, 1997.

Rawls, John, *The Law of Peoples: With, the Idea of Public Reason Revisited.* Cambridge: Harvard University Press, 2001.

Ray, Sibnarayan, ed., *Selected Works of M. N. Roy, Volume IV: 1932–1936.* New Delhi: Oxford University Press, 1997.

Ray, Sibnarayan, *In Freedoms Quest: Life of M.N. Roy.* Kolkata: Renaissance Publishers, 2005.

Robb, Peter, *A History of India.* New York: Palgrave Macmillan, 2002.

Rodrigues, Valerian, *The Essential Writings of B.R. Ambedkar.* New Delhi: Oxford University Press, 2002.

Round Table India, 'Dr Ambedkar Remembers the Poona Pact in an Interview on BBC', 2012, http://roundtableindia.co.in/index.php?option=com_content&view=article&id=3797:dr-ambedkar-remembers-the-poona-pact-in-an-interview-on-the-bbc-&catid=116:dr-ambedkar&Itemid=128.

Roy, M.N., *Revolution and Counter-Revolution in China.* Kolkata: Renaissance Publishers, 1946.

Roy, M.N., *Constitution of Free India: A Draft* (Radical Democratic Party [India], 1944).

Roy, Samaren, *M.N. Roy: A Political Biography.* New Delhi: Orient Longman Limited, 1997.

S.G. Sardesai, 'Gautam Buddha, Karl Marx and Dr. B.R. Ambedkar (1981)' in A.B. Bardhan, et al, ed., S. *G. Sardesai: Patriot and Communist.* New Delhi: People's Publishing House, 1998.

Sangharakshita, *Ambedkar and Buddhism.* London: Windhorse Publications, 1986.

Sawarkar, V.D., *Hindutva: Who Is a Hindu.* Bombay: Hindi Sahitya Sadan, 2012.

Shastri, Haraprasad, *Mahamahopadhyaya Haraprasad Sastri Memorial Volume*, edited by Narendra Nath Law (available in the National Library of India), cited in Ambedkar, *BAWS*, vol. 3, (1987).

Shourie, Arun, *Worshiping False Gods.* New Delhi: HarperCollins, 2000.

Siderits, Mark, *Buddhism as Philosophy: An Introduction.* England: Ashgate, 2007.

Singh, Upinder, *Political Violence in Ancient India.* Cambridge, London, Massachusetts and England: Harvard University Press, 2017.

Stroud, Scott R., 'Pragmatism and the Pursuit of Social Justice in India: Bhimrao Ambedkar and the Rhetoric of Religious Reorientation', *Rhetoric Society Quarterly*, vol. 46, no. 1, 2016, pp. 5–27, DOI: 10.1080/02773945.2015.1104717, https://www.tandfonline.com/doi/pdf/10.1080/02773945.2015.1104717?needAccess=true.

Syrkin, Alexander, 'On the Beginning of Sutta Pitaka (The Brahmajala Sutta)', in *Orthodoxy, Heterodoxy and Dissent in India*, S.N. Eisenstadt, et al. New York: Mouton publishing, 1984.

Talisse, Robert B., *On Dewey: The Reconstruction of Philosophy*. Belmont: Wadsworth Thomson learning, 2000.

Tartakov, Gary Michael, 'Art and Identity: The Rise of a New Buddhist Imagery', *Art Journal*, vol. 49, no. 4, New Approaches to South Asian Art, 1990, pp. 409–16.

Taylor, R. W., 'The Ambedkarite Buddhists', in T.S. Wilkinson and M.N. Thomas, ed., *Ambedkar and the Neo-Buddhist Movement*. Madras: Christian Literature Society, 1972.

Teltumbde, Anand, *Republic of Caste: Thinking Equality in the Time of Neoliberal Hindutva*. New Delhi: Navayana, 2018.

Thapar, Romila, *A History of India, Volume One*. New Delhi: Penguin History, 1957.

The Constitution of the Federal Republic of Germany, https://www.bundesregierung.de/breg-en/chancellor/basic-law-470510.

Universal Declaration of Human Rights, https://www.un.org/en/universal-declaration-human-rights/.

Vajpayi, Ananya, *Righteous Republic: The Political Foundations of Modern India*. Cambridge: Harvard University Press, 2012.

Viswanathan, Gauri, *Outside the Fold: Conversion, Modernity, and Belief*. Princeton: Princeton University, 1998.

Wilkinson, T.S. and M.N. Thomas, ed., *Ambedkar and the Neo-Buddhist Movement*. Madras: Christian Literature Society, 1972.

Yadav, K.C., ed., *From Periphery to Center Stage, Ambedkar, Ambedkarism & Dalit Future*. New Delhi: Manohar, 2000.

Yengde, Suraj, *Caste Matters*. New Delhi: Penguin, 2019.

Zelliot, Eleanor, 'Chokhamela and Eknath: Two Bhakti Modes of Legitimacy for Modern Change (1980)' in Eleanor Zelliot, ed., *From Untouchable to Dalit: Essays on the Ambedkar Movement*. New Delhi: Manohar, 1996.

Zelliot, Eleanor, 'Learning the Use of Political Means: The Mahars of Maharashtra (1970)' in Eleanor Zelliot, ed., *From Untouchable to Dalit: Essays on the Ambedkar Movement*. New Delhi: Manohar, 1996.

Zelliot, Eleanor, 'The Nineteenth Century Background of the Mahar and Non-Brahman Movements in Maharashtra (1970)' in Eleanor Zelliot, ed., *From Untouchable to Dalit: Essays on the Ambedkar Movement*. New Delhi: Manohar, 1996.

Zelliot, Eleanor, *Ambedkar's World*. New Delhi: Navayana, 2013.

Zelliot, Eleanor, *Dr. Babasaheb Ambedkar and the Untouchable Movement*. New Delhi: Blumoon Books, 2004.

Zelliot, Eleanor, *From Untouchable to Dalit: Essays on the Ambedkar Movement*. New Delhi: Manohar, 1996.

Index